India at the Time of the Mahabharata

Not all kingdoms, cities, etc., are shown.

GANDHARA

KAMBHOJA

KEKAYA

TRIGARTA

MADRA

BRAHMAVARTA

Kurukshetra

Mt. Gandhamadana
Mt. Kailasa

SINDHU

R. Sindhu

R. Saraswati

KURU

Hastinapura

Indraprastha

MATSYA

Vrindavan

Gokula

Virata

Mathura

PANCHALA

Himalaya Mountains

SAUVIRA

R. Yamuna

R. Ganga

KOSALA

VIDEHA

PRAGJYOTISHA

R. Brahmaputra

SHALVA

KASHI

Kashi
(Varanasi)

ANGA

AVANTI

MAGADHA

KARUSHA

Dwaraka

ANARTA

MAHISHMATI

CHEDI

Prabhasa

VIDARBHA

Kundinapura

MAHARASHTRA

KALINGA

Bay of Bengal

Sea of Surashtra
(Arabian Sea)

Kilometers

0   200   400   600   800

0   100   200   300   400   500

Miles

Indian Ocean

LANKA

THE
Hidden Story
OF THE
Mahabharata

WITH INNER MEANINGS FROM
PARAMHANSA YOGANANDA

Nayaswami Gyandev

CRYSTAL CLARITY PUBLISHERS Commerce, California

CRYSTAL CLARITY PUBLISHERS
1123 Goodrich Blvd | Commerce, California
crystalclarity.com | clarity@crystalclarity.com
800.424.1055

ISBN   978-1-56589-348-1 (print) | LCCN 2024024671 (print)
ISBN   978-1-56589-557-7 (e-book) | LCCN 2024024672 (e-book)
ISBN   978-1-56589-842-4 (audiobook)

Cover design by Tejindra Scott Tully
Interior design and layout by Michele Madhavi Molloy
Photo credit: Bishwambers Photography, Shutterstock.com

The *Joy Is Within You* symbol is registered by Ananda
Church of Self-Realization of Nevada County, California.

Contents

Dedication

To Paramhansa Yogananda and Swami Kriyananda,
through whom has come everything that
I understand of the spiritual life

Preface

FOR MORE THAN THIRTY YEARS, it has been my great joy and blessing to retell the story of the Mahabharata to audiences around the world. Many listeners have become so enthralled that they have implored me to offer a deeper dive into this ancient epic. I am delighted to provide this expanded version in response.

I had two purposes beyond that of telling more of the story. First, I wanted to share the Mahabharata's subtle inner meanings revealed by Paramhansa Yogananda, the celebrated author of *Autobiography of a Yogi*. His insights enrich the tale immeasurably. I have found them life-changing, and I believe you will, too.

Yogananda built upon an approach first given in modern times by Lahiri Mahasaya, his *paramguru* (guru's guru). These spiritual luminaries offered a unique perspective on the Mahabharata, showing how its rousing outward saga is a powerful allegory for the pursuit of lasting happiness and divine realization.

Over the centuries, others have pointed out hidden meanings within the Mahabharata. However, Yogananda's insights are especially relevant to the needs of today's restless, fractured world—and they are highly practical. From his own Self-realization, he knew the highest spiritual wisdom within the Mahabharata and how to apply it to modern life.

Yogananda said that, at the time of the historical Mahabharata, he and Babaji (Lahiri Mahasaya's guru) incarnated as the two principal characters of the story: the noble prince Arjuna and his guru, Sri Krishna. He and Babaji had attained *moksha* (final liberation, union with God) long before that time. However, as Arjuna, Yogananda played the role of a sincere seeker who still had much to learn. Who better to offer us deeper insight into this beloved epic than one who lived it?

As for my second purpose, I have seen many people feel inspired to dive deeper into the Mahabharata and eagerly begin reading some version of the epic. All too often, however, the story's length, complexity, countless digressions, and interminable speeches drain their energy and enthusiasm—and they quit. I wanted to provide a clear, uncluttered abridgment that avoids those pitfalls while remaining loyal to the original scripture. I hope this treatment will keep you engaged, entertained, and inspired to the very end.

I base my storytelling on K. M Ganguli's literal translation into English of the original epic by the ancient master Vyasa. First published in the 1880s, his translation spans five thousand pages of small type. I have faithfully adhered to the narrative of Vyasa and Ganguli. I have not invented or embellished any part of the story, nor have I included material from other versions of the Mahabharata. Vyasa's tale needs no improvement.

Naturally, I had to leave out a great deal, which required making many hard choices. But some were easy, such as sparing you most of the gory details of the Kurukshetra War. Also, I included only a little of what Bhishma taught King Yudhisthira after the war—his entire teaching constitutes almost a quarter of the original text! And I have excluded numerous minor characters and episodes that are peripheral to the central teachings of the story.

In addition, I have abridged or omitted countless lengthy monologues and digressions that bog down the action. In the full version, it is not unusual for a character to take two pages—or even twenty or more!—to say what they could easily have said in two sentences. I wanted to share some of that extravagant verbiage because it helps weave the magical aura of the Mahabharata. However, it is too much for most people, so I merely included a few delightful examples in Supplement 2.

Throughout the story, I have retained many of the translation's charming figures of speech, which help bring to life the unique culture of that long-ago era.

I pray that you will experience the potent spiritual vibrations of the original scripture in this retelling—and have a lot of inspiration, inner growth, and fun along the way.

Thank you for everything, Master Vyasa.

Let the adventure begin!

Nayaswami Gyandev
Ananda Village, California

Introduction

THE MAHABHARATA IS THE LONGEST POEM in world literature and the most beloved epic of the Indian spiritual tradition. It is a thrilling tale of *dharma* (right action), *karma* (choices and consequences), politics, human relationships, and above all, the quest for God. At its center is the Bhagavad Gita, the flower of Indian spiritual teaching.

The Mahabharata also has an important—and little-known—personal dimension: It offers practical insight into the interplay of psychological qualities within us, helping us navigate the process of spiritual growth. Therein lies the hidden story of the Mahabharata, and we will explore it as the outer story unfolds—from the celestial events that gave rise to the compelling earthly drama to its surprising conclusion back in Heaven.

First, some background on this treasured scripture: *Maha* means "great" in Sanskrit, the native language of the Mahabharata. Bharata was an ancient Indian king; the central characters in the story proudly claim him as their common ancestor. Bharata also means "giver of Divine Light" or "devoted to Divine Light." The great Light-giver in this tale is Lord Krishna, the best-known of India's spiritual masters.

The Mahabharata has everything we could wish for in an epic: heroes and villains, triumph and tragedy, intrigue, political maneuvering, rousing adventure, magical powers, angels and demons, romance, deep allegory, spiritual teachings, and even humor.

The story centers on a conflict between two sets of cousins over which clan will rule the kingdom. Their struggle has a historical basis in a war that was fought northwest of modern Delhi, probably early in the first millennium B.C.E. Paramhansa Yogananda stated that the main characters in the story were actual historical figures.

However, any genuine history in the Mahabharata is irrelevant to its higher purpose. The great master Vyasa, who was both the author and a character in the story, reshaped the historical events into a spiritual allegory for our search for true, lasting happiness.

Yogananda likened the mind to a kingdom, and our many psychological and spiritual qualities to the citizens of the kingdom. He taught that each main character in the Mahabharata represents one of those qualities, and that the Sanskrit root of their name suggests that quality. As with an external kingdom, our inner kingdom has good citizens (positive qualities that lead us toward true happiness) and not-so-good citizens (negative qualities that keep us caught in ego consciousness: the belief that we *are* the body and personality, and the inclination to seek happiness by gratifying the body and personality through outward attainments).

In the story, the characters' actions tend to be consistent with the qualities they represent. The "good guys" usually act righteously, while "bad guys" almost always behave badly. It is all about their underlying motivations and the corresponding choices they make—just as it is with us.

As each character appears in the story, I will point out the quality they represent. For some characters and episodes, I will share additional spiritual insights from Yogananda and his direct disciple, Swami Kriyananda.

> I will present the characters' qualities and additional spiritual insights apart from the main text, as in this example.

Even if you are familiar with the Mahabharata, those qualities and insights will increase the story's relevance to your quest for happiness and divine realization by helping you recognize more clearly your inner tendencies and how to work with them. It can be a doorway to personal awakening.

The Glossary of Characters will help you keep all the players straight through the many twists and turns of the story.

Although the events of the Mahabharata took place long ago, the era in which they occurred bears many similarities to our own. Both have positive aspects, as well as the blights of war, social injustice, and widespread *adharma* (unrighteous behavior). Those miseries persist in our era because human nature has not changed since the time of the Mahabharata. The vast majority of people still live in ego consciousness—and as Yogananda often said, that is the source of all our troubles.

The Mahabharata's timeless wisdom, both overt and hidden, shows us a way to overcome those troubles. Its solutions are relevant to any person and era, offering inspiration and practical methods for finding true, lasting happiness — for finding God. And that is what spirituality is all about.

So, let us now immerse ourselves in this thrilling exploration of how to live. To quote the Mahabharata's principal narrator:

> All sins that are committed by body, word, or mind immediately leave them who hear this history. They who hear it, without the spirit of fault finding, can have no fear of maladies, let alone the fear of the other world. It is excellent, productive of fame, grants long life, and is sacred and heavenly. He who hears it always attains to purity of heart. The gratification that one derives from attaining to Heaven is scarcely equal to that which one derives from hearing this holy history.

Prologue

Long ago, the Earth enjoyed a time of great prosperity and happiness. All the orders of humankind attended to their natural duties.

The Brahmins, or priestly caste, lived by the timeless wisdom of the Vedas and freely taught anyone ready to learn. The Kshatriyas, the caste of rulers and warriors, were virtuous, self-sacrificing, and generous. The Vaishyas were farmers and merchants; they raised bountiful crops and were always honest in their business dealings. And the Sudras, or peasants, willingly served others.

All persons followed the ways of *dharma* (virtue, righteousness). Consequently, Indra, the lord of the heavens, poured down his life-giving rain showers at proper times and places, blessing all creatures. Trees bore flowers and fruit according to their natural seasons. And no young person ever died.

Peace and tranquility also reigned in the celestial regions, for the Devas, the gods, had finally driven the Asuras, the demons, out of Heaven. The Asuras had to live in humiliating exile in the nether regions.

Tormented by this suffering and driven by the desire for power, the Asuras decided that if they could not rule Heaven, they would instead rule Earth. They used their celestial powers to take birth among the ruling families of Earth. From those positions of earthly power, they began to oppress others. Devoid of virtue, proud of their strength, and intoxicated with the wine of insolence, they even harassed the wise sages, the *rishis*, in their forest hermitages.

The evil influence of the Asuras spread among humankind, and many people fell from the ways of dharma. Ignorance, greed, dishonesty, and laziness became increasingly common.

Finally, the Earth could no longer endure that evil, and She begged Brahma, the Creator of worlds, for relief. In response, Brahma commanded the Devas, "Go forth and take birth among humans. Fight the evil Asuras and free the Earth of Her burden!"

Indra, the chief of the Devas, went directly to Lord Narayana,

also known as Vishnu, the Sovereign of all the deities. He implored
Narayana, "Do Thou incarnate also." And Narayana replied, "So be it!"
    Thus, the celestials began to incarnate among humans. Narayana
took the form of a humble cowherd named Krishna, who would bring
about all that the Earth had requested. He was the Divine Power behind the saga of the descendants of the ancient King Bharata—the
great story called the Mahabharata.

India's spiritual teachings declare that human consciousness is not
forever rising, as most modern minds believe. Instead, it rises and
falls in cycles — as a number of other ancient traditions also assert.
The above account allegorically places the events of the Mahabharata near the end of the descending portion of a cycle, in a *yuga* (era,
age) called Dwapara.

Swami Sri Yukteswar, Paramhansa Yogananda's guru, taught that each
cycle is 24,000 years long: 12,000 years of ascending consciousness
followed by 12,000 years of descending consciousness. He said the
historical Mahabharata occurred early in the first millennium B.C.E.,
a little more than a thousand years before the very bottom of a yuga
cycle. It had been more than ten thousand years since humans lived
at the top of a cycle in the happy era described at the beginning of
this prologue. Since then, the overall level of human consciousness
had steadily declined.

Now, the lowest age, Kali Yuga, was approaching. Knowledge was being lost, and lower consciousness (represented by the Asuras) was
gaining strength. Divine Light was as present on Earth as ever, but
fewer people could — or even wanted to — align themselves with it.

The caste system is one example of this decline. In higher yugas,
caste is a fluid and supportive concept, a way to understand each individual's level of development and how to help them rise to a higher
level. In lower yugas, caste can regress into a rigid and oppressive
social stratification based solely on heredity, as in the Mahabharata
era. We, too, live in a relatively low age, and many modern cultures
are similarly stratified, without a formal caste system.

In the Bhagavad Gita, Krishna states that at such times of dire need,
God helps humanity by sending avatars — souls that have attained
moksha (liberation, union with God). Speaking from that state of

oneness, he says, "Whenever virtue (dharma) declines, and vice (adharma) is in the ascendant, I incarnate Myself on Earth (as an avatar). Appearing from age to age in visible form, I come to destroy evil and to re-establish virtue." (Gita 4:7–8)

The Mahabharata — and Indian spiritual tradition generally — portrays Krishna as an incarnation of Narayana/Vishnu, but Yogananda called that a myth. He said the historical Krishna was a soul liberated long before the time of the Mahabharata and now reincarnated to help others find freedom. Allegorically, that meant keeping the evil Asuras from taking over the world.

Over the millennia, many great spiritual masters have come to Earth to help sincere seekers escape the pull of lower consciousness and experience their innate soul reality. And the above Gita verses assure us that the masters will continue to come, in Yogananda's words, "so long as one stray brother is left behind."

THE
Hidden Story
OF THE
Mahabharata

CHAPTER 1

The Loves of His Life

SHANTANU WAS THE KING OF the Kuru people. He was a descendant of the ancient King Bharata, and like most kings and princes, he was of the Kshatriya caste.

Shantanu was a noble king universally revered for his wisdom and virtue. Under his rule, the Kuru kingdom became the most powerful realm on earth, and the citizens enjoyed peace, harmony, and prosperity. His great virtue brought him both worldly riches and a wealth of good karma.

> Paramhansa Yogananda taught that Shantanu represents the Father aspect of God — the aspect that set the cosmic drama of creation in motion, but remains aloof from creation, uninvolved with it.

One day, Shantanu was hunting along the banks of the holy River Ganga. As he rounded a thicket, he beheld a maiden standing at the river's edge. The young woman's beauty stole his breath away. Her skin was the color of honey, and her black hair shone with a heavenly light. She turned toward him, and her eyes told him that she would happily feast her gaze on him forever.

He said, "I am Shantanu, king of the Kurus. O radiant one, marry me!"

Her smile melted his heart. "I will happily marry you, O King. But I have one condition: If ever you interfere with my actions or speak unkindly to me, I will leave you forever."

Shantanu was so enthralled by her that he could not imagine ever questioning anything she might do. He quickly said, "So be it." Together, they walked back to his chariot, and he took her to the royal palace in his capital city of Hastinapura. Their marriage marked the beginning of a beautiful love that uplifted all the Kuru people.

She soon conceived a child, and in due course, a son was born. When Shantanu heard the news, he was elated: Here was his successor to the Kuru throne! He rushed to her palace apartments, where one of her servants told him, "Sire, she took the child to the river."

His brow furrowed, and he thought, "That is very odd." He immediately set out for the river, arriving just in time to see his wife cast the newborn into the flowing current, smiling as she said to the child, "This is for your good."

Shantanu's eyes grew wide with horror. He was about to shout a protest, but he remembered their agreement and, with great difficulty, swallowed his words. As he watched the baby disappear beneath the swirling waters, he sank into despair. His beloved queen had drowned his successor!

She turned to him, and the look in her eyes said that she knew his torment and expected him to object. But despite his anguish, he said nothing, lest she leave him forever. They returned to the palace in an uncomfortable silence.

A year passed, and another son was born. Shantanu rejoiced, for surely this son would be his successor. But again, immediately after the birth, his queen took the child to the Ganga and cast him into its waters, saying, "This is for your good." Again, Shantanu endured his pain and said nothing.

Over the years that followed, the drama repeated itself on five more occasions. Shantanu's torment grew stronger each time. Still, he said nothing.

When his queen gave birth to an eighth boy and carried the baby to the river, Shantanu followed. As she was about to cast the newborn into the water, he could no longer restrain himself. "Stop!" he cried. "How can you do this? Murderer! Great is the weight of your sins!"

She paused and turned to him. "Very well, O King, this one shall not drown. I have lived happily with you for all these years, but by our agreement, I shall now leave you. First, however, I should tell you who I am, and why I have acted as I have. I am Ganga, the deity of this river.

"Your sons were the incarnations of eight celestial beings. They had committed a crime against the great rishi Vasishtha, who cursed them to incarnate on Earth. They begged me to give them birth and then help them return quickly to Heaven. I agreed to take human form and do that as your wife.

"However, one of those eight celestials was the main perpetrator of the crime, and Vasishtha cursed him to live a long life in a human form. This eighth child is that one. He shall be called Devavrata. I now take him with me to Heaven. Farewell, O King." And with those words, she vanished with his infant son.

Shantanu was beside himself with grief. He had lost both his successor and his beloved queen! With his heart as heavy as the earth itself, he slowly returned to Hastinapura.

> The AUM vibration is the eternal divine power that gives birth to and sustains creation. Ganga represents AUM's inward-drawing aspect, which attracts us back toward our home in Spirit — to the degree that we cooperate with it.
>
> This strange episode has a profound esoteric meaning, which we will explore in Supplement 1.

* * * * *

As the years passed, Shantanu's memories of Devavrata and Ganga slowly faded. Then, while hunting near the River Ganga one day, he noticed it was unusually shallow. He glanced upstream and was wonderstruck to see a dam where none had existed before. And it was no earthly dam; only celestial power could have created it.

Near the dam, he saw a young boy who glowed with heavenly radiance. Had he manifested the dam? The boy disappeared the moment he saw Shantanu, who began to suspect that this was his eighth son. He demanded, "O Holy Ganga, show me that child!"

In response, Ganga appeared in a large and beautiful human form, cradling the boy in her right arm. She said, "This excellent child is our eighth son, Devavrata. He has studied the Vedas with sage Vasishtha, as well as with Vrihaspati, the guru of the Devas. He became a mighty warrior under the training of the great warrior rishi, Parashurama. And he is fully conversant with all the duties of a ruler. Take him, O King, for he is yours." She then set the boy down and vanished.

Shantanu was thrilled. His successor had returned! With great joy, he took Devavrata back to Hastinapura and installed him as the Yuvaraja, the heir to the throne.

Devavrata was everything a father could wish for: intelligent, virtuous, courageous, humble, handsome, highly skilled, and utterly devoted to his father. Four years passed as Shantanu enjoyed to the fullest the return of his lost son, the finest son a king could imagine.

. . . . .

One day, Shantanu was hunting along the banks of the River Jamuna when he came upon a maiden of celestial beauty. She immediately captured his heart.

"Who are you?" he asked. "And who is your father?"

She replied humbly, "Sire, my name is Satyavati. My father is the chief of the fishermen."

> Satyavati represents AUM's outward-manifesting aspect: the material universe and its inherent power of *maya* (cosmic illusion). Maya is an intelligent, outward-moving force that strives to make us feel separate from all else and attracted to outward rather than inward fulfillment.

Shantanu went directly to the fisherman chief and asked for Satyavati's hand in marriage.

"I am honored that you ask, O King," said the chief. "I will consent on one condition: You must promise that your first son by my daughter will be your successor to the throne."

Ah, but Devavrata was his successor. He would never consider giving away his beloved son's birthright. With his heart torn by anguish, Shantanu returned to Hastinapura, where he remained deeply depressed for many days. Devavrata repeatedly asked him what was distressing him, but the king would not answer clearly. Finally, Devavrata consulted Shantanu's prime minister, who told him the cause of his father's grief.

Straightaway, Devavrata went to the fisherman chief and said, "O best of men, hear my vow: If my father weds your daughter, her son shall be our king!"

The chief replied, "I do not doubt your sincerity, O Prince. But what about any children you may have? As your lawful heirs, they will surely feel they should rule."

Without hesitation, Devavrata declared, "Then I shall father no children. From this day forth, I take the vow of celibacy."

At those words, celestial beings rained flowers from Heaven upon Devavrata, proclaiming, "Bhishma! Bhishma!" And from that day, he was known as Bhishma, which means "fearsome" or "terrible."

Indeed, that vow would be fearsome for any young man, especially for the sole heir to the Kuru throne.

The chief was delighted, and he readily consented to the marriage. When Shantanu learned what Bhishma had done, he was heartbroken for Bhishma's sake. But he was also deeply grateful for his son's sacrifice. He summoned Bhishma and told him, "My beloved son, in gratitude for your selfless action, I hereby bestow upon you all my good karma in the form of a boon: Death shall never come to you so long as you desire to live."

And that would prove to be a very, *very* long time.

Bhishma represents the universal intelligence that endows all beings with a sense of individuality. On the human level, that is ego consciousness, which Yogananda defined as the soul identified with the body and personality. Ego consciousness is our false sense of separateness from God. Bhishma's boon of never dying until he wished to die symbolizes that we will never "die" to this world — that is, lose that sense of separateness — until we transcend our identification with the body and personality.

The sincere decision to transcend the ego is the beginning of the spiritual path. Then the real work commences. Soul freedom requires overcoming the deeply ingrained habits, tendencies, desires, and karma of countless lifetimes in which we lived for the ego rather than the soul. The task can seem overwhelming, but God will help through His grace, and that grace is a central theme of the Mahabharata.

CHAPTER 2

Generations

SHANTANU AND SATYAVATI HAD TWO SONS. The elder son was named Chitrangada, and the younger was Vichitravirya. Shantanu died while his sons were still young, so Bhishma served as the regent for the throne until Chitrangada came of age and became the Kuru king. Sadly, Chitrangada was killed before he could marry and produce a successor, so his brother, Vichitravirya, became king.

> Chitrangada represents divine *chitta*, which Yogananda translated as "primordial feeling," the bedrock of consciousness. It is Absolute Bliss. Vichitravirya represents divine ego: identification with all creation, not merely the tiny body and personality.
>
> The deaths of Shantanu and Chitrangada symbolize that the divine realities they represent are hidden from us. Supplement 1 offers esoteric interpretations of these and other characters in this chapter.

Bhishma urgently sought wives for Vichitravirya to ensure that the Kuru dynasty would continue. As it happened, the King of Kashi's three beautiful daughters would soon celebrate their wedding. It would be a *swayamvara* wedding, a "ceremony of self-choice," meaning that the three princesses would choose their husbands from among the kings and princes whom their father, the king, had invited.

Would one of them select Vichitravirya as her husband? Bhishma decided to leave nothing to chance: He traveled to Kashi, and while the ceremony was underway, he abducted all three princesses in plain view of everyone.

The other kings and princes were outraged. They immediately took up their weapons and charged off after Bhishma, showering him with arrows as he took the princesses to his chariot. But Parashurama's training had given Bhishma formidable combat skills, and he defeated all his pursuers, then drove off with his three prizes.

As soon as he arrived in Hastinapura, he ordered that preparations be made for the three princesses to marry Vichitravirya. However, the eldest of the three, Amva, went to Bhishma and said, "Sire, I had already decided upon the king of Saubha as my husband, and he wished to have me as his wife. Wise as you are in the ways of dharma, please tell me what I should do."

Bhishma considered her request, then said, "You should do as you wish."

Amva replied, "I wish to go to Saubha and marry him."

"Very well," said Bhishma. "I will arrange for you to be taken to him." And so it was that Amva left Hastinapura.

· · · · ·

Upon reaching Saubha's kingdom, Amva went directly to the royal palace and received an audience. She said, "O King, I offer myself to be your wife if you will have me."

But Saubha was cold to her. "I will never accept a woman who was promised to another, especially not after she has been abducted. Leave me!"

Brokenhearted and furious, Amva returned to Hastinapura and confronted Bhishma. "You have ruined my life! *You* are obligated to marry me!"

"I cannot, O Princess," said Bhishma. "I must follow dharma. I vowed never to marry, and I will honor that vow."

Amva was enraged. "I *will* have my revenge upon you! That much is certain!"

She searched for a warrior who would avenge her ruined life by killing Bhishma. But none would agree to fight him, for his prowess was well known — as was his boon of never dying until he wished it.

So Amva sought out Bhishma's guru, the renowned warrior and rishi Parashurama, and asked him to help her get satisfaction. He agreed to do so. He journeyed to Hastinapura and confronted his disciple, saying, "Bhishma, as your preceptor, I command you to marry Amva."

Bhishma answered, "Forgive me, Guruji, but I must honor my vow."

Parashurama said, "If you refuse to marry her, I will kill you in combat."

"So be it," Bhishma replied.

They prepared for combat, then began fighting fiercely with consummate skill. They were so closely matched that the day ended with neither having prevailed. They resumed combat the following day and fought all day long, but again, neither was victorious.

They continued fighting for many days, yet neither could vanquish the other. Even though Parashurama was famed for his martial prowess, Bhishma had been a flawless disciple. He had absorbed all his guru's combat knowledge. With that, plus the boon of never dying until he wished for it, he was an unbeatable foe.

Finally, Parashurama had to accept the futility of further combat, and he declared the contest at an end. That infuriated Amva all the more. She could think of only one possible way to get what she longed for: She went to the forest to receive instruction from the monks who lived there. She hoped to learn ascetic practices that would give her the inner power to exact her revenge.

After twelve years of *tapasya*, severe austerities, Lord Shiva appeared to her. "O blessed lady, you shall have the boon that you seek. In your next life, you will kill Bhishma. And you will remember everything from this life, so you will enjoy the satisfaction you seek." Then Shiva vanished.

Amva immediately began gathering firewood and piling it high. Then she set it aflame. Her heart burned with wrath as she climbed atop the blazing pile, saying, "This I do for the destruction of Bhishma!"

*   *   *   *   *

More than twelve years earlier, Amva's two sisters, Amvika and Amvalika, had married Vichitravirya.

> Amvika represents negative doubt: intellect used to negate rather than understand. Amvalika represents the positive discriminating faculty: intellect used to deepen one's understanding. Yogananda did not attribute a quality to Amva.

Vichitravirya and his two wives were ideal partners. They lived together in perfect harmony and love. Under King Vichitravirya, the Kuru people enjoyed an idyllic period of peace and happiness.

But seven years after they married, tragedy struck: Vichitravirya, who had always been the very picture of health and vitality, contract-ed a dread disease and died—without having fathered children. So once again, Bhishma took on the burden of guiding the kingdom that had no king.

> Vichitravirya's passing symbolizes that divine ego is hidden from us. Rather than feeling ourselves one with all creation — which is the truth of our being — we identify with the tiny body and personality, symbolized by Bhishma once again becoming the interim king.
>
> Our human ego is not solely responsible for the feeling of sep-arateness that we experience. Maya strives to reinforce that feeling by keeping us fascinated by the endless variety of the outer world. Those two forces — one personal, the other universal — keep us identified with the body and personality.

With no heir to the throne, the great Kuru dynasty was in dan-ger of dying out, so Satyavati summoned Bhishma. "My son, the scriptures say that a king's royal lineage may continue through his widow and brother. You owe it to your ancestors to continue the Kuru line."

Bhishma replied, "Mother, I must follow dharma by holding to my vow of celibacy. However, the scriptures also declare that a high-souled Brahmin may continue the line through the widow."

Satyavati immediately thought of her other son, Vyasa, a Brahmin born before she met Shantanu. His father was Parashara; like his fa-ther, Vyasa was a great rishi and forest ascetic.

> Vyasa represents the consciousness of relativity, the power to "see through" the seeming diversity of this world and perceive the un-derlying unity of God's consciousness. He was both a character in the story and the author of the Mahabharata.

Satyavati summoned Vyasa and said, "My son, the Kuru lineage is in peril. You must continue it through the widows of my dear Vichitravirya."

"Very well, Mother," he replied. "First, the princesses should puri-fy themselves by observing for one full year the vow I shall give them."

"There is no time for that!" Satyavati exclaimed. "We must have a king, else the kingdom will perish!"

Vyasa replied, "Then they must be purified through a different austerity." He reflected briefly, then said, "I think that enduring my ugliness and odor will be austerity enough. Yes, let us proceed."

Vyasa was indeed ugly and unkempt. He rarely bathed, he wore only rags, and he smeared his body daily with ashes from the ceremonial fire. Moreover, his eyes blazed with the fearsome heat of many years of tapasya.

Satyavati arranged for Vyasa to come first to Amvika, the elder of the two princesses. His repulsive appearance, horrid odor, and fierce gaze caused her to close her eyes in revulsion and fear. She did not reopen them until he had departed.

Afterward, Vyasa told Satyavati, "She shall bring forth a son with great intelligence and the strength of ten thousand elephants, and he shall father one hundred sons. However, because she closed her eyes during our meeting, he shall be blind. His name shall be Dhritarashtra."

Satyavati gasped. "A blind man can never be a king! How could he protect his people? You must give the Kurus another son through Amvalika!"

So Vyasa went to Amvalika. She grew pale with fear when she saw him, but she kept her eyes open. Afterward, Vyasa told Satyavati, "She shall bear a son of pale complexion. His name shall be Pandu."

After Amvika gave birth to the blind child, Satyavati asked her to be with Vyasa again to produce another child. Amvika could not refuse her mother-in-law's request, but neither could she bear having to endure Vyasa's dreadful presence again. So she sent a maidservant to Vyasa in her place.

The maidservant was the very picture of decorum, which pleased Vyasa greatly. He blessed her, saying, "On account of your noble conduct, you shall no longer be a servant, and your son will be the most intelligent man on earth."

In time, a child was born to the maidservant. He was named Vidura. He, too, was considered a son of Vichitravirya, but because his mother was of a low caste, he was not in line for the throne.

Dhritarashtra represents what Yogananda called "blind mind" or "sense-mind" — that part of our awareness that receives sensory data and relays it to the intellect. However, it cannot discern what that data means, and it is easily swayed by the lure — and longtime habit — of sense indulgence.

Pandu represents discriminating intellect, the ability to understand what the senses perceive, differentiate right from wrong, and choose a course of action. Yogananda did not attribute a quality to the youngest of the three princes, Vidura.

Bhishma ruled as the regent for the throne as the three Kuru princes grew up. He raised them as though they were his sons, and they grew into fine young men, well-versed in the Vedas and many other subjects. Dhritarashtra was the strongest of all men, Pandu excelled everyone in archery, and in all the world, Vidura had no equal in devotion to dharma.

The Kuru kingdom flourished, the earth yielded a bountiful harvest, and the citizens adhered to dharma. Many people from other realms came to dwell among the Kurus. It was a time of great happiness and harmony.

By this time, Bhishma had become widely revered as the grandfather, not only of the three princes but of the entire Kuru people. Many called him by that title out of respect, even though he had fathered no children. He lived as though the only purpose of his life was the continuation of the Kuru lineage.

So it is with us: As long as we live in ego consciousness (symbolized by Bhishma), we think life's purpose is to cater to the body and personality. We do not try to realize our inherent oneness with God. In fact, we are not sure that is even possible.

When Pandu reached manhood, he became king of the Kurus, for although Dhritarashtra was the eldest prince, ancient custom dictated that a blind man could not be a proper king.

To ensure that the Kuru lineage would continue, Bhishma found wives for King Pandu and his brothers. He arranged for Dhritarashtra to marry Princess Gandhari of the northern hill country (modern Afghanistan). Bhishma had heard that Lord Shiva had given her the boon that she would have one hundred sons, which Vyasa had also predicted for Dhritarashtra. It was therefore a perfect match that would ensure the continuity of the Kuru lineage.

When Gandhari learned that her future husband was blind, she blindfolded herself so she would not appear superior to him. She wore a blindfold for the rest of her life. For that tapasya, she acquired much ascetic merit, which she would spend many years later in dramatic fashion.

Pandu married two princesses from separate kingdoms. The elder's name was Kunti, and she chose Pandu as her husband in her swayamvara. The younger princess was Madri. Bhishma secured her for Pandu through a combination of Kuru might (he marched his entire army to the gates of her city) and wealth (he gave Madri's brother, the king, vast riches in exchange for her hand). Shortly after that, Bhishma also obtained a wife for Vidura.

> Dhritarashtra's wife, Gandhari, represents the power of desire. Pandu's elder wife, Kunti, represents dispassion, the ability not to get caught up in emotional reactions. His other wife, Madri, represents attachment to dispassion. Swami Kriyananda pointed out that dispassion differs from attachment to dispassion in the degree of ego involvement. In attachment to dispassion, there is the feeling "I am dispassionate." Without such attachment, there is dispassion but no self-identification with it. One simply is dispassionate.

Immediately after his two marriages, Pandu led a mighty army on a military campaign that brought many other kingdoms under the sway of the Kuru throne. He was a warrior, with no taste for the administrative duties of a king. So he arranged for his blind brother, Dhritarashtra, to administer the kingdom, with Vidura as his chief advisor. Pandu then took his two wives to live in the forest for a time. There he could pursue his favorite pastime: hunting.

One day, while Pandu was hunting, tragedy again struck the Kuru kingdom. He came upon a large buck that was mating with a doe. He quickly pierced the buck with five arrows, and it fell to the ground with a human cry of anguish. After a few moments, it spoke to Pandu: "How could you, who are of such a noble and virtuous race, allow your passion for the hunt to so cloud your judgment that you would commit this crime?"

Pandu replied, "Clearly, you are no ordinary deer. But what I have done is not a crime. Hunting is what kings do."

The buck answered, "I do not fault you for slaying a deer—not even in this case, where the deer is myself, a rishi who has taken the form of a deer for sport. I fault you for violating all morality by shooting a deer engaged in the sacred act of union. Through my many years of tapasya, I have gained some spiritual power. I shall use it by placing a curse upon you: Just as I will now die, having been on the verge of physical ecstasy, so too will you die if ever you engage in sexual union."

With a final gasp, the buck collapsed in death.

Pandu was horror-stricken. Not only would sexual pleasure be forever denied him, but he did not yet have a successor to the throne. The Kuru dynasty was once again in peril.

Deep in despair, he lost all taste for worldly pleasure, power, and wealth. He returned to their encampment and declared to his wives, "I shall live the remainder of my life as a forest ascetic. You should return to Hastinapura and live out your lives there."

Kunti and Madri, however, would have none of it. Kunti said, "If you abandon us, O King, then we shall this very day abandon our bodies and depart from this world."

Pandu had to relent. The three of them gave their servants all their possessions, including their costly garments and jewels, to be taken back to Hastinapura and given to charity.

They then embarked upon their new lives. After living with every privilege and comfort, they would now live as wanderers, exposed to the elements and subsisting on the fruits of the forest and Pandu's hunting.

The graphic "Kuru Generations — Part 1" shows the genealogy described so far.

Kuru Generations—Part 1

The qualities that the characters represent are in italics.

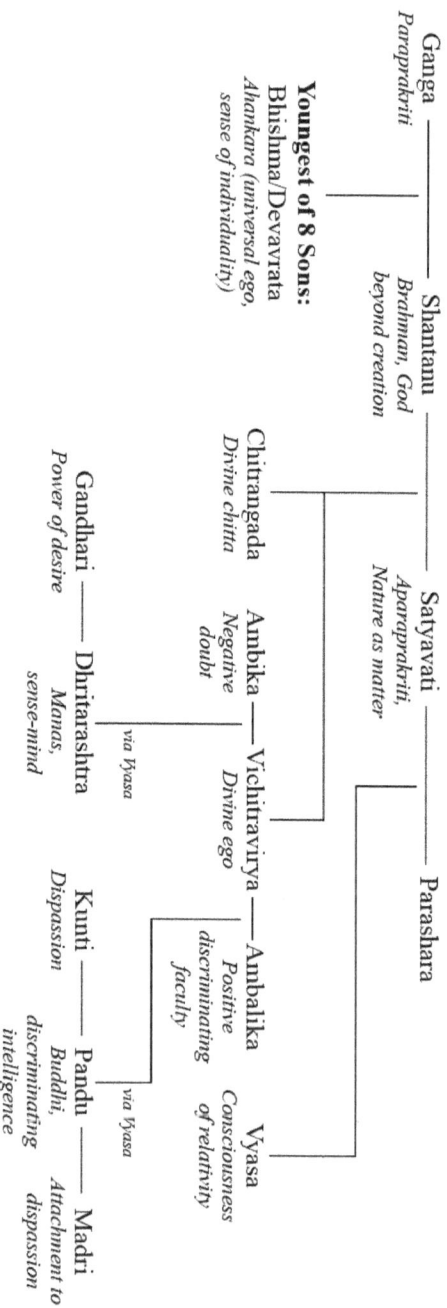

Ganga
Paraprakriti
— **Shantanu**
*Brahman, God
beyond creation*
— **Satyavati**
*Aparaprakriti,
Nature as matter*
— **Parashara**

Youngest of 8 Sons:
Bhishma/Devavrata
*Ahankara (universal ego,
sense of individuality)*

Chitrangada
Divine chitta

Ambika — **Vichitravirya** — **Ambalika**
*Negative   Divine ego   Positive
doubt   discriminating
                                faculty*

Vyasa
*Consciousness
of relativity*

via Vyasa

Gandhari — **Dhritarashtra**
*Power of desire   Manas,
                      sense-mind*

Kunti — **Pandu** — **Madri**
*Dispassion   Buddhi,   Attachment to
               discriminating dispassion
               intelligence*

via Vyasa

CHAPTER 3

Seeds of Destiny

Pandu was still the Kuru king, yet his new life was anything but royal. He, Kunti, and Madri roamed far and wide as forest ascetics. However, they lived much more comfortably than other ascetics, because many great rishis used their spiritual powers to provide them with invisible support and protection.

As time passed, Pandu even grew to enjoy this simple life. Still, one thing troubled him greatly: He had no son, no successor to the Kuru throne. That was as unfortunate for him as for his kingdom, for tradition declared that a man without sons could not attain Heaven. And due to the rishi's curse, he could not father a son without dying.

However, the other forest rishis assured him that he was fated to have offspring, and they urged him to think of how he would accomplish that. Reflecting on his own parentage, he realized that if his wives had sons by other men, he would nevertheless be considered their father. So he approached Kunti: "Beloved wife, I ask that you continue the royal lineage by being with some high-souled Brahmin."

She replied, "I am devoted to you alone, O King. I could not bear the thought of being with another man."

He repeatedly tried to persuade her—to no avail. But in her eagerness to please him, she remembered a possible solution. She said to him: "Many years ago, when I was a young princess in my home kingdom, the great rishi Durvasa visited us for a time, and I served him during his stay. He was an extraordinarily difficult guest, and he did many wrong things that could have upset me. But I refused to get angry; I simply served him with patience and respect. In gratitude for my service, he insisted on giving me a boon: He initiated me into a mantra that would enable me to have children with any of the Devas. O King, shall I summon one of the gods?"

Pandu was thrilled: Here was the solution to continuing his lineage! He asked her to invoke Dharma, the god of righteousness. She did so, and the Deva came to her. Later, when a son was born, a voice from the heavens proclaimed: "This child shall be the foremost of all virtuous persons. He shall live only for Truth, and he will rule the earth. His name shall be 'Yudhisthira.'"

A year passed, and Pandu told Kunti, "The wise say that a Kshatriya must be extraordinarily strong, else he is not a Kshatriya. Therefore, I ask that you use your mantra to bear a son of great strength."

So Kunti invoked Vayu, the god of the wind, the mightiest of the Devas. When a son was born, a voice from the sky declared, "This child shall grow to be the strongest of all men." They named the boy Bhima.

Pandu wanted a son to be fathered by Indra, the chief of the Devas. He asked Kunti to prepare for that by observing an auspicious vow for one year while he practiced many severe austerities. Their efforts bore fruit when a third son was born through Indra. Once again, a heavenly voice rang out: "This child shall stand supreme among all warriors. He will vanquish all foes and win great fame." They named him Arjuna.

Pandu wanted even more sons, but Kunti declined. She felt it would be immoral for her to be with anyone other than Pandu for a fourth time, even if it were a Deva. Now Pandu's younger wife, Madri, saw her opportunity. She was jealous of Kunti, for she had no children. So Madri asked Pandu to ask Kunti to use the mantra on her behalf.

Kunti was quite willing, and after reciting the mantra, she told Madri to bring to mind some Deva who would father a child. Madri thought of the twin Aswin gods, the gods of healing. When she gave birth to twin sons, a voice from the sky declared, "In energy and beauty, these boys shall transcend even the twin Aswins."

Their names were Nakula and Sahadeva. Nakula would become known for his beauty, and Sahadeva would be renowned for his wisdom.

Soon afterward, Pandu said to Kunti, "I ask that you use the mantra again, that Madri may deliver more children."

"O King," she replied, "Madri deceived me by invoking two Devas instead of only one. If she uses the mantra again, I fear she will soon have more children than I have. That is the way of all wicked women. I beg of you, do not ask this of me."

Pandu decided to remain content with five sons. And they were exceptional sons: handsome, strong, and virtuous, and their bodies bore every auspicious mark. Although fathered by Devas, they were considered Pandu's sons, so they were known as the Pandavas.

> Yudhisthira represents calmness in psychological battle. Bhima represents vitality. Arjuna symbolizes fiery self-control. Nakula corresponds to *niyama,* the power to channel one's energy in spiritually beneficial ways. Sahadeva symbolizes *yama,* the ability to refrain from acting in self-harmful ways.

. . . . .

Meanwhile, in the Kuru capital city of Hastinapura, Dhritarashtra and Gandhari had also brought forth children: one hundred sons and one daughter. This was the fulfillment of the boon that Lord Shiva had promised Gandhari years earlier. It also fulfilled Vyasa's prediction at Dhritarashtra's birth.

However, those children were born inauspiciously. Gandhari had conceived a full year before Yudhisthira was born, but her pregnancy lasted so long that Kunti delivered first. That so upset Gandhari that she violently struck her own abdomen. Out came a mass of flesh as hard as a ball of iron. Rishi Vyasa perceived the unusual birth through his spiritual sight. He rushed to her, crying, "What have you done?!"

Gandhari explained, "I could not bear that Kunti gave birth before I did, and in my grief, I struck at my womb." She looked with anguish at the mass of flesh and said, "Here is the fulfillment of my great boon: a ball of hardened flesh instead of one hundred sons."

Vyasa said, "Call for one hundred and one pots of ghee. Sprinkle cool water on this ball of flesh and divide it into one hundred and one parts, each the size of a thumb. Place each part in a pot and cover the pot. Keep all of them in a concealed place, and after one year, open the pots."

Gandhari followed Vyasa's directions, and at the end of that year, those pots contained one hundred boys and one girl. The first boy was brought out on the same day as Bhima, the second oldest Pandava, was born. He immediately began to cry and bray like an ass. Vultures, jackals, and crows also cried out. Violent winds began to blow. Fires erupted in the distance. Dhritarashtra became greatly alarmed, and he summoned Bhishma and Vidura.

He said, "Yudhisthira is by right the next king, having been born first. We cannot say otherwise. But what about my son? Shall he be the king after Yudhisthira?"

Again, jackals and other carnivores began to howl, and many frightful omens appeared.

Vidura said, "From these omens, I see that this boy shall be the exterminator of the Kuru people. You must not let him live. You will still have ninety-nine sons. You must do what is best for the world and cast him off."

But Dhritarashtra could not bring himself to abandon his first-born son, and he named the boy Duryodhana. Within a month, ninety-nine other sons and one daughter were born. Those one hundred sons were known as the Kauravas.

> Duryodhana represents material desire, the natural result of the union of sense-mind (Dhritarashtra) and the power of desire (Gandhari).
>
> The second oldest son was Dushasana. He represents anger, ever the close companion of desire because it tends to arise whenever desire is frustrated.
>
> Years later, in the Bhagavad Gita, Arjuna would ask Krishna, "What compels us to do wrong, even against our will?"
>
> Krishna would reply: "It is desire; it is anger. Know these to be mankind's greatest enemies." (Gita 3:36–37)
>
> The remaining ninety-eight sons correspond to ninety-eight other negative qualities, such as greed, jealousy, selfishness, and judgment. Those qualities bring only misery and keep us from knowing we are the soul. Yogananda did not suggest a quality for the daughter, Dussala, who plays only a minor role in the story.

· · · · ·

So the two sets of Kuru princes began to grow up. The Kauravas lived in the luxurious palace of Hastinapura, while their cousins, the five Pandavas, led a simple life in the forest.

Pandu's five sons gave him fresh enthusiasm for life. One fine spring day, he and Madri were roaming the woods together, enjoying the vitality of the forest as it came back to life after the winter. Madri was beautiful, and her clothing was revealing. The fire of desire sprang up within Pandu and soon overpowered him. He forgot about the rishi's curse and began to force himself upon her. Madri remembered the curse and resisted his advances. But she could not push him away, and soon he was dead.

Madri began to wail in grief, and upon hearing her, Kunti and the five boys ran toward where Madri and Pandu lay. As they approached, Madri called out, "Kunti, come here, but keep the children there." When Kunti saw what had happened, she, too, began to wail. "Madri, I have been watching over our husband to ensure this would not happen. How could you tempt him when you should have been protecting him?"

Madri replied through her tears, "I begged him not to do it, but he could not control himself."

After some time, Kunti calmed down and said, "As the elder wife, I shall follow our lord to the realms of the dead. Take care of our children, Madri."

Madri replied, "I should be the one to follow him to Heaven, as this calamity is my fault. Besides, I know that you could raise my two sons as your own, but I could never raise your three sons as my own. Please stay and be the mother of all five of them."

Kunti yielded to Madri's argument. Together, Pandu's wives and sons built a funeral pyre. Then Madri set it afire and joined her dead husband in the flames.

· · · · ·

The forest rishis advised Kunti to move with her sons to Hastinapura, and they accompanied the family on the journey. The citizens and Kuru elders eagerly came out of the city to greet the rishis. The holy men told everyone of Pandu's death, introduced the five boys, and explained their unusual births. They declared, "Receive these boys with due honor as the sons of King Pandu." Then the rishis vanished.

The elders and citizens performed the funeral rites for Pandu and Madri, then passed twelve days of mourning along with Kunti and the Pandavas. All the while, Bhishma grew increasingly depressed, for the Kuru dynasty had once again suffered a severe blow—and as before, the burden of leadership rested squarely on his shoulders.

Soon after the mourning period ended, Vyasa sought out Satyavati. "Mother," he said, "our days of happiness have ended. Sin is increasing by the day. Deceit and wrong will prevail. Do not stay to witness the annihilation of your people. Retire to the forest, and devote yourself to meditation."

Satyavati understood, and she began making arrangements to leave Hastinapura. When Amvika and Amvalika learned of her plans—and of Vyasa's dire prediction—they decided to join her. Together, the three mothers departed to live out the remainder of their lives in simplicity in the forest, far removed from what was to come.

> Vyasa's prediction speaks to us as well. Recall that Pandu represents discriminating intellect while Dhritarashtra represents the sense-mind. As long as we have both, we can get along in life for a time — but only "for a time" because both are faculties of the conscious mind, which can be led astray all too easily by desire and emotion. As Yogananda often warned, "Reason follows feeling."
>
> Indeed, passion led Pandu to his death, and soul intuition remains hidden from us (represented by Chitrangada's death years earlier). Our inner kingdom then relies only on sense-mind (Dhritarashtra) and ego (Bhishma). That is not merely a shaky situation; it is a recipe for disaster, as Vyasa pointed out in warning Satyavati. Supplement 1 elaborates on this point.

Kuru Generations—Part 2

The qualities that the characters represent are in italics.

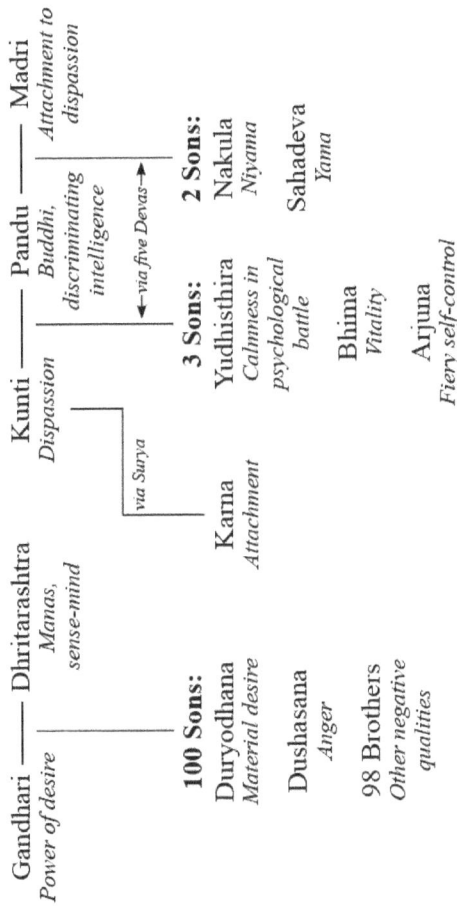

Gandhari ——— Dhritarashtra
Power of desire   *Manas, sense-mind*

Kunti ——— Pandu ——— Madri
Dispassion   *Buddhi, discriminating intelligence*   *Attachment to dispassion*

via Surya

←via five Devas→

100 Sons:
Duryodhana
Material desire

Dushasana
Anger

98 Brothers
Other negative qualities

Karna
Attachment

3 Sons:
Yudhisthira
Calmness in psychological battle

Bhima
Vitality

Arjuna
Fiery self-control

2 Sons:
Nakula
Niyama

Sahadeva
Yama

CHAPTER 4

Dawn of Conflict

AFTER KING PANDU DIED, his blind older brother, Dhritarashtra, became the acting king. Custom dictated that he would serve in that role until Pandu's eldest son, Yudhisthira, came of age and ascended the throne. Dhritarashtra welcomed the Pandavas to the palace, and they began to live alongside the Kauravas as proper princes of the Kuru dynasty.

The cousins often played games together, and as will happen with young boys, an intense rivalry soon developed. The Pandavas were always superior, especially Bhima, who was bigger, stronger, and faster than any of the Kauravas. Even as a young boy, he was very broad-shouldered and much taller than the other Kuru princes. And his appetite for food was staggering.

He was also mischievous. He loved to show off his strength by tormenting his cousins. He would sometimes hold two of them by the hair, one in each massive hand, and smash them together as though they were fighting. Or he would throw them to the ground and drag them through the dirt. Or he might hold their heads underwater until they nearly drowned. If some of the Kauravas climbed a tree to pick fruit, Bhima would kick the tree so hard that both the fruit and the Kauravas would fall to the ground. Always, he would laugh uproariously, even when he had injured his cousins. Bhima meant no harm — to him, it was merely childish mischief, pranks done without any feelings of malice.

But the eldest Kaurava, Duryodhana, *did* feel malice toward Bhima — not only because of this "mischief," but also because he saw Bhima as the main obstacle between himself and someday being king. Yes, Yudhisthira was the rightful heir to the throne. But Duryodhana was sure that if he could kill Bhima, it would be easy to dispose of the other four Pandavas — and seize the throne for himself.

Was it Bhima's size and strength that made him the main obstacle for Duryodhana? Yes, in part, but Bhima's physical prowess in the story is much less important than the quality he represents: vitality. The positive qualities represented by the other four Pandavas — calmness, self-control, niyama, and yama — can uplift consciousness only when we vitalize them. Unless we put abundant energy into expressing those qualities, the momentum of lifetimes of material desires (represented by Duryodhana) will rule our lives.

While the Kuru princes were still relatively young, Gandhari's younger brother, Shakuni, came to live in the palace. Shakuni had utter disregard for virtue, and he hungered for power within the Kuru court. He quickly realized that Duryodhana's jealousy and greed presented an opportunity to employ his evil means to gain such influence. So he befriended Duryodhana and soon became his closest ally and advisor.

Shakuni represents material attachment. He was the mastermind behind all the scheming that Duryodhana and others would do over the coming years. In the same way, worldly attachment is the stimulus behind material desire.

For their first plot against the Pandavas, Duryodhana and Shakuni arranged for Kuru laborers to build a small palace on the banks of the Ganga. When the palace was complete, Duryodhana approached Yudhisthira and said, "There is a beautiful new water-sport palace alongside the Ganga, not far from here. It has many excellent amusements. Let us all go there today to play in the water and enjoy the palace!"

Yudhisthira replied unsuspectingly, "We would be happy to go with you."

So all the Kuru princes mounted horses, elephants, and chariots, then rode out to the new palace. When they arrived, servants provided a sumptuous meal. The boys had great fun feeding each other and laughing. Duryodhana insisted on feeding Bhima, for he had mixed a deadly poison into Bhima's usual large portion of food. After eating, the boys played in the water until they were exhausted. Then, they all lay down for a nap in the palace garden.

Bhima quickly slipped into unconsciousness. When everyone else was asleep, Duryodhana got up and bound Bhima with vines from nearby plants. He then took hold of Bhima's feet, dragged him to the river's edge, and rolled him into the water. Bhima quickly sank out of sight, and Duryodhana happily returned to his nap.

Bhima continued to sink through the Ganga's waters, down and down, until he entered the kingdom of the snake-people. There, legions of poisonous snakes attacked and bit him all over his body. But by good luck, the snakes' poison was an antidote for the poison that Duryodhana had put in Bhima's food, and Bhima soon woke up. He quickly burst his bonds and fought off the snakes, who fled for their lives.

Happily, one of the snake-people was Kunti's great-grandfather. He embraced Bhima with love, then convinced the snake king to welcome Bhima with honor and allow him to drink from a pot of special nectar that would bestow the strength of a thousand elephants. Bhima drank and drank, emptying not only that pot but nine more as well. The snakes then prepared an excellent bed for him, and he lay down and fell into a deep sleep.

*   *   *   *   *

Back at the water-sport palace, when the other boys awakened, Yudhisthira looked around and said, "I do not see Bhima. Has anyone seen him?"

No one had seen him. The four Pandavas searched the palace, inside and out, but they found no trace of him. Yudhisthira said to the others, "He must have returned to Hastinapura. Let us go home as well."

When they arrived and discovered that Bhima was not at the Hastinapura palace, they began to worry. Kunti summoned Vidura and told him, "It is that wicked Duryodhana—I am sure of it. He hates Bhima."

Vidura hushed her. "Do not say that to anyone! If you accuse him, he may try to slay your other four sons. But do not worry; Bhima will return. Rishi Vyasa has said that all your sons will live long lives."

Bhima slept in the snake kingdom for eight days. When he awoke, he had the strength of ten thousand elephants. He had, after all, drunk ten pots of the nectar. Bhima saluted the snake-people and received their blessings. Then, they brought him back up from their realm to the garden of the water-sport palace. Bhima immediately ran all the way to Hastinapura, where he had a joyful reunion with his mother and brothers. He told them, "This was Duryodhana's doing. I am certain of it."

Yudhisthira said, "You may be right, brother, but we cannot accuse him without proof. From now on, we must be *very vigilant.*"

. . . . .

Soon after the episode of the water-sport palace, Duryodhana again poisoned Bhima's food. But Yuyutsu, Dhritarashtra's son by a Vaishya wife, was fond of the Pandavas, and he warned Bhima not to eat it.

Yuyutsu represents the desire to give psychological battle.

Bhima ignored the warning and happily ate the poisoned food. He was unaffected. Seeing this, Duryodhana and Shakuni resorted to other means of killing the Pandavas. But every attempt failed, often due to warnings from Vidura, who had eyes and ears all over Hastinapura.

Despite the continuing attempts on their lives, Vidura advised the Pandavas, "Say nothing. You are young, and you have few allies in the court. Without proof of Duryodhana's involvement, it would be unwise to make accusations against the eldest son of the acting king."

Meanwhile, Dhritarashtra had begun to notice increasing idleness and misbehavior among his sons and their cousins, so he decided it was time for them to receive formal training. He called upon sage Kripa, a Kuru elder well-versed in the Vedas and highly skilled with weapons. With Kripa as their teacher, the Kuru princes began training as proper Kshatriyas.

Kripa represents delusion, ignorance of what is real. Why, then, did Dhritarashtra choose him as the princes' teacher? Remember, the blind mind (represented by Dhritarashtra) does not have discrimination. Kripa was a respected elder with much knowledge and keen loyalty to the Kuru throne, so to blind mind, he would be a natural choice.

. . . . .

One day, the Kuru princes were playing outdoors with a ball when it fell into a well. As they milled about, trying to think of how to retrieve it, a lean and somewhat decrepit-looking Brahmin approached them. His clothing was ragged, and his hair and beard were long and white.

He asked, "What is the problem, young princes?"

They pointed to the well. "Our ball fell in, and we do not know how to get it out."

"Shame on your Kshatriya prowess!" the Brahmin scolded. "How is it that you cannot recover that ball? If you promise to give me dinner, I will retrieve it for you, using only the blades of grass that you see growing here."

The boys could not imagine how the grass could serve such a purpose. Yet they were eager to see whether he could make good on his claim, so they quickly promised him the meal.

The Brahmin plucked a long blade of grass, then closed his eyes and, with deep concentration, recited a mantra that infused the blade with celestial power. It became as rigid as a spear. The Brahmin opened his eyes and threw that spear to the bottom of the well, where it pierced the ball. That impressed the boys.

The Brahmin then infused a second blade with celestial power and threw it into the well, where it pierced the end of the first blade. That impressed the boys even more. He did the same with a third blade, then a fourth, and many more blades to form a chain. Once the chain was long enough, he easily pulled the ball out of the well.

The boys were speechless with awe.

The Brahmin next threw his ring into the well, picked up a bow, and shot an arrow through the ring. Then, through seeming magic, he recalled that arrow from the bottom of the well with the ring still around its shaft. The amazed boys clustered around him, babbling in admiration.

He said, "Find Bhishma. Describe me to him. Tell him of my skill. He will know who I am."

The boys rushed to tell the grandfather what had happened. Hearing this, Bhishma smiled, for he realized that the Brahmin could only be the illustrious Drona. And Drona was no ordinary Brahmin; he was also a famous warrior. It was rare for a Brahmin to engage in combat; it was even rarer for a Brahmin to be renowned for his warrior prowess. But like Bhishma, Drona had been a disciple of the famous Brahmin rishi and warrior Parashurama, who had given him knowledge of all weapons, including the astras, the magical celestial weapons.

> What are astras? Although most often used as weapons in this tale, they are not physical objects and are not always used as weapons. They are intelligent forces of nature. One invokes an astra by repeating its particular mantra with high energy, deep concentration, and intuitive attunement with the astra's unique qualities. In that way, one can infuse the astra's power into any desired object, transforming it into a weapon, a tool, or any number of other manifestations. One can even use astras to create things that have not previously existed.

> There is an astra that enables one to manifest fire out of thin air. Another astra can make rain fall from a cloudless sky. A third can cause powerful winds to blow. A fourth can put an entire army to sleep. Yet another astra can multiply a single ordinary weapon into countless similar weapons and shower destruction upon the foe. As a young boy, Bhishma had used an astra to dam the River Ganga. There are many other astras as well. Anyone trained in using astras is a formidable warrior!

> Astras may seem fanciful, but great spiritual masters have long used such powers to perform seemingly miraculous deeds. They can cure diseases, travel instantly from one place to another, know the future, raise the dead, or exercise various other powers. Such masters are simply working with natural laws that very few people understand.

Although Kripa was a capable teacher of both the Vedas and the science of weaponry, Bhishma wanted the Kuru princes to receive the very best training, and he was confident that Drona would provide it. Drona could even teach the science of astras to those with sufficient energy, dedication, receptivity, and intuitive understanding.

So Bhishma arranged for Drona to live in Hastinapura and train the princes. He gave Drona, his wife, and his son, Aswatthama, a spacious home filled with beautiful furnishings and expensive gifts.

It was a new reality for Drona, who had always been poor. He had been unable even to afford a cow so the young Aswatthama could drink milk. Years earlier, the boy's playmates had once added rice flour to water, making a drink that looked like milk. Aswatthama drank it and danced for joy, exclaiming, "I have drunk milk!" His playmates had smiled at the boy's simplicity, but Drona had been ashamed.

Now, those days of lack were gone, and Drona had the comfort, wealth, and prestige he had long yearned for. But he wanted one more thing, and he hoped that his position as guru of the Kuru princes would bring it to him.

> Drona represents the quality of habit. Just as he would train the Pandavas and Kauravas, habit trains both our positive and negative tendencies. Any action we repeat — even a thought or emotion — becomes a habit, regardless of whether it leads us toward or away from greater happiness. As Yogananda said, "Every action leaves a trace in the subconscious mind, and tends to repeat itself until it becomes a formidable, automatically performing habit."
>
> Clearly, we should choose our thoughts and actions carefully.

CHAPTER 5

The Way of a Disciple

D RONA BEGAN THE TRAINING BY calling together the Kuru
princes and making a strong demand of his new disciples: "I
have in my heart a deep desire. Promise me, as your guru, that you
will accomplish it when you have become skilled in combat."

All the princes remained silent, reluctant to commit to an unknown task — except Arjuna, who immediately said: "I will accomplish it, Guruji, whatever it may be!" Drona embraced Arjuna and
wept for joy, thinking of the long-awaited triumph he was now sure
would come.

The Kuru princes lived with Drona as a *gurukula*, the guru's extended family. With his disciples constantly under his watchful eye,
Drona could assess each one's aptitude, character, motivations, and
receptivity. That enabled him to discern the next step in the disciple's
growth, and how to help him take that step.

Although the training included the Vedas, statecraft, and other
subjects essential for a Kshatriya prince, the main focus was weaponry and combat — many a young boy's natural fascination, and a
necessity for any Kshatriya. Drona taught his disciples how to fight
with various weapons: bow and arrow, spear, sword, dart, and mace,
which was a heavy metal club with one end shaped like a large ball.
They learned how to fight on the ground, on horseback, and in a
chariot. Drona also taught his more accomplished disciples how to
use certain astras.

From the start, Arjuna's dedication was absolute. He was always
by Drona's side, eager to learn and ready to do whatever his guru
asked. His self-discipline and perseverance surpassed that of all his
fellow disciples.

> Self-discipline and perseverance can seem dull and unenjoyable.
> However, Paramhansa Yogananda called self-control "a spiritual busi-
> ness proposition calculated to bring the greatest happiness to man.

> Once self-control ripens, the soul begins to experience finer, happier perceptions, and enjoy itself far more than when it lived identified with sense pleasures."
>
> Of perseverance, he urged, "As often as you fail, get up and try again. God will never let you down, so long as you make the effort."

Drona was partial to his son, Aswatthama. He wanted to give certain advanced teachings to him—and *only* to him.

> Aswatthama represents the power of attraction. Drona's love for his son reflects that a habit is sustained by our attraction to its fruits. Without that underlying attraction, the habit would not persist.

For example, Drona would sometimes give each of his disciples a pot and a simple task: "Go to the river and fill your pot with water, then return to me." He would give Aswatthama a pot with a wide neck, whereas the other disciples' pots had very narrow necks. Aswatthama could fill his pot quickly and rejoin the guru, but it took the others much longer. Drona used the interval before the others returned to instruct his son in superior combat techniques.

Arjuna soon realized what was happening, but he did not complain about the guru's partiality. Instead, he invoked the Varuna astra, sacred to Lord Varuna, the god of all waters. That astra gave him control over water and enabled him to fill his pot as quickly as Aswatthama filled his. He then returned to Drona and received the same training as Aswatthama in superior combat techniques.

As another example of Drona's favoritism, he wanted to train Aswatthama—again, *only* Aswatthama—to fight in the dark. He told the cook, "Never give Arjuna food at night," fearing that if Arjuna ate in relative darkness, he might discover on his own the art of night combat.

Some days later, while Arjuna was eating dinner by the light of a lamp, a sudden breeze extinguished the flame. Nevertheless, from habit, he continued eating normally. That made him think, "If I can eat in the dark, surely I can shoot an arrow in the dark." So he began practicing at night.

But unlike eating, habit alone was not enough for success in nighttime archery; he needed to feel intuitively where the target was. And the more he practiced in the dark, the stronger his intuition became.

Night after night, Drona heard the twang of Arjuna's bowstring. He was thrilled by such dedication. One night, while Arjuna was practicing, Drona went to him and embraced him, saying, "Truly, I shall help you become the greatest archer in the world."

He taught Arjuna how to shoot arrows with pinpoint accuracy, and so rapidly that one could barely distinguish one arrow from the next. Drona gave him advanced instruction in the art of fighting on horseback, on the back of an elephant, in a chariot, and on the ground. He even taught Arjuna how to fight using many weapons at once and with many men at the same time. Arjuna was indeed becoming the greatest archer in the world.

> Swami Kriyananda pointed out how archery offers several useful metaphors for meditation. The rounded body of the bow represents the front of the meditator's torso, seen from the side. The bowstring represents a straight spine, which is vital for deep meditation. We aim the "arrow" of our concentration at the target: the spiritual eye, which resembles a modern archery target. When the mind is very calm, we see the spiritual eye in the forehead at the point between the eyebrows: a ring of golden light surrounding a field of deep blue, in the middle of which is a five-pointed, silvery-white star. Arjuna's nighttime practice symbolizes turning away from the distractions of the outer world and diving into the darkness behind closed eyes. As Arjuna discovered with nighttime archery, intuition is essential for deep meditation — and in turn, deep meditation helps us develop intuition.

> Paramhansa Yogananda said, "The best way [to develop intuition] is, every time you meditate, sit calmly for a long time after doing the techniques. It is during this period that you will be able to deepen your awareness of God's presence within you. Go ever deeper in your enjoyment of that presence. The longer and more deeply you enjoy the peace within, the more quickly will your intuition develop."

As time passed, the talents of Drona's other disciples also began to emerge. Yudhisthira became highly skilled in chariot warfare. Bhima and Duryodhana excelled everyone with the mace. Nakula and Sahadeva became expert swordsmen. Aswatthama nearly equaled Arjuna as an archer. Yet Arjuna surpassed everyone, not only in archery, but in overall mastery of the science of weapons.

• • • • •

One day, Drona decided to test his disciples' power of concentration. He placed a wooden bird on a branch high in a tree and told them, "You are to hit the bird with an arrow. Yudhisthira, come here and aim at the target."

Yudhisthira quickly stepped forward and knelt on one knee. He placed an arrow on his bowstring, drew the bow to readiness, and took aim.

Drona asked him, "Do you see the bird?"

"Yes, Guruji, I see the bird," replied Yudhisthira.

Drona asked, "Do you see the tree, myself, or your brothers?"

"Yes, Guruji, I see them all."

"Then move aside!" said Drona. "You cannot succeed. Duryodhana, come here and aim at the target."

When Duryodhana did so, Drona asked him the same questions and received the same answers. Duryodhana, too, had to move aside. It was the same with all the other disciples until finally, Drona commanded, "Arjuna, come here and take aim." Arjuna stepped forward, knelt, and fixed an arrow on his bowstring, then drew the bow and aimed at the target.

Drona asked, "Do you see the bird?"

"Yes, Guruji, I see the bird."

"Do you see the tree, myself, or your brothers?"

"No, Guruji, only the bird."

"Describe the bird to me."

"I see only the head of the bird, Guruji, not the body."

Drona was immensely pleased. He said, "Your concentration is perfect. Shoot!"

Arjuna released the arrow, and it neatly sliced off the head of the bird.

Drona clasped Arjuna to his bosom, thinking his secret desire was as good as fulfilled.

• • • • •

On another occasion, Drona took his disciples to the river. No sooner had he waded into the water than a giant crocodile seized him by the thigh. Although he could have freed himself easily, he called to his disciples, "Help! Rescue me!" While everyone else looked on helplessly, unsure of what to do, Arjuna pierced the crocodile with five arrows before Drona's plea for help faded away. The creature released its hold and rolled over, dead.

Drona embraced Arjuna, then took him aside and said, "I am highly pleased with you. You are my foremost disciple, dearer to me than my own son. I shall give you the Brahma weapon, the most powerful astra of all, and teach you how to launch and withdraw it. It will create an enormous fireball that will consume the very heavens. You must never use this astra against an ordinary human, for it would burn up the entire universe. Use it only against non-human foes."

Arjuna humbly received the weapon and his guru's instructions for its use.

Drona blessed him and said, "No adversary will ever be able to vanquish you, and your achievements will be great."

* * * * *

Reports of Arjuna's impressive skills drew many other kings and princes to Hastinapura to learn the science of arms from Drona. Among them was a young prince named Ekalavya, whose natural talent immediately became evident. But because the boy was of a low caste, Drona would not accept him as a disciple lest he outshine the high-born Kuru princes.

Ekalavya bowed his head in disappointment and departed. But he did not give up his hopes. He made a clay image of Drona in the forest near his home and worshipped it daily. Every day, he practiced archery before the image as though it were his living guru. As time passed, his attunement with Drona grew ever deeper, and he developed great skill as an archer.

One day, while the Kuru princes were hunting in the forest, their dog ran ahead of the group in search of prey. The dog soon came upon Ekalavya, who was dressed in rags and smeared with filth, his hair in matted locks. His appearance was so stark and fearsome that the dog began to bark furiously at him.

In a blur of motion, Ekalavya shot seven arrows that wove a perfect muzzle around the dog's mouth. Whimpering piteously, the dog returned to the Kuru princes, who were astonished to see such skill in archery. They immediately set out to find the person with such mastery.

When they came upon Ekalavya, they asked, "Who are you, and how have you attained such skill?"

"I am Ekalavya, a student of Drona, striving to master the art of archery."

Arjuna felt a sharp pang of jealousy in his heart over Ekalavya's skill. As soon as he returned to Hastinapura, he sought out Drona. "Guruji, you promised to make me the greatest archer in the world, yet this Ekalavya is superior to me."

Drona reflected for a few moments, then replied, "Take me to him."

They returned to the forest and soon found Ekalavya, who rushed to Drona and fell at his feet, exclaiming, "Guruji, you have come!"

Drona raised him upright and said, "If I am your guru, give me *gurudakshina*, the guru's fee for teaching."

"Anything, Guruji," said Ekalavya. "Name it, and I will give it to you if I can."

"Give me the thumb of your right hand," said Drona.

Immediately, Ekalavya drew his knife, cheerfully sliced off his right thumb, and presented it to Drona. Of course, that meant that Ekalavya would never again have the superlative archery skills he had developed.

As Arjuna witnessed this extraordinary act of self-offering, the fever of jealousy left his heart. He was happy, for he would still be the greatest archer in the world.

Ekalavya's attunement and self-sacrifice are inspiring, whereas Arjuna's jealousy is disappointing. But Drona's treatment of Ekalavya is positively disturbing. Why did he do it?

Much later in the epic, Vyasa explains that Ekalavya was an incarnated Asura, a demon who would have fought for Duryodhana in the war that came later. His superlative archery skills could have meant victory for Duryodhana. Krishna realized that, so he eliminated the threat by working through Arjuna's jealousy and Drona's partiality toward Arjuna.

Nevertheless, we cannot help but feel respect and deep sympathy for Ekalavya. We might ask ourselves, "Could I do what he did?"

· · · · ·

Drona had another highly accomplished disciple. Many people thought him the equal of Arjuna. His name was Karna, and he was a bit older than the Kuru princes. He was of the Suta caste, a low caste of charioteers and storytellers. Ordinarily, a Sutaputra—a son of a Suta—would not have been allowed to train with the Kuru princes. He might never even have met them. But Karna's father was a friend of Dhritarashtra's, and the king had allowed him to send his son to Drona for training.

Karna craved to be known as the greatest of all warriors. So naturally, he became jealous of Arjuna, and an intense rivalry sprang up between them. Karna was also jealous of Yudhisthira for being next in line for the throne. He even resented the noble nature of all the Pandavas. As a result, he fell in with Duryodhana, who was delighted to have such a mighty warrior as his friend. Karna joined Shakuni and Dushasana, the second oldest Kaurava, as Duryodhana's main allies in conspiring against the Pandavas.

Karna represents attachment. His attachment was not to material things but to fame and worldly respect.

Not long after Drona gave Arjuna the Brahma astra, Karna approached Drona privately. "Guruji, I ask that you give me the Brahma weapon, for I wish to be known as a master of the science of weaponry—and I wish to fight Arjuna."

Drona could see wickedness in Karna's nature—and he was partial toward Arjuna. So he said, "Only a Brahmin of high vows, or a Kshatriya who has practiced severe austerities, may receive this weapon. It is not for a Sutaputra."

Karna concealed his anger and bowed at Drona's feet, then rose and walked away. His desire to have the Brahma weapon and show himself superior to Arjuna was too intense for him to remain with Drona. He left his preceptor and journeyed far to the south in search of Drona's guru, Parashurama.

It was well known that Parashurama would accept only Brahmins as disciples, so when Karna found the master, he lied: He said he was a Brahmin, and the guru accepted him.

Karna was a model of self-discipline and dedication. In time, Parashurama gave him many astras, including the Brahma weapon. Karna was ecstatic.

But his ecstasy was short-lived, for while hunting one day, he accidentally killed a cow that belonged to a Brahmin—a cow that was essential for the Brahmin's fire rituals. Karna approached the Brahmin and said, "Please forgive me, sir, for I unintentionally killed your cow."

The Brahmin would have none of it. "O vile man, you deserve to be killed! Therefore, I curse you. When you meet your greatest enemy in battle, that foe whom you most wish to conquer, and when fear enters your heart, your chariot wheel will become stuck in the mud, and your foe will cut off your head!"

Karna pleaded, "Please, sir, withdraw your curse. I will give you many cattle and great wealth."

But the Brahmin was adamant. "Neither your words nor your gifts will falsify my curse. Leave me now!"

Karna hung his head and slowly returned to his guru's ashram.

Sometime later, Parashurama and Karna were walking together in the forest. The guru had been fasting for some days and began to feel very tired, so he lay down for a nap, affectionately resting his head on Karna's lap. Karna was highly pleased to be able to provide such a service to his guru.

Soon, an enormous worm crawled onto Karna's thigh and began to bite him. The pain was excruciating, but Karna endured it so his guru would not be disturbed. It was not long before blood from the bite began to flow so freely that it touched Parashurama. He awakened with a start. "What is this?! I have been defiled!"

Karna pointed at the worm. "Gurudeva, this worm was biting me. I did not want to kill it lest you be disturbed."

When Parashurama looked at the worm, he immediately realized its bite would have caused tremendous pain. He narrowed his eyes. "No Brahmin could have endured such pain. You have the patience and endurance of a Kshatriya. Is that what you are? Tell me the truth!"

Karna prostrated himself before the master. "Beloved Gurudeva, it is true that I am not a Brahmin. I am a Sutaputra. I came to you out of a desire to learn the science of weaponry. The scriptures say that the guru is one's father. That is why I told you that I am a Brahmin."

Parashurama was not sympathetic. "You came to me out of greed for weapons, then lied to me. You will therefore suffer the consequences of that conduct. I hereby curse you: When you find yourself in combat with one who is your equal, you will not remember the mantra for invoking the Brahma weapon. Now go away! My ashram is no place for a liar!"

Karna sadly left his guru and began the long journey back to Hastinapura.

What a difference between Karna's discipleship and Arjuna's!

Arjuna gave his complete obedience to Drona and trusted the guru to give him whatever was right for him. In contrast, Karna deserted the guru who would not give him what he wanted, and then lied to another guru to get it.

Obedience is not an imposition on our free will. Yogananda said, "Its aim is not to enslave the disciple, but to liberate his will from that which enslaves it truly: whims, and much more — bondage to likes and dislikes, and to desires and attachments.

"Most people consider it an affirmation of freedom to indulge their desires 'freely.' They don't see that desire itself is compulsive. It blinds their discrimination. Where is the freedom in any act that leads one more deeply into bondage?

"Cooperation with the guru strengthens the willpower immeasurably, for it attunes the disciple's will to the infinite will of God."

Arjuna lived that teaching. Karna lived for his attachments, and he would pay dearly for that — just as we do when we live for our attachments.

CHAPTER 6

Kshatriya Prowess

WHEN DRONA'S TRAINING OF THE Kuru princes was complete, he requested a public exhibition to show off their skills. The Kuru elders fully supported the idea, eager to take the measure of the next generation of Kuru leaders. To showcase the event, they commissioned a glorious new arena made of pure gold, decked with strings of pearls and stones of lapis lazuli.

On the appointed day, the Kuru citizenry flocked to the arena, buzzing with anticipation. Then the Kuru royalty and elders arrived, including Gandhari, Kunti, and the other ladies of the royal household. Drona entered next, accompanied by his son, Aswatthama.

Finally, the Kuru princes entered the arena, drawing loud cheers from the crowd. They began to perform astounding feats with swords, spears, and bows and arrows—on foot, on horseback, and in chariots. The exhibition was thrilling, and the spectators were in awe of their skills.

Drona then announced, "Let there now be a demonstration of mace combat between Bhima and Duryodhana."

The two princes walked to the center of the arena and stood glaring at each other with hatred, eager to fight. Bhima had tremendous strength, whereas Duryodhana had superior skill.

Drona gave the signal to commence, and they immediately began to fight fiercely. Blood soon began to flow, and the demonstration turned into mortal combat. The crowd had initially been enthusiastic, but now it became agitated with concern.

Drona watched with increasing disapproval as the two young men expressed their mutual animosity. Finally, he stood up and shouted an order, "Bhima! Duryodhana! Stop the demonstration!"

Reluctantly, Bhima and Duryodhana ceased fighting and began to move off the arena floor, still eying each other with loathing.

The late afternoon shadows were growing long when Drona

announced the grand finale: "Let us now see Arjuna, the master of all arms, the son of Indra himself!"

Amid much cheering from the crowd, Arjuna came to the center of the arena. He began performing many difficult feats—first with ordinary weapons, then with astras. His first astra was the Agneya weapon, sacred to Lord Agni, the god of fire. When he shot it into the sky, it turned into a mushrooming fireball that threatened to incinerate the entire arena. He then launched the Varuna astra, which enveloped that fireball with water that extinguished the fire. With a third astra, he covered the sky with heavy clouds. With a fourth, he caused a violent wind to blow the clouds away. With a fifth, he materialized an entire mountain range in the distance. And with one final astra, he made the mountains disappear. It was exceedingly wonderful, and the crowd roared its appreciation. Kunti's heart swelled with pride over her son's accomplishments.

But Arjuna had yet to finish. He used an astra to make himself extremely tall, then another to become extremely small. With still other astras, he made himself disappear, then reappear on the yoke of his chariot, then disappear and reappear in the chariot, then disappear again and reappear on the ground. Finally, he shot twenty-one arrows into the hollow of a cow's horn as it swung back and forth on the end of a rope.

The crowd cheered wildly for a long time. When the cheering subsided, there was a ripple of excitement near the gate. Everyone turned and saw a tall young warrior stride into the arena, making a sound like thunder by slapping his arms in challenge. His face was radiant with light and supreme confidence. The sun itself seemed to have arrived.

He bowed indifferently to Drona and Kripa as the spectators wondered, "Who is this young man?" But Kunti recognized him, and emotions flooded over her. She had not told Pandu, Madri, or anyone else the entire story behind the mantra she had received many years earlier.

*　*　*　*　*

After that long-ago initiation, the young girl Kunti had wondered, "Is it true? Could I use this mantra to summon one of the Devas?" Her girlish curiosity got the better of her, and she used the mantra to invoke Surya, the sun god, who came to her in a blaze of light.

The deity said, "Ask of me a boon, O gentle maiden."

Kunti was thrilled, yet also afraid. "Forgive me, my Lord. A rishi gave me this mantra. I summoned you only to test it." She bowed and said, "Please, Lord, return to the heavens."

"If you have summoned me for no reason," said Surya, "I will curse both you *and* that rishi. But I see in your mind a desire for a son like myself, a powerful son who will be a mighty warrior. I shall give you such a son."

"No, Lord, please forgive me," cried Kunti in sudden desperation. "I am just a girl. I have made a childish mistake. I fear my family will banish me if I sacrifice my virtue."

"Fear not, child," said Surya. "Your son shall be born this very day, and no one shall know."

A boy was indeed born to Kunti that day. He was as beautiful as one of the celestials, and he shone like his father, the sun. He had natural armor and earrings made of amrita, the divine nectar, which made him invulnerable to all weapons.

Kunti immediately felt great love for him. But fearing her family's reaction, she placed him in a basket, took him to the river, and set him afloat, praying to Surya that he protect his son.

· · · · ·

Kunti had not seen her son since then, and she had never spoken of him to anyone for fear of scandal. She did not even know whether he was alive. But when the tall young man entered the arena, with natural armor and earrings, his face glowing like the sun, she immediately knew him to be the son she had abandoned. Tears of joy streamed down her cheeks.

The young man was Karna, returning from his bittersweet time with Parashurama. So Karna was not a Sutaputra after all. Although a charioteer had adopted him, he was the son of a Kshatriya princess and a god! Yet only Kunti knew that secret.

Karna called out a challenge: "Arjuna, I shall perform all the feats you have performed—and more! With the guru's permission, I shall begin."

Drona consented, and Karna did what he had promised. He even duplicated Arjuna's accomplishments with the astras. The spectators were delighted, and Kunti's heart swelled with pride over her son's prowess.

Duryodhana was overjoyed, for his ally had returned with impressive new skills. He rushed to Karna. "Well done, O great warrior! It is my good fortune to have found you again! Stay here and live with us. How can I please you?"

> Duryodhana (material desire) knew that Karna (attachment) was central to his plans for taking over the kingdom. In the same way, a desire is only as strong as the power of its underlying attachment.

Karna answered, "I long only for your friendship." He then turned a spiteful gaze toward Arjuna. "And for single combat with Arjuna."

Arjuna flushed and angrily exclaimed, "You are an unwelcome intruder and an uninvited speaker! For that, I shall slay you!"

Karna shouted back, "This arena is not yours alone, Arjuna! Insults are the weapons of the weak. Let us fight with arrows, and I will kill you in front of the preceptor himself!"

As they approached each other for combat, Lord Indra, favoring his son, Arjuna, covered them with many dark clouds that emitted bright flashes of lightning, set off by a brilliant rainbow. Karna's father, Lord Surya, burned through the clouds that obscured Karna. The two warriors stood glaring at each other, one covered with clouds and illuminated by lightning, the other radiant in the sunlight.

Kunti fainted at the prospect of her two sons fighting to the death. Vidura immediately sprinkled water on her and spread sandalwood paste over her forehead. She soon recovered, but she could only sit frozen with fear over what might happen to her sons.

Then Kripa invoked the formalities concerning duels, saying to Karna, "Everyone knows the royal lineage of Arjuna. O mighty warrior, tell us your royal lineage. For sons of kings never fight with lowborn men."

Karna's face flushed. He hung his head and said nothing.

Duryodhana stepped forward. "If Arjuna is unwilling to fight with one who is not a king or prince, I shall exercise my privilege as the eldest son of King Dhritarashtra: I hereby install Karna as ruler of the kingdom of Anga."

Anga was a tiny kingdom, but Duryodhana's gesture was huge, and a murmur of approval went through the crowd. Brahmin priests performed a brief coronation ceremony amid loud cheers from the citizenry.

Karna said to Duryodhana, "O prince, what can I give you to compare with your gift of a kingdom?"

Duryodhana answered, "I wish only for your friendship."

As they embraced, Karna's adoptive father, the charioteer, entered the arena. Karna ran to him and fell at his feet, then stood and embraced him. His father's eyes were brimming with tears of joy. His son was now a king!

Bhima called out, "O Sutaputra, you do not deserve death at the hands of Arjuna. As befits your caste, take up the whip. You are not worthy to rule Anga, even as a dog does not deserve the ghee placed before the sacrificial fire."

Duryodhana shouted angrily at Bhima, "Look at this warrior, shining like the sun, born with natural armor! How can you doubt his lineage? Could a deer have given birth to this tiger? This prince among men deserves sovereignty over the entire world!"

There was confused whispering among the crowd, many of whom approved of what Duryodhana had said. Then, just as Arjuna and Karna were about to commence fighting, the sun went down, ending the exhibition—and the prospect of a duel.

The crowd breathed a huge sigh of relief, and Duryodhana left the arena arm in arm with Karna. The people, too, came away, some naming Arjuna, some Karna, and some Duryodhana as the victor of the day.

Kunti was immensely pleased that Karna had become a king. Duryodhana, too, was delighted, for his fear of Arjuna had vanished now that Karna was back with him. And Yudhisthira began to believe there was no warrior on earth to compare with Karna.

The confrontation between Arjuna and Karna has inner significance. They are the consummate warriors — and rivals. Arjuna represents fiery self-control, while Karna represents attachment. Every spiritual seeker experiences internal conflict between those two qualities.

Attachment is the mistaken belief that happiness depends on some outer condition: "I *must* have that!" It is reinforced by maya, the cosmic force that creates the illusion that everything is separate from everything else — and from God.

Self-control represents the view that happiness lies within, not in outward gratification. It doesn't always win its battles with attachment, which can be exceedingly powerful. But even resisting temptation is a valuable effort toward success. As Yogananda once reassured a disciple, "I don't ask that you overcome temptation. I ask only that you resist it."

The rivalry between Arjuna and Karna is not only personal. It also plays a role in the contest for the Kuru throne between Yudhisthira (who represents calmness in psychological battle) and Duryodhana (material desire). They, too, represent opposites: Desire is always accompanied by agitation, whereas inner calmness quenches desire.

In the Mahabharata, Yudhisthira often cites Arjuna as his most important asset: calmness relies upon self-control for its existence. Duryodhana sees Karna as his critical asset, for attachment is the foundation of material desire. So self-control and attachment are the powers behind the contenders for the throne of our inner kingdom of happiness.

·   ·   ·   ·   ·

Having completed his training of the Kuru princes, Drona decided it was time for the fulfillment of his longtime dream. He called the princes together and said, "You will remember that, at the start of your training, I told you I had a deep desire, and I asked who among you would satisfy it. Here is what I now demand of you as gurudakshina: Do battle with Drupada, the king of Panchala. Capture him, and bring him to me."

The disciples answered as one, "So be it." They gathered their weapons and armor while attendants hitched the horses to their chariots. Then they set out for Panchala.

·   ·   ·   ·   ·

Why did Drona want Drupada captured? Their story began when he and Drupada were boys in the kingdom of Panchala. Drupada was

the son of the king of Panchala, and he had often come to the hermitage of Drona's father, where he and Drona would play together. They
became such close friends that Drupada told him, "When I become
king of Panchala, I promise that my kingdom and wealth shall be as
much yours as mine."

Years later, Drupada became king as expected, while Drona lived
in severe poverty. So one day, Drona asked for and received an audience with Drupada. He did not remind the king of his promise. He
merely said to him, "I am your friend."

But Drupada was intoxicated with the pride of wealth and power,
and his temper flared. "O Brahmin, you are quite stupid to say that.
Yes, we were friends as mere boys, when we were equals, but time
changes everything. There cannot be friendship between those who
are unequal. The rich and the poor can never be friends. Heroes cannot be friends with cowards. Kings cannot be friends with those who
are not kings. But I will give you a meal, and you may stay here for
one night." He then dismissed Drona from his royal presence.

Drona was outraged, yet he held his anger in check. After
some reflection, he came upon a plan to avenge Drupada's cruel-
ty and arrogance. He moved to Hastinapura with his wife and son,
Aswatthama. They lived in the house of Kripa, his wife's brother, and
Aswatthama often gave the young Kuru princes basic lessons in the
use of weapons.

Then, one day, Drona found the young Kuru princes puzzling
over how to retrieve a ball that had fallen into a well. He dazzled
them with his astonishing feats with blades of grass and a ring. He
was confident that Bhishma would ask him to train the Kuru princes,
and they would be his instruments of revenge against Drupada. He
was correct on both counts.

· · · · ·

As the Kuru princes neared Panchala, the Kauravas began to vie
with one another for the honor of leading the attack. Arjuna told his
brothers, "Let us wait and attack after the Kauravas have displayed
their prowess." He shook his head. "The likes of them can never defeat King Drupada." The Pandavas remained well outside the city
while the Kauravas launched their attack.

When Drupada led his army out of the city to fight, the Kauravas showered him with arrows. But he was a great warrior, and he quickly began to rain arrows on the attackers. He fought with such speed and skill that he and his one chariot seemed to be many.

In response, the Kauravas intensified their attack. Drupada and his army countered with such ferocity that the Kauravas soon broke their ranks and fled back toward the Pandavas, with the Panchala army in hot pursuit.

Hearing the terrified Kauravas approach, the Pandavas saluted Drona and received his blessing on their attack. Arjuna asked Yudhisthira not to enter the fight, then mounted his chariot. Nakula and Sahadeva protected his flanks as he sped into the midst of the pursuing Panchala ranks and began to decimate them. Bhima, too, was soon crushing Panchala soldiers—and even their war elephants—with his massive iron mace.

Arjuna launched his arrows with such speed that one could not distinguish between when he took an arrow from his quiver, placed it on the bowstring, drew the bow, and shot the arrow. He attacked and quickly defeated Drupada's general, making him flee for his life. Then Drupada attacked Arjuna, but Arjuna soon got the better of the king and had him at his mercy. He jumped out of his chariot into Drupada's chariot and captured him. When the Panchala army saw that, they fled in all directions.

Arjuna called out to his brothers, "Stop your attack! We have accomplished our task. Let us now bring King Drupada back to Guruji." They soon reached the spot where Drona waited with a fierce gleam in his eye as he savored to the full the long-awaited humiliation of Drupada.

"My forces have laid waste your army," he said to Drupada. "But fear not, O King. I will not kill you." He smiled broadly. "We Brahmins are ever forgiving. Would you now like to be friends once again? You once told me that a king can never be a friend of one who is not a king. So I shall return the southern half of your kingdom while I reign over the northern half. Then we will both be kings—we will be equals, so we can be friends."

Drupada replied, "You are a noble soul of great prowess, and I am not surprised at this generous gesture. I am highly grateful, and I desire your eternal friendship."

"So be it," said Drona, and he released Drupada.

Drupada was alive, free, and still a king. But he was exceedingly angry. He had been defeated and humiliated by someone he felt was his inferior. And he had lost half his kingdom. Now, he was the one who wished for revenge.

Drupada did not believe he could kill Drona in combat, so he decided to have a holy man perform a sacred ceremony that would produce a son who could kill Drona. Every holy man he approached refused to support such an unworthy motive as revenge. He kept searching, however, and finally found one who agreed to conduct the ceremony. It was a success, for out of the sacred fire arose a magnificent son, full-grown and dressed in battle armor. His name was Dhrishtadyumna.

And Drupada was exceedingly happy.

> Drupada represents extreme dispassion, although he did not display that quality in this episode. His fire-born son, Dhrishtadyumna, symbolizes the calm inner light of superconsciousness. Only from that higher level of awareness can we truly overcome habit (Drona), which is of the subconscious mind.

CHAPTER 7

Escape from Fire

AFTER DEFEATING DRUPADA, THE PANDAVAS began to exercise their newly demonstrated prowess by conquering several neighboring kings who had previously taken territory from the Kurus. The Pandavas' popularity among the Kuru citizens increased by the day. The people especially loved Yudhisthira for his kindness, benevolence, and unswerving truthfulness. Sentiment was rapidly growing for him to claim his birthright: the Kuru throne.

That was worrisome for Dhritarashtra; he had always wanted Duryodhana to take the Kuru throne. The Pandavas' popularity was one concern; another was their Kshatriya prowess, for he suspected that his sons' rivalry with them would someday ripen into armed conflict. He became so anxious that he could hardly sleep, and his feelings toward the Pandavas turned poisonous. Still, he realized he could no longer keep Yudhisthira in the background, so he made the eldest Pandava the Yuvaraja, the next in line for the throne.

Dhritarashtra consulted his minister of politics and confided his fears about the Pandavas. The minister said, "There is no doubt that the Pandavas can conquer your sons in battle, O King. But there are ways to conquer a foe other than battle. One must draw upon one's strengths while concealing one's vulnerabilities. And one must find and exploit the vulnerability of the foe. What is your strength, Sire, and in what ways are the Pandavas vulnerable? Ponder these things, O King."

Duryodhana had already been pondering those things. He was painfully aware of the growing tide of public sentiment for Yudhisthira to be king. So he and his uncle, Shakuni, along with Karna and Dushasana, thought of a way to take advantage of the fact that Dhritarashtra still occupied the throne, whereas the Pandavas had no formal power.

Duryodhana went to Dhritarashtra. "Father, the people are saying you are not the rightful king because you are blind. They say it

is time for Yudhisthira to take the throne. You must eliminate the
Pandavas now, or we will live under Yudhisthira's rule forever."

"But how?" asked Dhritarashtra. "Yudhisthira is the people's favorite. If we kill him, the citizens will surely arise and slay us."

"We need not *kill* him," countered Duryodhana. "You should
merely find a reason to send him and his brothers away for a time. We
control the treasury. If we appease the people with wealth and honors,
they will soon forget the Pandavas. Meanwhile, you can invest me as
the next king."

Dhritarashtra said, "I have had the same thought, but I was afraid
to mention it because of its sinfulness. The elders will surely oppose
the idea."

Duryodhana replied, "The elders who *matter* will not oppose it.
Bhishma is neutral; he loves us as much as the Pandavas. Drona will
be wherever Aswatthama is, and Aswatthama is on my side. Kripa is
Drona's brother-in-law, so they will stay together. Vidura is the only
one who favors the Pandavas, and he is of no consequence."

"But where should we send them?" asked Dhritarashtra. "And
what reason can we give for sending them there?"

Duryodhana replied, "Send them to Varanavata so they can
take part in the festival of Shiva. O Father, I am in torment over the
Pandavas, and I cannot sleep! Send them away!"

Dhritarashtra said, "Very well. I will have my councilors regale
the Pandavas with the delights of Varanavata. Then I will suggest that
they go there."

They immediately put the plan in motion: Duryodhana and
his brothers set about increasing their popularity by bestowing
wealth and honors upon the Kuru citizens. And before the entire court—and the Pandavas—Dhritarashtra's councilors spoke
glowingly of the city of Varanavata and its upcoming festival of
Lord Shiva.

Dhritarashtra exclaimed, "What an excellent idea!" as though he
had never heard it before. He said, "Yudhisthira, if you and your
brothers would like to experience the festival, then you should go
to Varanavata. When you have enjoyed it as much as you like, then
return to Hastinapura."

"So be it," said Yudhisthira, who understood very well that another plot was afoot—this time with Dhritarashtra's involvement. Yet

one could not refuse the king's suggestion, so he, his brothers, and Kunti prepared for an extended absence from Hastinapura.

Meanwhile, Duryodhana summoned one of his trusted agents. "Quickly, take a crew of workers to Varanavata and build a beautiful mansion. Make it out of hemp, lacquer, and ghee so it will be highly flammable. It should have only one exit. We will invite the Pandavas and their mother to live there. You should live there as the caretaker. Some night, when they are all asleep, you must set fire to the mansion near the exit. Then, all of them will burn to death."

"So be it," said the agent, and he set off to gather a crew and go to Varanavata to build the mansion.

. . . . .

On the morning of their departure for Varanavata, the five brothers and Kunti saluted Bhishma, Vidura, and the other Kuru elders, then mounted their chariots and began traveling slowly toward Varanavata. Vidura followed them on foot, as did many Kuru citizens, who suspected villainy was afoot—villainy supported by the blind king.

But Yudhisthira told the citizens, "The king is our father. We must do with unsuspicious hearts whatever he asks of us. He has asked us to go to Varanavata, so we will go. Your presence here makes us happy, but please return home."

As the citizens reluctantly turned back toward Hastinapura, Vidura took Yudhisthira aside and spoke in a foreign language that only Yudhisthira would understand: "That which consumes wood and straw cannot consume the occupants of a hole in the forest. Knowing this, protect yourselves from death."

Yudhisthira nodded and said, "I understand, Uncle." Vidura then returned to Hastinapura.

. . . . .

When the Pandavas and Kunti arrived in Varanavata, they received a joyous welcome from the residents. They stayed in local lodgings until Duryodhana's laborers finished building the mansion. Then, the brothers and Kunti moved in.

As Yudhisthira toured the mansion, he immediately recognized danger. He said to his brothers, "Can you smell the lacquer? This mansion is highly flammable, and I am sure you have noticed there is only one exit. It is a death trap. We should appear unsuspicious, lest Duryodhana take even bolder steps to kill us. But we must constantly stay alert and ensure there is never a time when all of us are asleep. Also, we should spend our days hunting in the woods to familiarize ourselves with the forest paths in case we need to escape quickly."

Vidura soon sent help in the form of a miner. Following Vidura's hint, Yudhisthira instructed the miner to dig a tunnel from out in the forest to a point directly under the center of the mansion. When the miner finished the tunnel, Yudhisthira sent a secret message to Vidura, saying that, on a particular night, the Pandavas would make their escape from Varanavata.

On the chosen night, a mighty windstorm came up. The Pandavas waited until they were sure Duryodhana's agent was asleep inside the mansion. Bhima then set fire to the front door of the mansion — the only door — trapping the agent inside. He also lit the mansion afire in several other places while his brothers and Kunti climbed into the tunnel. Finally, Bhima squeezed into the tunnel and closed its trap door.

The strong gale quickly turned the mansion into a roaring inferno as the Pandavas and Kunti escaped through the tunnel into the forest. They needed to get far away fast and in total darkness lest anyone recognize them. So Bhima summoned his tremendous strength, picked up his mother and four brothers, and carried them through the forest as swiftly as the wind, knocking down any trees that blocked his path.

They soon reached the Ganga, where a boat, arranged by Vidura, waited to take them across the river. From there, they proceeded south into a dense forest, where they would be safe from Duryodhana's spies.

Meanwhile, the roar of the blazing fire had awakened the residents of Varanavata. The flames were far too intense for them to extinguish; they could only watch the mansion burn to cinders. The next day, the charred ruins told them that the Pandavas and Kunti had died in the flames. They felt sure that Duryodhana was behind this tragedy, but what could they do? The Pandavas were dead. When they sadly turned away and went home, the miner quickly filled the tunnel entrance so no one would suspect the Pandavas had escaped.

In Hastinapura, Dhritarashtra and his sons made a dramatic show of grief over the Pandavas' tragic deaths. Now, with his enemies dead and his father easy to manipulate, Duryodhana would be, more than ever, the king of the Kurus.

> Outwardly, this episode symbolizes how, in the absence of discrimination (Pandu), material desire (Duryodhana) can push higher consciousness (the Pandavas) into the background of our lives. It then has free rein because the only "authority figure" — sense-mind (Dhritarashtra) — habitually favors material realities.
>
> On a deeper level, the Pandavas' escape through the tunnel symbolizes what must be our primary strategy for spiritual freedom: We must withdraw our life force from the senses, which are located at the periphery of the body, into the *sushumna*, the deep astral or energy spine in the center of the torso, just in front of the physical spinal column. Only when our energy and consciousness rise through the tunnel of the sushumna can we realize the true Self.

. . . . .

After escaping from the fire in Varanavata, the Pandavas wandered in the forest for a time as they pondered what to do next. One day, a Rakshasi—a demoness—saw Bhima walking through the woods and instantly fell in love with him. Through her powers of illusion, she changed her appearance into that of a beautiful human woman. Bhima married her, and they soon had a son whom they named Ghatotkacha.

Although Ghatotkacha was half-human, he looked like a Rakshasa, with a gaping mouth, sharp teeth, and pointed ears. He grew into a youth in the very first hour of his life. He quickly became a great favorite with his uncles, and he was, in turn, very devoted to them. All too soon, however, it was time for him to go with his mother to grow up in the realms of the Rakshasas. At his departure, he promised Bhima, "Father, if ever you need me, I will come."

That day would indeed come.

Soon after Ghatotkacha departed, Vyasa used his spiritual sight to locate the brothers and Kunti, and he came to visit them. He advised them to stay in hiding and let everyone continue to think them dead.

So they disguised themselves as Brahmin ascetics to keep Duryodhana's spies from recognizing them. Vyasa took them to a village where they could stay for a time. He assured them that, unlikely though it might seem, everything was happening for their ultimate happiness.

● ● ● ● ●

The Pandavas remained in the forest for nearly a year, moving from place to place, living as Brahmin ascetics. They supported themselves as Brahmin ascetics would: by begging for alms. Whatever food people gave them, Bhima ate half, while his four brothers and mother shared the other half.

In their wanderings, they often encountered fellow travelers who shared news of events in the outside world. One such traveler gave them some highly unusual news: "There will soon be a swayamvara for the daughter of King Drupada of Panchala. Draupadi is her name, and she is said to be the most beautiful maiden in the world."

> Sometimes, when a princess was to marry, her father, the king, would invite other kings and princes who might make proper husbands, and she would place a garland around the neck of her chosen husband. Such a *swayamvara*, or "ceremony of self-choice," had been how Amva, Amvika, and Amvalika were to marry — until Bhishma abducted them. At other times, the king would arrange for his daughter to wed a specific king or prince for political alliance. Although the princess had no choice in such a case, her wedding was nevertheless called a swayamvara.

The traveler continued, "King Drupada has decreed that Draupadi's swayamvara will be different from other swayamvaras. His new son-in-law will be the man who can win a highly demanding archery contest."

At those words, Arjuna suddenly became keenly interested. The traveler went on, "Draupadi is extraordinary, not only because of her beauty, but because of how she was born. King Drupada had retained a holy man to perform a sacred fire ceremony that would produce a son. That son was born full-grown from the flames; his name is Dhrishtadyumna.

"But to everyone's surprise, a full-grown daughter also rose from the flames, and a voice from the heavens declared, 'This maiden will be the foremost of all women. She will cause the destruction of countless Kshatriyas, and she will accomplish the purpose of the gods.'"

Even just hearing about Draupadi, all five Pandavas lost their peace of mind over her. So, still disguised as Brahmin ascetics, they and Kunti began the long trek to Panchala.

> Draupadi represents Kundalini, the reservoir of *prana* (life force) at the base of the astral spine. Any thought, emotion, or action that reinforces our false sense of separateness from other people and God — for example, selfishness, judgment, anger, or greed — causes energy to flow down the spine and feed that reservoir. That is why Swami Kriyananda described Kundalini as "the entrenched vitality of our mortal delusion."
>
> Kundalini is not bad; it is simply energy. But its entrenchment at the base of the spine exerts a downward magnetic pull on our consciousness, inclining us toward behavior that reinforces feelings of separateness and thereby feeds the reservoir.
>
> Our job is twofold: We need to withdraw our outward-directed energies into the spine, as symbolized by the Pandavas' escape through the tunnel in Varanavata. We must also lift those energies — led by Kundalini (Draupadi) — to the spiritual eye, the center of superconscious awareness, located just interior to the point between the eyebrows.
>
> Meditation is the main tool for accomplishing those two aims. In addition, every thought, feeling, or action that expresses unity and harmony — such as kindness, generosity, humility, or sympathy — helps lift our energies toward the spiritual eye and weaken Kundalini's downward pull. Eventually, we will bring enough energy to the spiritual eye that its magnetism will raise the Kundalini energy up the spine.
>
> The entire spiritual path is an inward and upward movement of energy. However, it is not merely a mechanical process. We must ally self-effort with right attitude and divine attunement to receive God's grace, the only power that can take us to freedom. Then Kundalini will rise in earnest. Swami Kriyananda said of that experience, "You feel so much joy you cannot stand it!"

CHAPTER 8

Turning Point

WHEN THE PANDAVAS AND KUNTI reached Panchala, they found shelter in a potter's house. They remained disguised as Brahmin ascetics and supported themselves by begging for alms each day.

Soon, famous kings and princes began to arrive from far and wide, eager to win Draupadi's hand in marriage. Among them were Duryodhana, Dushasana, and their brothers. Their maternal uncle, Shakuni, came. Karna also came, for as king of Anga, he too could compete.

Two other illustrious persons also came: Krishna and his brother, Balarama, had journeyed from their home in the kingdom of Dwaraka, far away on the west coast of India. Krishna was a prince, not yet a king. But because of his prowess, virtue, kindness, and wisdom, his people regarded him even more highly than a king.

Krishna represents God or the guru.

Krishna and Balarama had not come to Panchala to compete for Draupadi's hand. Krishna wanted to meet his cousins, the Pandavas, for his father was Kunti's brother. Almost everyone thought the Pandavas had perished in the fire at Varanavata. But Krishna's divine sight told him they were still alive and would come to compete for Draupadi.

· · · · ·

On the day of the contest, thousands of people thronged into a grand arena adorned with countless wreaths of fragrant flowers. The royal contestants entered and took seats of honor around an elegant central stage. The Devas also came, along with a large contingent of other celestials and divine rishis — all of them invisible to mortal eyes. When the Pandavas arrived, still in disguise, they sat in the section reserved for Brahmins.

Finally, Draupadi entered. Dressed in elegant silks and sparkling jewels, she was endowed with every auspicious feature. She was slender-waisted and of medium height. Her eyes were large as lotus petals, and her complexion was faultless. Her black hair was thick and curly, and it shimmered with light. She carried a golden plate, on which was a garland of flowers that she would drape around the neck of whoever won the contest and would, therefore, be her husband.

Draupadi was indeed the most beautiful maiden in the world, and her beauty transfixed all the kings and princes. They became so intoxicated with desire that they began to regard even their best friends with jealousy. And they set their hearts so firmly upon winning Draupadi that they did not notice the five rather unusual Brahmins, who resembled bull elephants more than ascetics.

But Krishna noticed them as they, too, gazed longingly at Draupadi. Though he had never seen the Pandavas, he immediately realized who those five Brahmins were. He tapped Balarama on the shoulder and pointed at the Brahmin section. "Do you see those five sturdy-looking Brahmins? That one is Yudhisthira. The huge one is Bhima. Next to him is Arjuna. The other two are the twins." Balarama surveyed the five, then turned to Krishna and smiled. They both sat back to watch the contest.

Prince Dhrishtadyumna, King Drupada's fire-born son, mounted the stage and said, "Welcome, O great kings and princes. Here is your challenge: The target is revolving atop the tall pole in the center of this stage. It is hidden behind the screen that you see near the top of the pole. Your task is to string the ceremonial bow and shoot an arrow through the small hole in the screen into the target. Here are five arrows; you have five chances to hit the target." He gestured toward Draupadi and said, "Whoever succeeds shall have my sister, Princess Draupadi, as his wife."

As if that task were not challenging enough, the target was not revolving at a uniform rate because a man, not a machine, was operating the mechanism. That meant that hitting the target would require good luck—or perfect intuition.

An additional difficulty was that the bow was extremely hard to string. That was intentional, for King Drupada suspected the Pandavas might still be alive. He had greatly admired Arjuna ever since being defeated and captured by him, and he harbored a secret desire that Draupadi would marry Arjuna. Therefore, he had stipulated that the bow should be so stiff that only the mightiest archers could string it.

The contest began, and one after another, the kings and princes proudly stepped onto the stage as a herald proclaimed their ancestry and achievements. Each one struggled to bend the bow to string it, but it was so stiff that it sprang out of his grip. It even threw a few of them down. They could not string that bow, even in their imagination.

Finally, Karna's turn came. He was so strong that he quickly strung the bow. A hush came over the arena as he placed the first arrow on the bowstring, drew the bow into a full circle, and aimed upward at the hole in the screen.

Seeing Karna's strength and evident skill, Draupadi grew alarmed at the prospect of him succeeding. She called out for all to hear, "I will not have a Sutaputra as my husband!"

Karna angrily threw down the bow and arrow, then stormed off the stage. No king or prince had won Draupadi.

Then Arjuna stood, stepped out of the Brahmin section, and walked toward the stage. The crowd began to buzz with astonishment. How could a Brahmin even think to succeed when all the mighty Kshatriya warriors had failed?

The Brahmins, too, wondered about that, and they began to argue among themselves. Some declared loudly, "No Brahmin should be allowed to compete! He will certainly fail, making all Brahmins a laughingstock." Others disagreed, saying, "No, look at him! He moves with such grace and strength. He could well win the princess. Let him try."

Arjuna mounted the stage and picked up the ceremonial bow. He strung it in the twinkling of an eye, instantly quieting the crowd. He nocked an arrow, drew the bow to full circle, and carefully aimed at the tiny hole in the screen. The spectators held their breath in suspense as Arjuna concentrated intensely, waiting to feel intuitively the perfect moment to shoot. A vibrant stillness filled the arena.

Suddenly, he unleashed the arrow. It flashed through the hole just as the target was passing by and ripped the target away from the mechanism. Together, the arrow and target fell onto the stage, accompanied by loud cheers from the crowd.

All the Brahmins stood and waved their upper garments in celebration. One of their own had won the princess!

Arjuna put down the bow and walked over to Draupadi. With a gleam in his eye, he presented himself to be garlanded. Draupadi glanced over at her father, who nodded as if to say, "So be it." With a slight smile, she gave the golden plate to an attendant, took the garland, and draped it around Arjuna's neck. The Brahmins cheered even louder as Arjuna brought her back to the Brahmin section.

The visiting kings and princes were furious. Bad enough that a Brahmin had succeeded when they had failed, but now Drupada was sanctioning the victory.

One of them bellowed, "This is an outrage! A Kshatriya princess should marry a Kshatriya!"

Another king shouted, "Drupada, you have insulted all of us!"

A third growled, "And we will kill you for that!"

They took up their weapons and began to advance upon the Panchala king, to the horror of everyone. But Arjuna leaped back onto the stage, picked up the ceremonial bow and remaining arrows, and stepped between Drupada and his attackers. Bhima jumped out of the Brahmin section and uprooted a tree. (Remember, he had the strength of ten thousand elephants!) He joined Arjuna on the stage, brandishing the tree like a giant mace, and their combined presence discouraged the angry kings and princes from attacking Drupada—to the amazement of all, for everyone thought Arjuna and Bhima were Brahmin ascetics.

After the arena quieted down and Drupada seemed safe, the Pandavas took Draupadi back to the potter's house where they were staying. As they entered, Arjuna called to Kunti, "Mother, come see the alms we collected today!"

Without looking at him, Kunti replied as she always did when her sons came home with alms: "All of you should share what you received."

The brothers were stunned. Share Draupadi? All five of them? It seemed unthinkable. And Kunti was horrified when she learned what—or rather, whom—Arjuna had been calling "alms."

It was a very delicate situation. Everyone looked to the wise and virtuous Yudhisthira to guide them safely through it. He said decisively, "The mother's word is sacred. We have never disobeyed her, nor shall we do so now. All five of us shall marry the princess."

Soon, Dhrishtadyumna arrived at the house, having secretly followed them. He stood outside a window and eavesdropped on their conversation, which had turned from marriage to topics only Kshatriyas would discuss: weapons, kingdoms, and war. He quickly returned to the palace and told Drupada, "Father, I have no doubt that those five Brahmins are the Pandavas, and the successful archer was Arjuna." Drupada was thrilled: his dream was coming true.

Later, the Pandavas escorted Draupadi to the palace for the wedding ceremony. When Yudhisthira revealed who he and his brothers were, Drupada glowed with happiness: his daughter would marry Arjuna. Yudhisthira then announced that all five Pandavas would marry Draupadi, and Drupada's dream became a nightmare. Surely, he could not consent to such a sin!

The entire court was in an uproar until the rishi Vyasa spoke. "O King, there is scriptural sanction for one woman marrying several men. And in your daughter's case, there is more."

Vyasa had the power to see both the past and the future, and he explained, "In her previous life, Draupadi was the daughter of a forest rishi. Though she was beautiful and chaste, she had no husband, so she performed severe austerities for a long time, hoping to gratify Lord Shiva that he would grant her the boon of a husband.

"At last, Shiva appeared and told her, 'Child, you shall have five husbands.'

"'But my Lord,' she said, 'I have asked only for one!'

"Shiva replied, 'Yes, but you prayed for a husband five times. However, this shall happen in your next life.'"

What could Drupada say? The marriage had both scriptural sanction and Lord Shiva's blessing. Furthermore, Arjuna would be one of her five husbands. So he ordered that the wedding take place.

The evening became a joyous celebration of both the marriage and the resurrection of the Pandavas, whom nearly everyone had feared dead. Drupada, Krishna, and many other kings and princes gave extravagant gifts to the new bride and her five husbands. It was exceedingly wonderful.

But it was not at all wonderful for Duryodhana. Yet another of his plots to kill the Pandavas had failed—worse than failed, for the Pandavas were not only alive but had married Draupadi, whom he had wanted to wed. Worse still, they had gained powerful allies in their cousin Krishna and their new father-in-law, King Drupada. And as a crowning blow, he felt utterly humiliated by his public failure even to string the bow!

In frustration and despair, Duryodhana began the long journey back to Hastinapura, accompanied by Shakuni, Karna, and Dushasana. They would have to do something about this new state of affairs!

> The spiritual qualities represented by the five Pandavas — yama, niyama, fiery self-control, vitality, and calmness in psychological battle — are positive qualities of the first five chakras, the centers of subtle energy in the astral spine. Those chakras govern the five senses, whose energies we must withdraw into the astral spine to meditate deeply.

> The Pandavas' marriage to Draupadi represents the rising Kundalini energy magnetically withdrawing the sense energies into the corresponding chakras and up the spine toward the *Kutastha* (the spiritual eye, the positive magnetic pole of the sixth chakra). In the astral anatomy, Krishna symbolizes the Kutastha. As the energy rises, we begin to come into our spiritual power — our sense of who we truly are — just as the Pandavas gained power by acquiring such mighty allies as Drupada (who represents extreme dispassion) and Krishna (who symbolizes God or guru).

. . . . .

As soon as news of the events in Panchala reached Hastinapura, Vidura went to Dhritarashtra and announced, "O King, I bring glad tidings from Panchala: By good luck, the Kurus are prospering!"

Dhritarashtra clapped his hands in glee and said, "So Duryodhana has won Draupadi! Such wonderful news! Invite the couple to come for a grand celebration and have many excellent ornaments made for her."

Vidura smiled broadly as he corrected the blind king's assumption. "O King," said Vidura with a smile, "Draupadi has married the five Pandavas, who are alive and well. King Drupada and many other powerful kings with large armies have received them with great respect."

Dhritarashtra was stunned, but he recovered quickly. "Ah, Vidura, the Pandavas are so dear to me, even dearer than they were to Pandu. How fortunate that they are well and have gained many strong allies."

Vidura gave him a penetrating look. "O King, may your understanding remain so for a hundred years." He then departed.

Duryodhana and Karna had been eavesdropping, and they burst in upon Dhritarashtra. Duryodhana exclaimed, "Father! How can you speak fondly of the Pandavas and be happy about their prosperity? You are not acting rightly. We must find a way to stop them before they gain more allies and swallow us all!"

Dhritarashtra replied, "I agree with you, my son. I applauded them only so Vidura would not know my thoughts. Now that he has gone, we can talk openly about your ideas."

Duryodhana said, "We could conspire to make them jealous of one another. Or send spies to assassinate Bhima; they are completely dependent on him. Or murder all five of them. Or tempt them with beautiful women so Draupadi will turn against them. Or bribe Drupada to abandon them. Or—"

Karna interrupted. "Duryodhana, you tried many clever ways to kill the Pandavas: poison, fire, and all the rest. Cleverness failed then, and it will fail now. We could never make them jealous of one another now that a common wife unites them. And Draupadi accepted them when she thought they were poor Brahmins. Will she leave them now that she knows they are the mighty Pandavas? And we could never tempt Drupada to abandon them. He is a virtuous man; we cannot bribe him.

"No, the time for cleverness has passed. We must attack the Pandavas and Drupada before Krishna brings his army to restore the brothers to their paternal kingdom. Prowess is the cardinal virtue of the brave. We must show our prowess and exterminate them!"

Dhritarashtra applauded. "Well said, Karna! But let us seek the counsel of Bhishma, Drona, and Vidura."

He summoned those elders, and when they arrived, Dhritarashtra raised the possibility of attacking the Pandavas.

Bhishma said, "I can never approve of a quarrel with the Pandavas, O King. They are as dear to me as your sons and equally deserving of the kingdom. You are fortunate that they are alive, for it saves your good name. Now, we must consider how to save Duryodhana from any more such foolishness. King Dhritarashtra, there is but one action worthy of the Kuru race: Give half the kingdom to the Pandavas!"

Duryodhana stamped his foot and shouted, "No! Never!"

Drona said, "Yes, send them great wealth and good wishes, and invite them to Hastinapura."

Karna said to Dhritarashtra, "O King, you have pampered Bhishma and Drona with your wealth, and you regard them as your trusted friends. How amusing, then, that they advise you against your welfare. I say, no, it is time to fight!"

Vidura said, "O King, Bhishma and Drona do indeed seek your welfare. The Pandavas' claim to the kingdom supersedes yours. The stain of evil is upon you because of the Varanavata plot, but you can wash it off with kind and virtuous behavior toward the Pandavas. Do not think of fighting with them; they now have powerful allies in King Drupada and Krishna. Know this: Where Krishna is, there is victory. Remember what I told you at Duryodhana's birth, O King: he will be the death of you all."

Dhritarashtra's greatest fear was that his sons—especially his beloved eldest, Duryodhana—might be killed. He began to tremble: "Y-yes, we are f-fortunate that the Pandavas are alive. Let us welcome them back to Hastinapura. We shall divide the kingdom. Then, no more hostilities will arise between my sons and their cousins."

Duryodhana snorted angrily and stormed out of the court, followed by Karna.

Dhritarashtra sent Vidura to Panchala to invite the Pandavas to return to Hastinapura with their new wife. They gladly accepted the invitation, and with Krishna and some of his clan, they set out for Hastinapura. When they arrived, the Kuru citizens gave them a joyous public welcome and many lavish gifts. And the blind king kept his word: He gave Yudhisthira half the Kuru kingdom—the half that was a barren desert wilderness. He gave Duryodhana the fertile and prosperous half.

Still, Yudhisthira was content with this, for he valued peace second only to Truth itself. He felt this decision would prevent future conflict, for surely Duryodhana would never go to war over such a worthless wilderness. So the Pandavas, Draupadi, and Kunti left Hastinapura with cheerful hearts, bound for their new kingdom, accompanied by Krishna.

Why did Bhishma (ego), the wise grandfather who treasured dharma, want to divide the kingdom when he knew Yudhisthira (calmness) was the rightful king? Was he thinking that having two Kuru kingdoms would better ensure the continuation of the Kuru dynasty? That is like the seeker who thinks, "I believe in the spiritual path, but it has not yet brought me the happiness it promises. I should also pursue my material desires, so I will be certain to have at least *some* happiness."

Paramhansa Yogananda said of such an attitude, "This only amounts to wanting to enjoy a poisonous drink and also an invigorating tonic at the same time." He often likened material habits to poisoned honey, saying, "They promise happiness but bring only misery."

Or perhaps Bhishma, like Yudhisthira, saw division as the only possible route to peace, unfair though it was. Was that why neither he nor Yudhisthira insisted on Yudhisthira's right to rule the entire kingdom?

In everyday life, we may face dilemmas similar to, though much smaller than, Yudhisthira's. We may wonder, "Shouldn't I stand up for my rights?" In his book *Sadhu, Beware!*, Swami Kriyananda offers this possible response for the sincere spiritual seeker:

> When you move to a new position in your work or living situation, carry no mental "baggage" with you. Have no expectations. Visualize receiving no recognition for anything you've done, and perhaps being shoved to the bottom of whatever ladder you must now climb. Then visualize yourself accepting that status cheerfully and willingly. It isn't that you are likely ever to receive such treatment. It is very freeing, however, to be able to feel that you need *nothing* from anyone. Make God your only support and joy.

That is what Yudhisthira did. It might not seem much fun — unless you can see the "fun" in freeing yourself from ego consciousness.

CHAPTER 9

Better Times

THE PANDAVAS WERE HAPPY WITH their new kingdom despite its barrenness. Krishna helped them select a site for a capital city and lay out a plan for its development. Together, they began to transform that portion of the desert into what would eventually be a beautiful city—so beautiful that it would become known as Indraprastha, meaning that it resembled the heavenly city of Lord Indra.

Soon after their arrival, the celestial rishi Narada paid a visit. He had come for but one reason, which he stated plainly: "Now that Princess Draupadi is your common wife, the five of you must establish a rule to avoid any brotherly conflict over her."

Indeed, all five of them felt strongly attracted to Draupadi. After some discussion, they decided that each Pandava would live as her husband for a time, then give way to the next brother. And if one of them intruded when Draupadi was with her current husband, the intruder would have to go to the forest and live as a *brahmachari*, a renunciate, for twelve years while purifying himself through ascetic practices. All five brothers vowed to abide by that rule.

During Krishna's stay with them, the Pandavas and Draupadi grew ever more aware of his spiritual stature. Before long, they took up the spiritual quest as his disciples. And when Krishna had to return home to Dwaraka, they stayed closely connected inwardly.

As the transformation of the new kingdom continued, many people from other realms came to dwell there, attracted by the Pandavas' great virtue. The Pandavas also brought several neighboring kings under their sway through their prowess. Little by little, their domain grew and prospered.

* * * * *

Time had been passing pleasantly when, one day, a Brahmin came to the palace in distress. "Robbers have stolen my cattle. You must help me get them back!"

Without hesitation, Arjuna said, "I will recover them for you."

To fulfill his promise, he would need his weapons. But Draupadi and Yudhisthira, her current husband, were in the room where the Pandavas kept their weapons. Entering that room would violate the Pandavas' marital rule.

Arjuna decided that helping the Brahmin was more important, even if it meant spending twelve years in the forest. So he entered and found Yudhisthira and Draupadi sitting on a royal couch, talking quietly. With a few words of apology, he quickly gathered his weapons and set out after the robbers.

It was a simple matter to recover the Brahmin's cattle, and Arjuna quickly succeeded. When he returned to the palace, he went to Yudhisthira and said, "I have violated our rule. Give me leave to observe my vow and live in the forest for twelve years."

Yudhisthira replied, "I know why you entered that room. You did not violate dharma or dishonor me in any way. Stay with us."

Arjuna said, "I have heard, even from you, that one must not quibble about dharma. I made a vow, and I must honor it. Truth is my weapon."

Yudhisthira had to allow him to go, so Arjuna soon departed amid rivers of tears from all five Pandavas, Draupadi, and Kunti. It was extremely painful to think of being apart for so long.

· · · · ·

During his twelve-year absence, Arjuna traveled widely and made pilgrimages to many sacred sites. But he did not always live as a brahmachari, for he had "encounters" with several princesses from other kingdoms. He even spent three of those years with one of them as her husband!

In the eleventh year, Arjuna journeyed to visit Krishna in Dwaraka, where the residents gave him a hero's welcome. Shortly after his arrival, he attended a grand festival where he saw Krishna's favorite sister, Subhadra, for the first time. Her beauty immediately enthralled him.

Krishna sensed what had happened, and he laughed. "How is this, Arjuna? Can the heart of a forest brahmachari be agitated by the god of desire?"

Arjuna answered, "Who would not be fascinated by her? Tell me, how can I obtain her? I will do anything!"

Krishna smiled. "She will have a swayamvara soon. One never knows whom a princess will choose. The wise say that, for a brave Kshatriya, a forcible abduction is an honorable alternative."

Arjuna understood, and one day soon after, as Subhadra was returning from worship, he spirited her away in his chariot. Her kinsmen felt insulted by the abduction, and they wanted to give chase and attack Arjuna.

But Krishna told them, "Yes, you should pursue him, but not so you can punish him — if you are even capable of that. Instead, invite Arjuna and Subhadra to return to Dwaraka for a proper wedding."

And so they did. Arjuna spent the twelfth year of his purification in Dwaraka as Subhadra's husband. When the year ended — and with it, his time as a supposed brahmachari — he brought her back to Indraprastha.

Draupadi was not at all pleased. She was exceedingly jealous, even before meeting Subhadra. When Arjuna went to greet Draupadi for the first time, she snapped, "Why come to me? Why not go to her? When a man gains a second wife, he throws the first wife into the fire."

Draupadi carried on in this way for quite some time despite Arjuna's repeated attempts to appease her. And that was before Draupadi discovered that Arjuna had not just one other wife, but two!

So Arjuna tried a different approach: He asked Subhadra to exchange her elegant red silk garments for the simple garb of a cowherd woman, then present herself to Draupadi with great humility. Subhadra consented and went to her, saying, "I am your servant." Draupadi's heart melted, and her anger evaporated. She rose from her seat and embraced Subhadra with sincere affection.

From that time forward, the Pandavas, their wives, and Kunti lived together in happiness and harmony.

•　•　•　•　•

Subhadra soon gave birth to a son, Abhimanyu, who immediately became everyone's favorite. Krishna returned to Indraprastha with many of his relatives to celebrate the birth of his nephew.

One day, as he and Arjuna were strolling in the woods, Lord Agni, the fire god, appeared and asked a favor, saying, "I wish to burn down the Khandava Forest. I tried to burn it several times, but each time, Lord Indra sent mighty rainstorms to extinguish my flames. It seems he is partial to certain of the forest's inhabitants, even though many Asuras, Rakshasas, snakes, and other undesirable beings live there. So I ask that the two of you fight Indra and keep him from interfering with my plans."

Agni was asking Arjuna to fight his own father. Nevertheless, Arjuna replied, "O Lord Agni, I have excellent astras with which I can fight many Indras, but I have no bow strong enough to bear the energy I will put forth in battle. I also require an inexhaustible supply of arrows and a chariot to carry such a load. I want white celestial horses to pull the chariot. Krishna, too, has no weapon suited to his power. It behooves you to give us the means to thwart Indra's rain showers."

Agni asked Varuna, the Deva who rules all waters, to help him. Varuna gave Arjuna a famous celestial bow and two divine quivers that would never run out of arrows. He also gave him a magnificent chariot and four heavenly horses that were white as fleecy clouds and fleet as the wind — or even the mind.

The celestial bow was called Gandiva. It was the foremost of all weapons and the destroyer of them all — six cubits tall with the power of a hundred thousand ordinary bows. It was so strong that no other weapon could ever break it. And it was beautiful to behold, variegated with excellent colors and nary a blemish.

The chariot, too, was celestial. It was equipped with every weapon and delighted the hearts of all who beheld it. A fierce divine ape on its banner seemed bent on burning everything in sight.

Krishna received a mighty divine mace and a celestial chakra — a disk five cubits in diameter with sharp blades all around its edge. One could command it to be larger or smaller — or even invisible — then start it spinning and launch it at the foe. It was a devastating weapon, and it would return to its wielder after each use.

Arjuna and Krishna assured Agni, "With these weapons, no one can stand against us, not even the Devas or Asuras. Therefore, O Lord, set the forest ablaze! We will help you."

> Agni's reason for burning the forest is peripheral to the overall story, but the burning itself and the weapons he gave Arjuna will prove significant.

Agni then set the forest afire. As before, Indra sent legions of rain clouds to extinguish the flames. Krishna and Arjuna battled fiercely against Indra to keep the clouds away, and they succeeded: Indra was unable to extinguish the forest fire.

Afterward, Indra was not at all angry. On the contrary, he said, "I am highly pleased with your efforts. Each of you may have a boon."

Arjuna said, "My lord, I request all of your astras."

Indra replied, "My son, I will grant that boon when Lord Shiva becomes pleased with you. Krishna, what boon do you desire?"

Krishna answered, "I ask that my friendship with Arjuna be eternal."

"Let it be so," said Indra.

During the battle, Arjuna had spared the life of an Asura named Maya, who was trying to escape the burning forest. Maya was the architect of the Asuras, and in gratitude, he built a wondrous assembly hall for the Pandavas. Composed entirely of gems and precious stones, it emitted both celestial and terrestrial light, making it seem like it was on fire. Its brilliance made even the bright rays of the sun appear dark.

That hall held all manner of illusions: walls that looked like doorways, doorways that appeared to be walls, crystal floors that resembled pools of water, and pools of water that seemed to be crystal floors. It was magnificent and genuinely magical.

· · · · ·

As the years passed, the Pandava family expanded. Draupadi gave birth to five sons — one through each of the five brothers. Subhadra's son Abhimanyu grew tall and strong, and Arjuna taught him the science of weapons, both ordinary and astral. He was his father's pride and joy.

> Abhimanyu represents the quality of self-mastery. The offspring of self-control (Arjuna) is self-mastery.

The Pandavas' kingdom continued to grow and prosper. The citizens were happy, for King Yudhisthira was more like a kind and generous father than a ruler. Peace, truth, and fairness were his guiding principles. The kingdom experienced no droughts, floods, fires, or premature deaths. The clouds poured as much rain as the people desired, and the cities and towns prospered. Even robbers and cheats never lied—among themselves, at least. Other kings never attacked Indraprastha; they came only to offer service or give tributes. Yudhisthira amassed great wealth, and his status rose ever higher among the world's kings.

One day, the celestial rishi Narada returned to Indraprastha and said to Yudhisthira, "O King, I bring a request from your father, Pandu. He has attained a heavenly region of felicity. However, he wishes for an even higher realm: that of Lord Indra. He asks that you perform the sacred Rajasuya ceremony so he can dwell there.

"But I must caution you, O King. To perform this ceremony is to declare yourself emperor of the entire earth, so you must make all other kings subservient to you. That is likely to cause a war, perhaps many wars. It might even destroy the entire Kshatriya caste. Reflect on this, O King, and do what seems best."

Yudhisthira was horrified by the prospect of such destruction. Yet the idea of the Rajasuya appealed to him—partly because his father wanted him to do it, and partly because tradition held that those who perform it will attain regions of felicity in the hereafter. His brothers also favored performing the ceremony.

After much soul-searching, Yudhisthira decided to proceed. He invited all the other kings to participate and pay him tribute. The Kurus and Drupada, being relatives, would be honored guests, not tributaries. But any other kings who refused to offer tribute would have to be conquered.

To that end, Yudhisthira's four brothers took four mighty armies north, south, east, and west to ensure that all other kings would be tributaries. It was extremely difficult to subjugate some of the kings, but the brothers eventually succeeded in their missions. Brahmin priests then chose an astrologically auspicious date for the climactic ceremony, and preparations began.

Before long, kings from all over the world began to arrive in Indraprastha to offer tribute and take part in the ceremony. Yudhisthira wished to show goodwill toward Duryodhana, so he offered his cousin a position of high honor as the official receiver of the tribute brought to Yudhisthira. Duryodhana did not want to attend, for he wanted to perform the Rajasuya himself. But having been offered this honor, he could not refuse. Day after day, he had to endure the anguish of receiving vast quantities of gems, gold, silver, and pearls from the tributary kings and depositing them in Yudhisthira's treasury.

The ceremony took place in the magical assembly hall, and it was a success: Yudhisthira was now emperor of the entire world. Still, Narada's warning weighed heavily on his mind, so when the rishi Vyasa came to take his leave, Yudhisthira said to him, "Rishi Narada warned me that performing the Rajasuya could cause the ruin of the entire Earth. Tell me, O Holy One, will that come to pass?"

Vyasa replied, "Indeed, O King, when thirteen years have passed, you will be the cause of the destruction of all Kshatriyas because of the sins of Duryodhana and through the might of Bhima and Arjuna."

That distressed Yudhisthira so severely that he vowed, "Then, for thirteen years, I will practice perfect virtue. I will not fight with anyone or even speak a harsh word, and I will live under the command of my relatives. There will be no disagreements, *and there will be no war!*"

* * * * *

After the other kings departed, Duryodhana and his contingent stayed in Indraprastha for a time. He was fascinated by the magical assembly hall, and he spent many hours marveling at beauties he had not imagined could exist. He was sorely jealous of Yudhisthira's new eminence and of all the Pandavas for having such a magnificent structure.

Duryodhana also fell victim to the hall's illusions. He mistook a crystal floor for a pool of water and lifted his garments to keep them dry. Seeing that, Bhima laughed uproariously. The next time Duryodhana saw a pool of water at floor level, he assumed it must be a floor, but it was indeed a pool of water, and he fell in. Bhima, Arjuna, and Draupadi laughed and laughed. Another time, thinking that a crystal wall was a doorway, he bashed his head, knocking himself nearly senseless. Nakula and Sahadeva—and even the servants—joined in the boisterous laughter.

So, while the Rajasuya was a grand success for Yudhisthira, it was yet another disaster for Duryodhana. He was deeply depressed over Yudhisthira's prominence and his own public humiliations in the magical assembly hall. He lamented to Shakuni, "Seeing the Pandavas' prosperity, I am dried up like a shallow pond in summer. It is all fate; self-effort is useless. I shall kill myself."

Shakuni replied, "Duryodhana, the Pandavas achieved prosperity through their efforts. So can you. Do not think of fighting them, for even the Devas cannot defeat them in battle. But I know another way to conquer them. They have a glaring weakness that we can exploit." During the journey home, he explained his idea. Duryodhana found it very encouraging, and together, they devised a strategy for carrying it out.

• • • • •

Upon reaching Hastinapura, they went directly to Dhritarashtra to set the plan in motion. Duryodhana began pacing back and forth in front of the blind king, apparently in great agitation, sighing repeatedly.

Shakuni said, "O King, Duryodhana seems extremely depressed and emaciated. Perhaps you should ask him what is wrong."

Dhritarashtra was puzzled. "Duryodhana, you have everything a man could want. What is wrong?"

Duryodhana fumed, "I am burning with jealousy—that is what is wrong! All those kings paying homage to the Pandavas, all that splendor and wealth. My hands grew tired from receiving the treasures brought to Yudhisthira!"

"My son," said Dhritarashtra, "you have as much wealth as Yudhisthira, yet he is not jealous of you. Why be jealous of him? The jealous person is never happy. Contentment with your lot in life is the way to happiness."

Duryodhana seethed with anger. "What man can be content when his foes are prospering? No, I shall seize their wealth or else die trying!"

Dhritarashtra began to tremble at the thought of his firstborn son's death.

Shakuni had known that would happen, and he leaned in close. "O King, I know how we can take their wealth *without* fighting them, for I am the greatest dice player in the world. I know many clever ways by which I can win every play. Yudhisthira is very fond of dice, but he has little skill. Duryodhana should challenge him to a friendly game, and I will compete on Duryodhana's behalf." He rubbed his hands in glee and declared, "I will win all of Yudhisthira's wealth, and it will be yours, O King!"

Dhritarashtra shook his head. "That would be dangerous. It could cause a war. I must consult Vidura. He will know the right thing to do."

Duryodhana countered, "Vidura always favors the Pandavas. He will surely persuade you to reject this plan. And if you do, Father, I will surely kill myself. When I am dead, you and Vidura can enjoy the whole earth. What need have you of me?"

Dhritarashtra briefly pondered the situation, then sighed deeply and said, "Oh, very well, let it be as you wish. Your plan is unwise, Duryodhana, and you will regret it. Immorality never brings prosperity. But I shall send Vidura to convey the challenge. Indeed, as he foretold at your birth, the calamity destined by fate is upon us."

With great reluctance, Vidura set out for Indraprastha, certain that the game of dice would lead to the destruction of the Kurus. When he arrived, he met with Yudhisthira and said, "O King, Duryodhana challenges you to a game of dice. And I must tell you: Shakuni will play on his behalf."

Yudhisthira shuddered. "Shakuni! He is adept at dice—and a cheater. I do not wish to gamble, yet a Kshatriya can never refuse a challenge." He shook his head in resignation. "There is no freedom in this world. God has ordained the fate of every creature, and we, as if bound by a rope, can do nothing to change it. Very well, Uncle. We shall go to Hastinapura for the game of dice."

So the five brothers, Kunti, Draupadi, and Vidura departed Indraprastha, bound for Hastinapura and a "friendly" game of dice.

How could such a wise and virtuous person as Yudhisthira fall into such an obvious trap? The answer goes deeper than the Kshatriya code of honor, which dictates that one must never refuse a challenge. Deeper also than the explanation that Yudhisthira would offer much later: that he had hoped to win Duryodhana's kingdom in the dice game.

Swami Kriyananda explained that there comes a time in our spiritual progress when we attain a state of profound calmness (symbolized by Yudhisthira) that we know intuitively is our true nature. We can think, "This is who I am, so I can never lose it."

However, until we attain soul freedom, lingering material tendencies (represented by Shakuni and Duryodhana) can tempt us to "gamble" by engaging too much with low-consciousness people, activities, or environments. Although we can never lose our soul's innate calmness, such gambling can pull us down and keep us from experiencing that calmness.

Commonsense discrimination will save us from such carelessness — only a little will suffice! But without discrimination (symbolized by Pandu being dead), our inner kingdom will be ruled by sense-mind (Dhritarashtra), which blindly follows material desire (Duryodhana).

CHAPTER 10

The Game of Dice

WHEN THE PANDAVAS, DRAUPADI, and Kunti arrived in Hastinapura, they were given elegant apartments in the Kuru palace. With cheerful hearts, they settled in and enjoyed a delightful evening of pleasure and sport before being lulled to sleep with sweet music and other entertainments.

The next day, they rose at dawn and performed their customary worship. The brothers then went to the Kurus' grand new assembly hall, which had been built expressly for this occasion. It was truly magnificent—constructed entirely of gold and lapis lazuli, intended to rival the Pandavas' wondrous hall of illusions in Indraprastha.

The Kuru elders and many visiting kings were present, as were the Kauravas, Shakuni, and Karna. King Dhritarashtra occupied his throne upon a raised platform; Queen Gandhari sat beside him. Bhishma and Drona sat to their right, Kripa and Vidura to their left. The dice board was directly in front of the royal couple; Shakuni and Duryodhana stood to one side of it.

After the Pandavas paid their respects to the Kuru elders, Shakuni said to Yudhisthira, "Gaze about you, O King. The assembly is full. We have all been waiting for you. Let the game begin!"

Yudhisthira answered, "Deceitful gambling is sinful. There is no Kshatriya honor or prowess in gambling, and certainly no morality."

Shakuni replied, "Why speak of morality, O King? Morality is not in question here. It is merely a matter of winning and losing. Is a great warrior immoral when he defeats a weaker warrior? Is a wise person immoral because he knows more than an ignorant person? In any contest, the strong confronts the weak, and there is nothing immoral about it. Of course, if you are *afraid* to play, then by all means, you should not play."

Yudhisthira said, "Challenged, I will never withdraw. Who am I to play?"

Duryodhana answered, "I will match your wagers. Uncle Shakuni will play on my behalf."

"A surrogate player is contrary to rule," said Yudhisthira. "Will a warrior not fight his own battles?" Duryodhana gave no response as he and Shakuni sat down at the dice board. They looked expectantly at Yudhisthira until he sat down opposite them.

Yudhisthira gathered himself, then said, "I will stake my entire wealth of flawless pearls."

Duryodhana nodded, agreeing to match the wager, and Shakuni began his play. Soon, he exclaimed, "Lo, I have won!"

Yudhisthira said, "I will stake my vast treasury of gold and silver."

Duryodhana nodded, and Shakuni played again. "Lo, I have won."

Yudhisthira continued, "I now stake my glorious chariot, the equal of a thousand ordinary chariots."

Duryodhana nodded, matching Yudhisthira's wager with a thousand ordinary chariots. Again, Shakuni played. And again, "Lo, I have won."

So the game began, and so it continued. Shakuni won every play of the dice. Yudhisthira's brothers longed to stop him, but they could say nothing, for he was their eldest. Caught up in a gambling fever, Yudhisthira lost his wealth, his city, his army—his entire kingdom. When he had no other possessions, he said, "I now stake my brother, the valiant Nakula."

All the Kauravas' eyes went wide at the prospect of winning one of the Pandavas as their slave. Shakuni played. "Lo, I have won!" The Kauravas shouted in glee.

In quick succession, Yudhisthira wagered—and lost—Sahadeva, Arjuna, Bhima, and finally himself.

Shakuni said, "You have lost yourself into slavery. That is very sinful. Still, there is something you can wager: Stake the Princess of Panchala and win yourself back."

The gambling fever raged on, for Yudhisthira said, "Full of compassion and sweetness, as beautiful as the goddess Lakshmi herself, Draupadi is now my stake."

Those words shook the entire assembly. The Kauravas cheered, whereas many others were ashamed of Yudhisthira and cried, "Fie! Fie!" Bhishma, Drona, and Kripa remained silent, drenched with perspiration. Vidura sat holding his head between his hands, looking at the floor and sighing like a snake.

But Dhritarashtra was glad, and he eagerly asked, "Has the stake been won? Has it been won?" Karna and Dushasana laughed aloud.

One more time, Shakuni began his play. And one more time, "Lo, I have won!"

Duryodhana shouted for joy, then said, "Vidura, bring hither the Pandavas' dearly beloved wife. Let her sweep the assembly hall before she moves in with our other servant women."

Vidura responded, "O wretch, do you not know that you hang on the edge of a precipice? Will you insist on destroying the Kuru race? Do not provoke the Pandavas into killing you. In my judgment, Draupadi is not a slave, for Yudhisthira staked her only after losing himself."

"Fie on you, Vidura!" shouted Duryodhana. He commanded a servant, "Go quickly and bring Draupadi here!"

The servant hurried to the Pandavas' apartments in the palace and said to Draupadi, "O Princess, Yudhisthira was intoxicated with gambling, and Duryodhana has won you. Come with me to the assembly hall. I will assign you to some menial work."

Draupadi's eyes grew wide with horror. "What royal Kshatriya would ever stake his own wife?! The king must have been drunk, or he surely would have staked something else."

The servant explained, "He had nothing else to stake. Before he staked you, he had already lost his wealth, his kingdom, his brothers, and even himself."

Draupadi considered that, then said, "If he lost himself before staking me, perhaps I am not a slave after all. Go back and ask the elders whether I am free or not. Tell them I will do whatever they say."

The servant returned to the assembly and conveyed Draupadi's request. But the elders all sat in silence, their eyes fixed on the floor.

Duryodhana had no patience for that, and he said to his brother, "Dushasana, bring Draupadi here forcibly."

Dushasana hurried off to the Pandavas' apartments, his eyes blood-red with anger and eagerness. He found Draupadi alone, wearing only a single piece of cloth. He demanded, "Come with me, O Princess!"

In great distress, Draupadi turned and ran to the place where the ladies of Dhritarashtra's household were. Dushasana roared with anger and ran after her. He quickly caught her, then dragged her by her hair through the palace and into the assembly hall. Her single piece of cloth became loosened as he kept dragging her in front of everyone.

She cried out in misery, "How can this disgraceful thing be happening? Truly, Bhishma and Drona have lost their energy, as have Vidura and the king."

She glanced at her husbands and shot them a look of fiery anger—a look that pained them more than the loss of their kingdom or even their freedom.

Seeing this, Dushasana laughed aloud and dragged her all the more forcibly, shouting, "Slave! Slave!" Karna and Shakuni joined him in laughter.

Draupadi said in a feeble voice, "I ask this assembly, full of virtuous persons, whether I am a slave since King Yudhisthira lost himself before he wagered me. Who will answer me?"

Bhishma replied, "Dharma is subtle, O Princess, and I cannot answer your question. One with no wealth—who does not even own himself—cannot stake anything. Yet it is said that wives always belong to their husbands. And Yudhisthira has not accused Shakuni of dishonesty. Therefore, I cannot decide."

Draupadi cried piteously, "But the king was forced to play against a cheater! I ask again: Am I a slave? Who will answer?!"

Dushasana began to insult her even more harshly, causing Bhima to boil with anger until he could no longer contain it. He said to Yudhisthira, "Gamblers have many loose women in their houses, but even they do not stake those women. You have caused the innocent Draupadi to be mistreated by the despicable Kauravas. I shall burn your hands for that. Sahadeva, bring me fire!"

Arjuna was horrified. "Bhima, how can you berate your eldest brother like this? He was challenged, and as a Kshatriya, he had no choice but to play."

Bhima accepted Arjuna's response and calmed down, but only slightly.

Vikarna, one of Duryodhana's brothers, asked the assembly, "Why do our elders not answer Draupadi's question?" Bhishma, Drona, Kripa, and Vidura bowed their heads in shame and said nothing. Dhritarashtra also remained silent.

Vikarna asked repeatedly, but the elders spoke not a word. At last, he said, "Then I will speak: King Yudhisthira lost himself before Shakuni lured him into staking Draupadi. Therefore, I say she is not a slave!"

Many of the visiting kings roared their approval, but Karna shouted, "Vikarna, you do not know what dharma is. You are just a boy, speaking as if you were old. Yudhisthira staked all his possessions. His wife was one of them — a whore who sleeps with five men. The Pandavas have been silent, so they obviously regard her as having been won." He turned to Dushasana and commanded, "Take the Pandavas' robes and Draupadi's cloth!"

The Pandavas took off their robes and threw them on the floor. Dushasana took hold of Draupadi's single piece of cloth and began to pull. She desperately cried out, "O Lord Krishna, save your devotee! You are my only refuge!"

Krishna was in far-off Dwaraka, but her desperate plea was answered, for when Dushasana pulled off Draupadi's single piece of cloth, another piece took its place. He pulled off that piece, and a third piece appeared. And so it continued, hundreds of times, with cloths of many excellent hues. The pile of fabric grew higher and higher, yet Draupadi always remained covered.

Others in the assembly began to jeer at Dushasana, and Bhima swore a terrible oath: "Let me not obtain the realms of my ancestors if I do not tear open in battle the breast of this wicked-minded Dushasana and drink his lifeblood!"

Many of the visitors applauded Bhima's oath. Meanwhile, Dushasana stopped trying to disrobe Draupadi, for he was tired and ashamed for having failed.

Karna sneered at Draupadi. "Even a Sutaputra is better than a slave, I think. Your husbands have sunk into eternal hell. The Kauravas are your masters now. Choose a new husband from among them," and he turned toward Yudhisthira with a nasty smile, "one who will not gamble you into slavery."

Duryodhana leered at Draupadi and pulled up his garment to reveal his thigh.

Bhima leaped to his feet and thundered another oath: "Duryodhana! May I not attain the regions of my ancestors when I die if I do not break that thigh of yours in the great conflict to come!"

Karna ignored him. "Dushasana, take her to the slave quarters."

As Dushasana began to drag Draupadi away, she wailed, "Wait, you wretch! I have a high duty to perform, and you have not allowed me to do it. I must salute our elders."

Dushasana replied by dragging her with even greater force. She cried out to the entire assembly. "I have put a question to all of you, and you have not answered. Tell me now, O Kurus: What is the dharma? Am I a slave or not? I will cheerfully accept your decision. Grandfather?"

Bhishma replied, "I have already said that I am uncertain whether you are a slave, Princess. But I *am* certain that the Kauravas are slaves—slaves of jealousy and folly, and their destruction will soon come." He paused and reflected, then said, "Yudhisthira is an expert on dharma. Let him say whether you are a slave."

Duryodhana's eyes lit up with an idea, and he smiled. "Yes, let the Pandavas speak. If one of them will say that Yudhisthira is not his master, then Draupadi will be freed."

That caused a buzzing throughout the assembly—some applauded his words, while others recoiled in horror at the suggestion. The Kauravas, however, were delighted, for if a younger brother denied the eldest's authority, it would split the Pandavas, destroying their power.

Bhima waved his massive arms for silence and said, "Yudhisthira will forever be our master, and if he commands me, I will slay the wicked Kauravas this very moment, like a lion slaying many small animals."

Duryodhana ignored him and said, "I say again, let Arjuna or one of the twins say that Yudhisthira is not his master. Then Draupadi will be freed."

Arjuna answered, "Yudhisthira was certainly our master before he began to play. But let the Kauravas judge whose master he could be after losing himself."

At those words, a jackal howled in the worship room of the palace, and asses brayed in response. Terrible birds cried out from all sides.

Vidura turned to Dhritarashtra. "O King, do you hear that? Those sounds are omens of the destruction of the Kurus."

Gandhari said, "Vidura speaks the truth, O King. Our realm will be utterly devastated."

The blind king suddenly began to fear for his sons' lives, and he clutched Duryodhana's arm. "You wicked fool, destruction is already upon you when you insult such a one as Draupadi." He turned toward her. "O Princess, forgive this outrage. Ask of me a boon."

Draupadi answered, "If you will grant me a boon, then I ask that King Yudhisthira be freed from slavery."

Dhritarashtra declared, "Let it be so. You do not deserve only one boon. Ask another."

She replied, "I ask that his four brothers also be freed."

Dhritarashtra said, "O blessed daughter, let it be so. Ask a third boon, for two boons have not honored you sufficiently."

Draupadi responded, "Greed always brings about a loss of virtue. I do not deserve a third boon, so I dare not ask for one. Free from bondage, my husbands will achieve prosperity by their virtuous acts."

Karna sneered. "Oh, how wonderful! The Princess of Panchala has rescued her powerless husbands, who were sinking in an ocean of distress."

Those words outraged Bhima, for it was a grave insult to say that the Pandavas were saved by their wife. He began to burn with anger. Fire and smoke poured out of his eyes and ears. He asked Yudhisthira, "Shall I slay all our foes right now? Then you can rule the entire earth!"

But Yudhisthira embraced him and said softly, "Have peace, Bhima."

Then Yudhisthira turned and bowed to Dhritarashtra. "O King, tell us what to do. We shall always remain obedient to you."

Dhritarashtra replied, "Take back your wealth. Take back your kingdom. You are virtuous and intelligent. Such persons see only their enemies' merits and good deeds, not their faults and hostile actions. They never retaliate for the hurts they receive.

"I allowed the game of dice to take place only that I might see my friends and assess the strengths and weaknesses of my sons. Go home now. Let there be brotherly love between you and your cousins. Fix your heart ever on dharma."

The Pandavas bowed to Dhritarashtra and the other Kuru elders. Along with Draupadi, they left the assembly and called for their chariots. As soon as Kunti joined them, they left Hastinapura with cheerful hearts, bound for Indraprastha.

Draupadi had been unable to fight, run away, or argue her way to
freedom. So she did the only thing she could do: surrender totally
to God in the form of Krishna, who rescued her from further humiliation. Krishna later highlights this attitude in the Bhagavad Gita,
where he says: "O Arjuna, with all eagerness of heart, make God
alone your refuge. By His grace you will attain the uttermost peace,
and find shelter for all eternity." (Gita 18:62)

• • • • •

After the Pandavas departed, Duryodhana, Dushasana, Karna,
and Shakuni went privately to Dhritarashtra. Duryodhana said,
"Father, the Pandavas will never forgive us for this! I have heard that,
even now, they are preparing to annihilate us, your sons! Call them
back. Let there be one more throw of the dice, with a different stake,
one that will give us time to consolidate our hold on the kingdom
and gain many powerful allies."

When he explained his idea, Dhritarashtra consented and sent a
messenger to recall the Pandavas.

The Kuru elders and visiting kings soon heard about that, and
they implored Dhritarashtra, "Do not do this, O King! Let there be
peace!"

Aswatthama, Yuyutsu, and Vikarna agreed, pleading, "Let the
Pandavas return to their kingdom, O King!"

Gandhari said, "Remember what Vidura said about the omens
at Duryodhana's birth. He will be the destruction of the Kurus! Do
not rekindle a fire that has been extinguished. You must abandon that
wretch. You could not do so before, but you must do so now. O King,
let virtue and peace guide you!"

Still, Dhritarashtra would not change his mind. "If destruction is
upon us, let it take place freely. I cannot prevent it. Let the Pandavas
return for a second game of dice."

• • • • •

The Pandavas had gone quite some distance by the time the
messenger caught up with them and conveyed the king's summons.

Everyone knew what this meant: Shakuni would again cheat, resulting in some dreadful outcome.

Yudhisthira said to his brothers, "What must happen will happen, whether I play or not. This summons is both a challenge and a royal command. I have pledged obedience to the king, so I cannot refuse, though I know it will prove destructive."

He told the messenger, "Return to Hastinapura and tell King Dhritarashtra that we are on our way."

When the brothers arrived in Hastinapura and entered the assembly hall, they again paid their respects to the elders. Shakuni said to Yudhisthira, "Let there be one more throw of the dice, O King. The losers will go into exile in the forest for twelve years, where they must live in strict poverty, dressed in deerskins, while the winners take over their kingdom. In the thirteenth year, the losers must live in some inhabited region without being recognized. If they succeed in that, the winners will return their kingdom. But if they are discovered during the thirteenth year, they will be exiled to the forest for twelve more years."

Yudhisthira agreed to those terms, as if knowing that the destruction of the Kurus was at hand. Shakuni again began to play, and he soon said, "Lo, I have won!"

The Kauravas cheered loudly and began to celebrate. The Pandavas and Draupadi immediately cast off their royal robes and started to dress in deerskins.

Dushasana smiled broadly and proclaimed, "The absolute sovereignty of the illustrious King Duryodhana has commenced! The Pandavas have sunk into eternal hell, having lost happiness and kingdom forever. They who laughed at Duryodhana will now go into the woods, defeated and deprived of all their wealth. They are no better than eunuchs!" He leered at Draupadi and said, "It is not too late to choose a husband from among the Kauravas, who have wealth aplenty."

Then he danced around Bhima, laughing and shouting, "Fat cow! Ugly cow!"

Bhima stepped up to Dushasana like a mighty lion confronting a jackal. "O wicked-minded villain, you boast here before all the kings and pierce our hearts with your words. But I say again, let me not reach the regions of blessedness when I die if I do not pierce your heart in battle and drink your lifeblood!"

Arjuna called out for all to hear, "And I vow that, when the fourteenth year arrives, I shall slay that wicked and vain fool, Karna!"

Sahadeva promised, "In the great battle to come, I shall kill the crooked and foul Shakuni … if that coward does not run from the fight!"

Nakula added, "Remembering the wrongs done to Draupadi, I shall make the earth destitute of the sons of Dhritarashtra!"

Yudhisthira said to the onlookers, "I bid you all farewell. I *shall* see you again."

The Pandavas and Draupadi touched the feet of Bhishma and Drona. Their children and other wives would move to Dwaraka when the Kauravas took over in Indraprastha. Kunti would stay with Vidura and his wife in Hastinapura during the exile.

As the brothers and Draupadi departed for the forest, leaving their comforts and riches behind, Yudhisthira wore a cloth over his head so his angry eyes would not burn everything and everyone. Bhima continually flexed his mighty arms as if crushing the Kauravas. Arjuna scattered grains of sand, symbolizing the countless arrows he would shower upon his foes. And Draupadi wept as she walked, with her hair still disheveled, signifying the grief that would come to the Kaurava wives after the thirteen years had passed.

Later that day, many evil omens were again seen and heard. Narada, the celestial rishi, appeared before the Kuru assembly and proclaimed, "In the fourteenth year hence, Bhima and Arjuna will destroy the Kauravas because of Duryodhana's behavior!" He then vanished.

Hearing this, Duryodhana, Karna, and Shakuni quaked with fear. In desperation, they offered the kingdom to Drona, who said, "As you have sought refuge in me, I will do my utmost to protect you. But remember: No one can kill the Pandavas. Do not think that you have accomplished everything by sending them into exile. Your happiness will last but a moment. In the fourteenth year hence, a great calamity will overwhelm you!"

Dhritarashtra trembled with anxiety as he turned to Vidura and said, "What Drona has said is true. Go and recall the Pandavas. If, out of honor, they will not come back, then let them go with respect and affection, with weapons and chariots and every good thing."

Sanjaya, the king's charioteer and trusted advisor, then spoke. "All of this is your own doing, O King. Destruction does not come as an upraised club to smash one's head. He whom the gods wish to destroy, they first deprive of reason, so he sees evil in good and good in evil. Once that is accomplished, destruction is certain."

Dhritarashtra replied, "O Sanjaya, the Pandavas will never forgive the dragging of Draupadi into the court. I should have made peace with them. That would have been the path of virtue and profit. But out of affection for Duryodhana, I did not follow that path."

> Sense-mind (Dhritarashtra) is always inclined to follow the path of material desire (Duryodhana), even when that means abandoning "the path of virtue and profit." As Krishna later emphasizes repeatedly in the Gita: "The unquenchable flames of inner desire are the constant enemy even of the wise." (Gita 3:39)

> When we look back, we can see our errors. That is introspection, represented by Sanjaya. If we impartially examine our actions and underlying motives, and if they do not align with our aspirations, we can make corrections. Dhritarashtra looked back and saw his error, but his desire was so strong that he could not bring himself to make corrections. That failure ensured the calamity that Narada and Drona had foretold.

CHAPTER 11

Into Exile

A s the Pandavas and Draupadi left Hastinapura and headed toward the forest, the Kuru citizens sank deep into grief, and they harshly condemned the Kuru elders and Duryodhana over the dice game. Many followed the Pandavas and pleaded, "Do not forsake us! We are your loving friends. The whole world is doomed when the sinful Duryodhana rules it. All virtues reside in the five of you, and we wish to live with you. Take us with you."

Yudhisthira responded, "You have blessed us with your affection. If you truly seek our welfare, please remain in Hastinapura and care for Grandfather and King Dhritarashtra, Vidura, and my mother. That would give me great happiness, for they are overwhelmed by sorrow over what has occurred."

Hearing those words, the citizens began to wail in despair. Reluctantly, they turned back toward Hastinapura while the Pandavas proceeded into the forest, accompanied by many Brahmin ascetics who refused to abandon them.

The Pandavas decided to begin their twelve years of exile in an area frequented by many rishis. They set up a modest hermitage and commenced their new lives of simplicity.

Back in Hastinapura, Dhritarashtra was consumed by guilt over his role in the dice game—and terrified of its karmic consequences. When he had asked Vidura to give the Pandavas "respect and affection and every good thing" during their exile, he had hoped somehow to mitigate the calamity that Narada foretold.

Nevertheless, he continued to vacillate. When he sought Vidura's advice, and Vidura told him to return the Pandavas' kingdom, he became so angry that he banished Vidura from the Kuru realm. But not long after Vidura departed, Dhritarashtra sank into great remorse over the banishment, and he sent a messenger to ask Vidura to return.

Still, the Pandavas had some good things in their new forest life: their weapons, chariots, horses, and some servants. Early in their exile, Yudhisthira received a boon that would prove invaluable. He had been distressed that he could not feed the many Brahmins who were following the Pandavas. So he decided to worship the sun god, Lord Surya, and ask for his help, for the sun is the ultimate source of all earthly sustenance.

His worship gratified Surya, who appeared to Yudhisthira and gave him a copper vessel. "O King, I shall provide you with food for twelve years through this vessel. When Draupadi fills it with food she has prepared, the food shall be inexhaustible until she has eaten." Surya added, "And in fourteen years, you shall regain your kingdom." Then he vanished.

Surya's boon enabled the Pandavas to feed not only the Brahmins, but also the many great rishis who came from far and wide to inspire them and raise their spirits. It also helped them satisfy Bhima's enormous appetite. All in all, life was not nearly as difficult as it might have been.

After a time, Krishna and a large contingent of his kinfolk came to visit the Pandavas. He had only recently learned of the dice game, for he had been fully occupied defending Dwaraka from attack. He was outraged and said fiercely, "The earth shall drink the blood of Duryodhana and Karna, of Dushasana and Shakuni, and we will install Yudhisthira on the throne. The wicked deserve to die!" He began to talk about the coming war, his eyes ablaze with a fiery light. He became so passionate that he seemed bent on incinerating the entire universe.

Arjuna hastened to soothe him by telling stories of Krishna's miraculous achievements in former lives. After a time, Krishna became his usual calm self once again, and he said with great affection, "You are mine, Arjuna, and I am yours. We are the ancient rishis Nara and Narayana, born now for a special purpose. You are from me, and I am from you. No one can tell the difference between us." Hearing those sweet words, everyone sat in a powerful silence for a time.

Draupadi broke the stillness by launching into a passionate account of all her miseries. She began to weep over the Pandavas' failure to protect her from humiliation. "Fie on Arjuna's prowess!" she cried. "Fie on Bhima's strength! Why do those great heroes, even now, not kill the Kauravas? Why do they not care what has happened to me? Truly, I have no husbands!"

Krishna replied, "Weep not, lady. The heavens might fall, the Earth might split in two, the oceans might dry up, but I promise that you shall once more be the queen of kings."

. . . . .

As time passed, Yudhisthira began to find his simple life in the forest rather pleasant. He was free of the burdens of being a king, food was abundant, and he was profoundly grateful for the regular visits of the rishis.

But Draupadi remained *extremely* impatient to regain their lost kingdom. When she could no longer restrain herself, she confronted Yudhisthira. "My lord, seeing you suffering in this horrible place, my heart knows no peace. How can you not be angry?! He who purposely harms another should be punished. You should slay your foes, not forgive them!"

Yudhisthira replied, "Anger is the cause of all distress. He who conquers it earns prosperity. He who gives way to it reaps adversity. How, then, can I indulge in it?

"It is the forgiving person who is ever victorious. Forgiveness holds the very universe together. Forgiveness is holiness. It is the might of the mighty. It is honor and Truth. It is peace of mind. He who can forgive everything attains God. Forgiveness is the greatest virtue.

"Do not be angry, Draupadi. The Kuru elders will surely persuade Dhritarashtra to return our kingdom. And if he does not, he will be destroyed. Because I deserve to rule, forgiveness has taken possession of me. Forgiveness and gentleness are the qualities of the self-possessed. They represent eternal dharma. Therefore, I shall adopt those qualities."

Far from persuaded, Draupadi countered, "I bow to the Creator of Delusion, who has thus clouded your reasoning! The wise say that the king protects dharma, and dharma protects him in return. But dharma has not protected you, though it has always been dearer to you than the kingdom, dearer than your brothers and myself, dearer than life itself! You are generous, humble, truthful—"

Yudhisthira interrupted, shaking his head. "It is true that good actions should bear good fruit. But I never act with desire for the fruits of my efforts. He who does so is merely a merchant in virtue.

I give because it is my duty to give. To the best of my ability, I do whatever a person in my position should do — not for the fruits of dharma, but for the sake of dharma itself.

"Why good actions go unrewarded is a mystery even to the gods. Yet, though you may not see the fruits of dharma, you should not doubt its workings. If dharma had no fruits, darkness would envelop the universe. No one would seek knowledge or salvation — men would live like beasts. Why would the Devas and rishis, who are above all human conditions, cherish dharma as they do? He who doubts dharma is full of anxiety and attains neither prosperity nor happiness."

His wise words still did not pacify Draupadi, so she took another approach: "I do not think God behaves like a loving parent. He is like a child playing with toys, creating and destroying his creatures at whim. I do not speak highly of a God who permits such injustice!"

Yudhisthira admonished her, "Do not slander God, Draupadi. Learn how to know Him. Bow down to Him. Never disparage Him through whose grace mortals may attain immortality."

She countered, "I never slander God! It is this suffering that causes me to rave. But listen, I will speak further. Only those who act will succeed. He who leaves life to chance meets with destruction. Do not depend on divine favor to restore your kingdom!"

Bhima had been listening nearby, and he joined the debate. "O King, what do we gain by this deprivation? It was not by virtue or might that Duryodhana snatched our kingdom. Why do you suffer this distress for the trite merit of keeping a promise? No one applauds you for this."

Bhima swelled with frustration and fury. "Your carelessness led to this calamity! We submitted to it only out of respect for you. I deeply regret that we did not slay the sons of Dhritarashtra then and there! They regard our forgiveness as impotence. That grieves me more than death in battle, for then we would attain Heaven rather than this miserable exile."

Yudhisthira sighed. "What you say is true, brother. This calamity is due to my folly alone. I thought I could win Duryodhana's kingdom in the dice game, but I was no match for Shakuni's deceptions. It is all Fate."

That admission did not pacify Bhima. "You cry, 'Dharma! Virtue!' But that which tortures one's self and friends is not dharma. Might and energy are the dharma of a Kshatriya! Do not forsake the duties of your caste, O King. You are a mighty warrior. Arjuna is the greatest of all archers. And I am the foremost with the mace. Let us seize the kingdom from the unworthy Duryodhana!"

Yudhisthira shook his head. "I accepted the terms of the dice game. Now, we must live out this exile. Death itself would be better than breaking my word. Kingdom, fame, even high regions of Heaven—all these do not come up to even a sixteenth part of Truth. Wait, brother, for better days. We shall have our revenge and thus win eternal fame."

Bhima trembled with anger. "We may not survive these twelve years to avenge ourselves! And even if we do, how can we conceal ourselves during the thirteenth year? All the world knows us. The kings we have conquered will surely help Duryodhana discover us and send us back to this dreadful place for twelve more years. We must fight! There is no higher dharma for a Kshatriya!"

"Yes, we will fight," replied Yudhisthira. "But we must proceed with caution and forethought—that road alone leads to success. Duryodhana has many powerful allies. As for Bhishma, Drona, and Kripa, I am certain they will give up their lives in battle to repay the royal favors they enjoy."

He began to pace anxiously back and forth. "All of them are masters of the astras. Even the gods could not defeat them! And Karna is invincible in his natural armor. When I think of his prowess, I cannot sleep!"

Those words so alarmed Bhima and Draupadi that all conversation ceased. After a time, the sage Vyasa entered the clearing. He said to Yudhisthira, "I know the fear in your heart, O King, and I have journeyed here to dispel it. The time of your prosperity will come when Arjuna will slay all your foes in battle. Toward that end, I shall initiate you into a high spiritual science. When you have mastered it, teach it to Arjuna and send him to the Himalayas for deep meditation and tapasya. Tell him that he should strive to gratify the Lord Shiva, for the Devas will give him many astras when he succeeds. Through Arjuna's prowess, you will defeat your enemy."

Yudhisthira purified himself by bathing in the nearby river, and then received initiation into that spiritual science. After some time and diligent practice, he became adept at it. He summoned Arjuna and said, "You are our sole refuge. You alone can defeat Bhishma, Drona, Karna, and Aswatthama. You alone can counter all their astras. A great burden is upon you, Arjuna. Vyasa has taught me a high spiritual science, and I wish to teach it to you. It will enable you to receive the grace of the gods."

Arjuna purified himself and received the teaching. Then, Yudhisthira said, "Now, go to the Himalayas, observe severe austerities, and practice this science."

Then, amid many tender and tearful farewells from all five Pandavas and Draupadi, Arjuna set off toward the sacred mountains of the north.

* * * * *

After a long journey, Arjuna reached the foothills of the Himalayas and began to ascend. In time, he entered a region where many great rishis lived and meditated. He chose a site near the River Ganga and began to practice severe tapasya. Clad in rags and a black deerskin, he ate just once every three days for the first month — and even that was only fruit. Whenever he was not meditating, he constantly chanted the great mantra, "AUM Namah Shivaya," which means, "I bow to Lord Shiva" or "Adoration to Lord Shiva."

Arjuna continued his practices in the second month while eating just once every six days — again, only fruit. In the third month, he ate only every two weeks as the mantra repeated itself ceaselessly in his mind: "AUM Namah Shivaya, AUM Namah Shivaya, AUM Namah Shivaya."

After three months, Arjuna began to eat only air as the mantra penetrated still deeper inside him. He stood on the tips of his toes with upraised arms for weeks at a time. His body became emaciated, but his face glowed with an inner radiance.

Arjuna's austerities grew so intense that the earth around him began to smoke. The rishis in the area became worried that it might ignite a fire that would consume the entire forest. Still, he continued to practice with ever-increasing devotional intensity: "AUM Namah Shivaya, AUM Namah Shivaya, AUM Namah Shivaya."

· · · · · ·

One day, while Arjuna was meditating, a Rakshasa, a demon, assumed the form of an immense wild boar and charged at him. Its crashing hooves shook the earth, and that caused Arjuna to open his eyes. He shouted, "Why do you attack me in this holy region? I have done you no injury." The boar continued to charge. Arjuna said, "Very well, then I will send you to the realm of the dead."

He nocked an arrow on his celestial bow, Gandiva, and was about to shoot the boar when a nearby hunter called out, "Stop! I aimed at that boar first!"

Arjuna ignored him and unleashed his arrow. Simultaneously, the hunter shot an arrow. The two arrows struck the boar in the same instant. With a sound like thunder, the massive animal crashed to the ground in death.

Arjuna was outraged at the hunter's action. "How dare you shoot at my target when I was the first to aim at it?! That was not honorable. Prepare to die!"

The hunter countered, "*I* aimed first, and *my* arrow killed the boar. It was you who behaved unrighteously. It is you who should prepare to die!"

Without replying, Arjuna began to shower arrows upon the hunter, who in turn rained arrows upon Arjuna. Arjuna easily destroyed the hunter's arrows before they could reach him, but he was astonished to see that his arrows were not harming the hunter. They were not even striking him.

"How could this be?" wondered Arjuna. "Who is this person?" He gritted his teeth and narrowed his gaze. "If it is anyone but Lord Shiva, I shall soon slay him!"

Arjuna redoubled his efforts. Still, his arrows failed to strike the hunter. After a time, he was shocked to see that his inexhaustible quivers had become empty.

He charged forward and swung Gandiva at the hunter, who grabbed the bow and snatched it from Arjuna's hands. Arjuna drew his sword and brought it down on the hunter's head with great force. The blade shattered.

Arjuna attacked with stones and large branches, yet the hunter was unfazed. He began to pummel the hunter with his fists, but to no effect. He grasped the hunter in a wrestling hold, intent on squeezing the life out of him. The hunter did the same, and Arjuna soon collapsed unconscious.

When he recovered, he saw the hunter standing nearby, watching him. Arjuna said, "Hold a moment." He made a clay image of Lord Shiva and decked it with a flower garland. Then he closed his eyes and prostrated himself before the idol. After a short time, he stood and turned toward the hunter to continue the fight — only to see that the garland was now on the hunter's head. That man could only be Lord Shiva Himself!

Arjuna was ecstatic, and he prostrated himself at the hunter's feet. He said, "O god of gods, I came here to behold you. I fought you only out of ignorance. It behooves you to forgive me."

Instantly, the hunter transformed into Lord Shiva. "I am greatly pleased with you, Arjuna. No one can equal your courage and patience. Your prowess is nearly equal to my own. You will conquer all foes, even the celestials themselves."

He took Arjuna's hands into his own, dispelling whatever evil had been in him. "I have forgiven you. Now, I will give you my favorite and most powerful weapon, the Pasupata, and teach you how to invoke it. First, you must purify yourself."

Arjuna immersed himself in the Ganga, then approached Shiva with rapt attention and said, "Instruct me, O Lord!" Shiva imparted the knowledge of that mighty weapon and the mysteries of launching and withdrawing it. After the lesson, the earth trembled as the mighty Pasupata remained by Arjuna's side, constantly emitting sparks and flames amid the sound of thousands of conches, drums, and trumpets. Great whirlwinds began to blow.

Then, Shiva returned Gandiva to Arjuna, saying, "Your quivers will again be inexhaustible. Go now to Heaven, where you will need them."

Arjuna bowed low, then lifted his gaze to watch Shiva rise into the sky and vanish. Shortly after that, the four Devas who govern the four directions arrived. Yama, the god of death and righteousness, also known as Dharma, rules the south. Varuna, the ruler of all waters, governs the west. Kuvera, the god of wealth, controls the north. And Indra, the chief of the Devas, reigns over the east. The four gods gave Arjuna many powerful astras.

As the Devas departed, Indra's divine charioteer landed his flying chariot nearby. He said, "Arjuna, step into the chariot. I am here to take you to Heaven."

Arjuna purified himself again by bathing in the Ganga, then said his customary prayers and offered oblations of water to his ancestors. He thanked the mountains where he had been dwelling, then mounted the chariot, which swiftly rose into the sky, bound for Heaven.

How many of us have Arjuna's level of dedication? To know God, we need not eat only air and stand on the tips of our toes for weeks on end. And thank goodness we need not fight Lord Shiva! But we do need to give our all to the quest.

However, many seekers are reluctant to commit fully to the spiritual path. They want spirituality, but other desires keep them from giving it their all. Paramhansa Yogananda said that such indecisiveness paralyzes the will, which he extolled as our most important human faculty.

True will power is not grim determination and strain. It is dynamic *willingness*, which attracts more energy, opens up new possibilities, and draws divine grace into the process. It is also more fun!

Arjuna exerted such will. It might not seem to have been much fun, but it drew Lord Shiva's grace — and that means divine joy, not mere fun. As Yogananda said, "A strong will, by its dynamic force, creates a way for its fulfillment. By its very strength, the will sets into motion certain vibrations in the atmosphere. Nature, with its laws of order, system, and efficiency, then creates circumstances favorable to the individual who exercises will power. Will derives its strength from an honest purpose, lofty motives, and the noble concern to do good for the world at large. A strong will is never stifled — it always finds a way."

CHAPTER 12

Higher Realms

As Indra's chariot took Arjuna up through the heavenly realms, he passed many Devas and great sages, as well as heroes who had sacrificed their lives in battle. Finally, he reached Indra's celestial city of Amaravati and marveled at its otherworldly beauty. His father, Lord Indra, received him affectionately and called for a grand celebration in Arjuna's honor, with entertainment by the Gandharvas and Apsaras, the celestial musicians, singers, and dancers.

Soon afterward, Indra summoned Arjuna and said, "My son, now that you have pleased Lord Shiva, I shall fulfill the promise I made after you and Krishna defeated my efforts to keep Lord Agni from burning the Khandava Forest. I shall give you all my astral weapons, even the Vajra, the mighty thunderbolt."

He taught Arjuna how to use those weapons, then gave him a task: "I want you to destroy certain of our enemies. We Devas have been unable to accomplish that because of a boon that Lord Brahma gave them. But with my astras and Lord Shiva's Pasupata weapon, you can do it."

"I will do it, my Lord," said Arjuna. And in the fierce campaign that followed, he succeeded. In gratitude, the Devas gave him all the mightiest astras, and Arjuna was greatly pleased.

Indra then told him, "Now, it is time for you to learn the arts of music and dance. Chitrasena will be your teacher and friend. He is the king of the Gandharvas."

Arjuna and Chitrasena quickly developed a close friendship, and Arjuna soon became accomplished in those gentle arts.

One day, Indra summoned Chitrasena and said to him, "I have often noticed Arjuna gazing upon the Apsara named Urvasi." He smiled and said, "And I sense it was not only because she was dancing so beautifully. Go and tell her this: 'As Arjuna has now mastered all the weapons, as well as music and dance, Lord Indra asks that you teach him how to acquit himself with a woman and taste the joys of Heaven.'"

Chitrasena went straightaway to Urvasi, who smiled broadly upon hearing Indra's command. "I am already under the influence of the god of love because of Arjuna. I shall gladly go to him."

She bathed and adorned herself with charming ornaments and splendid garlands of celestial flowers. Her beauty rivaled the full moon shrouded—only slightly—by fleecy clouds. The other celestials were enthralled, feeling she was the most beautiful sight they had ever beheld.

As soon as Arjuna saw her enter his palace, he closed his eyes in modesty and said, "O thou foremost of the Apsaras, I bow to thee and await thy command."

"O Arjuna," she replied, "many times I have seen you gazing at me as I danced. The arrows of the god of love have pierced my heart. Lord Indra has commanded that I come to you, and I do so gladly, for I am more than ever attracted by your virtues. You know my cherished wish."

Arjuna covered his ears with his hands. "O blessed lady, it is true that I have gazed at you as you danced, but it was not with lust, beautiful though you are. It was because you were the consort of King Puru, the ancient founder of our Kuru race. Therefore, you are our mother—to me, the equal of Lord Indra's wife. It behooves you not to entertain other feelings toward me."

Urvasi reassured him, "As immortals, we Apsaras are free to choose as we will. Therefore, do not regard me as your superior. Puru's descendants have sported with us without incurring sin. Neither will you incur sin. You should not send me away."

When Arjuna continued to resist her tempting advances, she became impatient. "I am burning with desire. You *must* accept me!"

"O beautiful lady," said Arjuna, "I know you are displeased with me, but I look upon you as I look upon my human mothers, Kunti and Madri. How, then, could I do what you ask? I prostrate myself at your feet. It behooves you to protect me as a son."

Urvasi began to tremble with rage. "How dare you reject a woman who has come to you at the command of your father, with her heart pierced by the shafts of the god of love?! I curse you: Henceforth, you shall spend your days as a dancer, destitute of your manhood and scorned as a eunuch!" She then swept out of the palace like a sudden storm.

Arjuna was horrified. He went straight to Chitrasena and told him what had happened. Chitrasena then related those events to Indra, who summoned Arjuna.

He said, "Today, Kunti has become a truly blessed mother, for you have surpassed even the rishis in patience and self-control. Fear not. I shall modify Urvasi's curse so it will be to your benefit. You will be a eunuch only during the thirteenth year of your exile, when you must avoid recognition. Your new skills in music and dance will serve you well throughout that year. After that, you shall regain your manhood. For now, stay here and enjoy Heaven's myriad comforts and delights."

Arjuna was greatly relieved. From that moment, he ceased to think about the curse as he sported happily in Heaven for five years. Still, he had no true peace of mind, for he could not forget Duryodhana's evil and the sorrowful plight of his brothers and Draupadi. He longed to return to Earth and fight for dharma.

● ● ● ● ●

From the moment Arjuna left the forest hermitage to go to the Himalayas, his brothers and Draupadi missed him dearly—and their miserable mode of life made them suffer even more. Yudhisthira felt especially wretched for having brought those trials upon his family. Time dragged on very slowly for everyone. Before long, they could not endure living in that forest anymore without Arjuna, so they decided to go elsewhere.

As they were considering where to go, the great rishi Lomasa arrived for a visit. He said, "I have recently been to Heaven, and I bring you greetings from Lord Indra. He asked me to tell you that Arjuna has acquired many astras, and he will soon provide a great service to the Devas. Afterward, he will rest for a time before returning to you. Meanwhile, all of you should go on pilgrimage to sacred places and purify yourselves through tapasya."

The four brothers and Draupadi were deeply honored that Indra was interested in them, and they were thrilled to receive news of Arjuna. Together with Lomasa, they embarked on a journey that took them all around India over a number of years. When they reached Mount Gandhamadana, Lomasa told them that Arjuna would soon rejoin them further up that mountain. So they eagerly began to climb to meet him.

After some days, they came to the ancient hermitage of Nara and Narayana, where they decided to rest for a time. One day, a magnificent thousand-petaled celestial lotus wafted to Draupadi on a gentle breeze. Its unearthly fragrance utterly enchanted her. "Bhima," she said, "I shall give this lotus to Yudhisthira. I wish to take many more of them back to our forest hermitage. Do bring some to me."

Bhima readily agreed. He detected that same fragrance coming from higher up the mountain, so he began to climb. Moving with the strength of a mad elephant and the swiftness of the wind, he shook the entire mountain with each step. Animals howled in terror and fled from him—not only birds and deer, but even tigers and elephants.

Gandhamadana was the dwelling place of Hanuman, king of the monkeys and son of Vayu, the god of the wind. He knew that Bhima was coming and why. So he laid his gigantic, copper-colored body across Bhima's path and began lashing his long tail repeatedly against the earth, making thunderous sounds and shaking the entire mountain. Then he stopped and went to sleep.

Bhima quickened his pace, eager to find the source of those deafening sounds. Very soon, he came upon the enormous monkey, whose body was so radiant that it seemed to be on fire. Seeing his path obstructed, Bhima gave an ear-splitting shout. Hanuman merely opened his bloodshot eyes slightly. "Why did you wake me? I am ill, and I was sleeping sweetly. Men should be kind to animals. Clearly, you do not know dharma. Who are you, and where are you going?"

Bhima thumped his chest and replied, "I am one of the Pandavas. My name is Bhima, the son of Vayu. Who are you?"

Hanuman answered, "I am just a monkey. Only celestials may pass this point, but you may rest here before returning down the mountain."

Bhima answered, "Get out of my way, O monkey, or else you will regret it."

Hanuman said, "But I am ill and too weak to get up. Do jump over me."

Bhima replied, "I could do that in an instant, even as Hanuman leaped over the ocean to rescue Rama's queen, Sita. But it would be unrighteous of me to jump over the Supreme Soul that resides within all bodies."

"Hanuman?" repeated Hanuman sleepily. "Who is that Hanuman?"

Bhima swelled with pride. "He is the king of monkeys. And he is my brother, for he too is a son of Vayu. Hanuman has great intelligence and strength, and I am his equal. So get out of my way, O monkey, else I shall send you to the realm of Yama."

"But I am old, my child," said Hanuman, "and too weak to get up. Please, you can get by if you move my tail."

Bhima thought, "Yes, I will move his tail. I will take hold of it and throw him all the way to Yama's realm." He grabbed the tail with one hand, only to find — to his great surprise — that he could not lift it. He gripped it with both hands but still could not lift it. Bhima was bewildered, but he resolved to try harder. He struggled and strained until he was covered with sweat and drained of his enormous strength. Still, he could not move the monkey's tail.

Bhima realized he was beaten, so he went near the monkey's head once again and bowed low. "O foremost of monkeys, forgive my harsh words. Surely you must be one of the celestials. Please tell me who you are."

"I am Hanuman, servant of Rama," said the monkey. "This path leads to the lake you seek. I blocked it lest you be cursed or defeated by the powerful creatures that lurk along the way."

"You have done me a great favor," said Bhima, close to tears. "Today, I have beheld my great elder brother."

He bowed even lower, and Hanuman contracted his colossal body and embraced him with love, fully restoring Bhima's strength. Hanuman said, "Ask of me a boon. If you wish, I will destroy the Kauravas. Or I can bind Duryodhana and bring him before you."

Bhima replied, "I feel you have already granted us those boons. I ask only this: Be pleased with me and become our protector so we may conquer our foes."

Hanuman said, "I shall remain on the banner of Arjuna's chariot, shouting fiercely to weaken your foes, that you may easily slay them."

Hanuman then pointed up the path and vanished. Straightaway, Bhima set off in that direction.

· · · · ·

Back at the hermitage, Yudhisthira saw omens that a great battle was imminent. He said, "We must arm ourselves. Where is Bhima?"

Draupadi replied, "He has gone up the mountain to find more celestial lotuses like the one I gave you."

The four brothers quickly gathered their weapons and, along with Draupadi, set off in haste along the path Bhima had followed.

Meanwhile, Bhima came upon a beautiful lake filled with the celestial lotuses he was seeking. But Rakshasa guards warned him, "Stay away, mortal. This lake belongs to Lord Kuvera. It is for celestials only."

Bhima ignored the guards and began to gather lotuses, so they attacked him. In a furious battle, Bhima defeated them all, for Hanuman's embrace had restored his great strength—that of ten thousand elephants. He then gathered more lotuses while the surviving Rakshasas fled in panic to Kuvera.

Upon hearing what had happened, Kuvera smiled and told his guards. "Let Bhima take as many lotuses as he likes."

When Yudhisthira and the others arrived at the lake, they were shocked to see the aftermath of the great battle that the omens had foretold. The bodies of countless Rakshasas were strewn all around the lake.

Despite having lost so many of his guards, Kuvera graciously received the five brothers and Draupadi in his palace. After their visit, they hiked back down the mountain to the hermitage of Nara and Narayana.

One day, soon after that incident, a blazing light appeared high in the sky. As it came nearer, they saw it was a chariot—Indra's chariot—and it was carrying their beloved Arjuna! When the chariot touched the earth, their hearts leaped with delight as he stepped out. Amid tears of joy, they celebrated a loving reunion filled with laughter and tales of everyone's adventures.

> Swami Kriyananda explained the inner meaning of the Pandavas' exile: "Yudhisthira — that is to say, our soul calmness — gets shattered by the dice game, and our inner nature is banished into the forest of delusion. In this case, it is no ordinary wilderness. You were kicked out of your birthright, your inner kingdom, and you are living in delusion for twelve years, which is to say, until you have finished that particular outward phase.

"Those twelve years have an astrological significance. The Indian scriptures say that we progress by twelve-year cycles, which relate to the cycles of Jupiter: It takes Jupiter twelve years to go once around the zodiac. I have seen in many lives, and certainly in my own, that every twelve-year cycle represents some stage of spiritual growth — if you are growing! The years twelve, twenty-four, thirty-six, and forty-eight are important stages in your spiritual life. You can do much with them if you make the most of that time.

"Kriya Yoga is a means of hastening those cycles by rotating the energy around the spine. Jupiter represents the guru; it is called *Guru* in Vedic astrology. With the help of the guru rotating that energy around the spine, we can achieve the same thing inwardly and quicken our spiritual growth. We can do nothing about how long it takes Jupiter to go around the zodiac. But with the help of Kriya Yoga, we can bring this same process to fruition more quickly by working with our *internal* zodiac."

During their exile, the Pandavas embraced many of the qualities that the Bhagavad Gita extols as vital for anyone who seeks God: forgiveness, truthfulness, freedom from anger, renunciation, spiritual practice, courage, devotion, perseverance, self-discipline, humility, and more. (Of course, Bhima had little choice but to be humble when he could not even lift Hanuman's tail!) Such qualities are signs that one has achieved some spiritual depth. So the Pandavas' exile was not only the bitter fruit of Yudhisthira's gambling. It was also a time to practice and strengthen spiritual qualities within them in preparation for what was to come.

It is the same for us in our quest to regain our inner kingdom: As we cultivate spiritual qualities, we live in ever-greater harmony with — and receptivity to — God's grace, the only power that can take us to soul freedom.

CHAPTER 13

Plans and Counterplans

A s THE PANDAVAS' EXILE DRAGGED ON, King Dhritarashtra frequently and openly lamented their unfair plight. He also praised their prowess in battle, especially that of Arjuna. It was all an attempt to banish his guilt over his role in exiling the Pandavas—and somehow, he hoped, diminish its consequences.

Duryodhana found his father's conduct extremely annoying, for he had no such qualms. The Pandavas' miserable existence did not rouse feelings of guilt or sympathy in him, nor did their absence from his life diminish his antipathy toward them. All that made his father's newfound tenderness toward them quite unbearable.

In the hope of lifting Duryodhana's spirits, Shakuni suggested, "Why not take your army to the forest near where the Pandavas are staying and make a great display of wealth, comfort, and luxury? Think how delightful it will be to mock the Pandavas in their adversity. You will laugh to see Arjuna clad in tree bark and deerskins. And Draupadi, also wearing bark and skins, will see your wife dressed in costly robes. Her anguish will far exceed what she felt during the dice game."

Duryodhana replied, "That would be most excellent, but if Father knows our intention, he will never allow it."

Karna said, "Then give your father a different reason for the expedition. The royal cattle stations are near the Pandavas' hermitage. Tell him that you plan to hunt deer and inspect the cattle stations. It is a normal thing for a king to do. He will certainly approve it."

But Dhritarashtra did not like the idea. He said, "That would be unwise, Duryodhana. It could result in a conflict with your cousins."

Bhishma, too, opposed the expedition. He told Duryodhana, "I am sure that would result in disaster. Do not go!"

Shakuni, however, argued, "There is nothing to worry about. Yudhisthira would never go back on his vow to live out the exile."

In the end, Dhritarashtra reluctantly gave his permission.

Duryodhana ordered his servants to equip the expedition with every imaginable convenience and comfort. Then he and his army set forth, accompanied by Karna, Shakuni, the other Kauravas, and all their wives. They were in high spirits, relishing the thought of tormenting the Pandavas.

They encamped near a large lake, a short distance from the Pandavas' tiny hermitage. Duryodhana ordered his workers to build pleasure houses along the lakeshore. But as they approached the lake to begin work, they found their path blocked by legions of heavenly Gandharva warriors.

The Gandharvas said to them, "Our king has come to this place for merriment. He has closed it to anyone else. You should go back to where you came from."

When the workers told Duryodhana what had happened, he sent a few warriors to command the Gandharvas to give way. But the Gandharvas only laughed. "Your wicked king must be exceptionally stupid, thinking he can command celestials as though we were his servants. You are very near death, having dared to bring us this message. Begone or die!"

The warriors scurried back to Duryodhana, who was outraged that he, the king of the Kurus, was being treated this way in his own kingdom. He commanded the entire Kuru army to attack, and they quickly began slaughtering the Gandharvas.

But then the Gandharvas began to use their powers of illusion, and the tide of battle turned dramatically. Kaurava warriors fell in great numbers, and most of the survivors fled the field of battle. Karna was severely wounded and had to run away as well. Duryodhana stayed and fought, but he was soon captured and put in chains, as were Dushasana and many other Kauravas. The Gandharvas then went to the Kaurava camp, where they seized the Kaurava wives and put them in chains, too.

Some of the Kuru troops who had fled sought out the Pandavas and implored them to rescue the Kauravas. Hearing of Duryodhana's disaster, Bhima roared with laughter. He exclaimed, "This is exceedingly wonderful! The Gandharvas have done what we *should* have done. Duryodhana came here to mock us, but now he is in disgrace!"

Yudhisthira admonished him, "This is no time for cruel words, Bhima. The honor of the Kurus is at stake. Are you high-souled enough to help our foe when he seeks our shelter? Besides, what greater joy than to see Duryodhana sunk in distress, with his very life depending on your prowess?"

He told his four brothers, "Try peaceful means to get the Gandharvas to release their prisoners. If that fails, try to rescue the Kurus by lightly skirmishing with the foe. If the Gandharvas still do not release their prisoners, then we must crush them. I cannot fight because I vowed nonviolence after the Rajasuya. But take up your arms, brothers, and get ready to fight!"

The Gandharvas did not respond to peaceful negotiations, nor did light skirmishing convince them to release their prisoners. So the four brothers began to fight fiercely against the thousands of Gandharvas, who used their celestial powers to rise into the air and attack from above. Nevertheless, Arjuna killed many of them with his arrows and many more with his astras. Bhima and the twins, too, slew many Gandharvas. Still, the outcome of the battle remained in doubt.

Then the Gandharva general attacked Arjuna from above with his celestial mace. But Arjuna cut it to pieces with his arrows. The general launched astras at Arjuna, who quickly countered them with other astras. The general made himself invisible and launched more astras, but Arjuna neutralized them also. Finally, Arjuna used an astra to reveal the general and attacked him. Before long, the general was exhausted and shouted, "Stop, Arjuna! It is I, Chitrasena!"

It was indeed Chitrasena, the Gandharva king, who had become Arjuna's dear friend during his years in Heaven. Arjuna withdrew his astras, and all conflict quickly ceased. Soon, the Pandavas and Chitrasena were sitting peacefully, side by side on their chariots, pleasantly inquiring about each other's welfare, while Duryodhana lay in chains in Chitrasena's chariot.

Arjuna asked, "Chitrasena, my friend, what led you to leave Heaven and cause such distress for the Kauravas?"

The Gandharva king replied, "I perceived Duryodhana's plan to humiliate you with a great show of wealth and luxury. Lord Indra, too, perceived the plan and commanded me to come here and foil it." He rattled Duryodhana's chains. "The wicked wretch is now our captive. I will take him to Heaven for proper punishment."

Arjuna said, "If you will, please set him free, for Duryodhana is our brother."

Chitrasena replied, "This sinful rogue is full of vanity. He does not deserve to be set free. But very well, let Yudhisthira decide the fate of this wretch."

So they took Duryodhana, still in chains, to Yudhisthira and explained all that had happened. Yudhisthira said to Chitrasena, "You have done us a great kindness by not slaying this wicked creature, for the honor of my family is saved by liberating him. Please, do set him free."

Yudhisthira's gracious gesture pleased Chitrasena, who then freed Duryodhana, the other Kauravas, and their wives as well. Yudhisthira affectionately told Duryodhana, "Go back home now, child. Never again do such a rash act." Duryodhana and the others skulked away in disgrace.

Soon, Lord Indra descended from Heaven and sprinkled amrita, the divine nectar, on all the fallen Gandharvas, restoring them to life. Then, Indra and the Gandharvas returned to Heaven.

* * * * *

Duryodhana burned with shame as he trudged back to his camp. Later, Karna also returned, and when he saw Duryodhana, he exclaimed, "By good fortune, O King, you are still alive! I was badly wounded and had to flee the battle. Who else but you could have defeated the mighty Gandharvas?"

Duryodhana shook his head and replied in a voice choked with tears, "O Karna, you do not know what happened. I was captured, along with my brothers and all our wives. It was the Pandavas who came to my rescue and defeated the Gandharvas. When the Gandharva king told the Pandavas that he had seen our plan and had come to foil it, I wanted the earth to split open and swallow me. I have always persecuted the Pandavas, and now, wretch that I am, I owe them my life!

"Better that I should have died in battle—at least my fame would have been great, and I would have obtained eternal bliss in Heaven. But, puffed up with vanity and insolence, I have done a highly improper and wicked act, and my enemies have laughed at me in my helplessness. How can I return to Hastinapura after this? What will the elders say? Proud as I am, I cannot bear to live after such humiliation. I will starve myself to death! Dushasana, you are now the king of the Kurus."

"No!" wailed Dushasana. "You alone can rule us! Relent, O King!" He threw himself at his brother's feet and grasped Duryodhana's ankles in supplication.

Karna scolded Duryodhana, "O King, this is childish! Do not delight the enemy by such conduct! A dead man cannot conquer his foes. Besides, the Pandavas have done nothing remarkable. They were only doing their duty to protect their king. It was highly improper that they did not follow you into battle at the outset! If you starve yourself to death, all the other kings will laugh at you. And your enemies, the Pandavas, will still be alive!"

Shakuni added, "Why would you foolishly give up the high prosperity I won for you? It seems to me that you have never learned to accept adversity. He who cannot weather life's sudden joys and sorrows is lost, like an unfired clay pot plunged into water. Do not undo this gracious and virtuous act on the part of the Pandavas. Be pleased for the favor they have done you, and reward them — then you will win both fame and good karma. Become friends with the Pandavas and give back their kingdom. Then you will be happy!"

All that made Duryodhana feel even more ashamed. He vowed, "I shall have nothing more to do with sovereignty, wealth, friendship, or virtue. Leave me alone, all of you! My resolution to die is firm!"

He broke free of Dushasana's grip on his ankles, then walked away and sat down. He quickly went into meditation, intending to leave his body once and for all.

The Asuras had seen all this from their place of exile in the nether regions, and they were gravely worried. Duryodhana was their chief instrument for taking over the world. If he died, it would be a devastating blow to their plans. Using their celestial powers, they entered his meditation and said, "Why do you seek death, O King? Suicide is sinful and not in your best interests. You are of celestial origin. Lord Shiva Himself made your body. You have many brave and mighty allies who will certainly slay the Pandavas. We will help you. We will enter the minds of Bhishma and Drona, and they will no longer be so affectionate toward the Pandavas. Karna will kill Arjuna, and you *will* triumph. You will rule the entire world! Go, O mighty one, and obtain victory!"

When Duryodhana returned to outward consciousness, he felt

greatly uplifted. He was now confident that he would defeat the Pandavas in battle. With great joy, he led his surviving army back to Hastinapura.

· · · · ·

Upon arrival, Duryodhana and Karna went to the royal court. Bhishma immediately began to scold Duryodhana: "O child, I told you this venture was foolish, but you would not listen. Are you not ashamed? And Karna fled the battlefield in panic! He is not worth even a quarter of the Pandavas, whose prowess freed you. He is nothing but a lowly coward!"

But Duryodhana only laughed, then left the court and met with Karna, Shakuni, and Dushasana. He asked them, "What shall we do now? What is good for me?"

Karna was eager to redeem himself, and he made a promise: "O King, Bhishma is forever praising the Pandavas and criticizing me. I shall make him change that behavior. Yudhisthira had his brothers conquer the world for his Rajasuya, but I shall conquer it single-handed and give it to you."

And in a fierce military campaign, that is what he did. As a result, Duryodhana now controlled the entire world. He wanted to perform the Rajasuya ceremony that had elevated Yudhisthira to emperor. However, his Brahmin priests told him that no one else could conduct the Rajasuya so long as Yudhisthira was alive. Instead, they recommended a different ceremony that they said was equal to the Rajasuya. Duryodhana accepted their suggestion, and the priests performed the ceremony.

Afterward, there was a grand celebratory banquet. Duryodhana loudly proclaimed to everyone, "When we have slain the wicked Pandavas, I shall perform the Rajasuya!"

Karna announced: "Hear my vow, O King: Until I slay Arjuna, I shall allow no one to pay me honor, I shall abstain from all wine, and if anyone asks a gift of me, I shall give it!"

Upon hearing that mighty vow, all the Kauravas gave a loud cheer, thinking the Pandavas were as good as dead.

From that time, Duryodhana began to rule the world, ever intent on increasing the welfare of other kings so they would be his allies.

He showered the Brahmins with abundant gifts, hoping they would bless him. And he constantly strived to do good to his brothers, certain that giving and enjoying were the only valid uses of riches.

. . . . .

In Heaven, Lord Indra, Arjuna's father, had heard Karna's vow, and he resolved to use it against him. Karna's father, Surya, learned of Indra's plan and came to his son in a dream, saying, "Karna, listen to me. Indra knows of your vow. Tomorrow, he will come to you, disguised as a Brahmin, and ask for the gift of your natural armor and earrings. Do not give them away, child! Offer him other kinds of wealth instead, or else you will lose your invulnerability—and your life."

Karna was consciously aware in his dream, and he replied, "My Lord, truly I am blessed that you would seek my welfare. But I will never break my vow. If Indra takes my armor and earrings for the good of the Pandavas, then great will be my fame, and great will be *his* disgrace. I wish for fame above all, even if its price is death. For fame will extend my life in this world and take me to high regions of bliss in the next."

Surya countered, "My son, I speak for your good. Only the living can enjoy fame. What good is fame to a dead man? So long as you have your divine armor and earrings, Arjuna and Indra *together* cannot defeat you. Do not give them away!"

But Karna was firm. "Forgive me, O Lord, but breaking my vow holds more terror for me than death itself. Do not worry about me on account of Arjuna. I will surely defeat him in battle. Permit me to observe my vow."

Surya sighed. "If you insist on giving away your protection, you must impose a condition. Indra has a magical spear that will slay any foe. Tell him he must give you that spear in return."

When Karna awakened, the dream was fresh in his mind. He went to the Ganga and performed his morning worship. Afterward, he waited for Indra, who soon arrived disguised as a Brahmin.

"What shall I give you?" asked Karna. "Gold, necklaces, fair damsels, villages with plenty of cows?"

Indra said, "Give those things to people who ask for them. I ask that you cut off your armor and earrings, and give them to me."

Karna replied, "I can give you gold, damsels, and villages, but I cannot give my armor and earrings. I was born with them, and no one can slay me as long as I have them. Do accept instead the entire kingdom of the earth."

But Indra refused those offers, as well as every alternative that Karna proposed. Karna smiled and said, "I know who you are and your purpose. I will give you what you ask. In exchange, you must give me your magical spear."

Indra replied, "I will give you the spear, but you can use it only once. Then, it will return to me in Heaven."

Karna answered, "Once will suffice, for there is only one enemy for whom I might need such a weapon. I ask only that my body not become scarred or unsightly when I cut off my armor."

Indra nodded. "So be it."

Karna drew his knife and slowly, painfully cut off his earrings, then his armor, which was his very own skin, smiling fiercely all the while. Seeing this incredible act of courage, the Devas in the heavenly realms let out a great roar, as did the Asuras in the nether regions. Celestial drums began to beat, and heavenly flowers rained upon Karna. Then, he gave his armor and earrings to Indra.

Indra smiled as he gave Karna the magical spear, thinking that the Pandavas' victory was now assured.

Divine intervention through Lord Indra was involved in both the Gandharvas' descent and the cutting of Karna's armor and earrings. The Pandavas had been doing their inner work, and that drew God's grace. As Sri Ramakrishna, a modern-day avatar, said, "The winds of God's grace are always blowing; it is for us to raise our sails." During their exile, the Pandavas were raising their sails.

Those two episodes — and many others in the Mahabharata — are allegories for one of Krishna's central teachings in the Gita, in which he says (speaking from the state of oneness with God), "To those who meditate on Me as their very own, (their hearts) ever united to Me by incessant (inward) worship, I supply their deficiencies and make permanent their gains." (Gita 9:22)

The more we give ourselves to God, the more we open a channel to receive divine grace, which will supply our deficiencies and make permanent our gains.

CHAPTER 14

The Twelfth Year

A T LAST, IT WAS THE final year of the Pandavas' exile in the forest. Great rishis came regularly to their hermitage to offer support and inspiration. The brothers and Draupadi had fully adjusted to their simple life. They were very happy—as happy as if they were living amid the comforts of city life.

But their happiness made Duryodhana very unhappy. So he summoned Shakuni, Karna, and Dushasana, and together they tried to think of a way to harm the Pandavas.

As they considered the possibilities, an unexpected opportunity arose: The great rishi Durvasa arrived in Hastinapura, accompanied by ten thousand of his disciples. Durvasa was known for being quick to anger, so Duryodhana and the others decided to try to make him so angry with the Pandavas that he would curse them.

> Recall that it was Durvasa who had insisted on giving Kunti the mantra that enabled her and Madri to have children through the Devas.

Duryodhana warmly welcomed Durvasa and humbly served him, day and night. Durvasa was a very difficult guest. He often demanded food on short notice—even at midnight for himself and all his disciples. He tested Duryodhana in many ways, but Duryodhana always remained even-minded and pleasant. Finally, Durvasa said to him, "I am pleased with you, O King. Ask of me a boon."

That was what Duryodhana had been hoping for. He knew about the magical copper vessel Surya had given Yudhisthira, and he said, "O Holy One, please take your disciples to the Pandavas in the forest, and be sure to arrive just after Draupadi has finished eating. That is all I ask."

"I shall do that," replied Durvasa.

Duryodhana was sure the plan would work because Surya's copper vessel held food only until Draupadi had finished eating. When the Pandavas could not feed Durvasa and his disciples, the great rishi would surely curse them.

The ascetics arrived at the Pandavas' hermitage while everyone was relaxing after a meal. The Pandavas graciously received Durvasa. Custom demanded that they feed that multitude, so Yudhisthira said, "Come back with your disciples, O Holy One, after all of you have performed your ablutions. Give us the honor of feeding you."

Durvasa said, "So be it," then led his disciples to the river to purify themselves.

Draupadi was distraught. She was responsible for providing food, but without the magic of the copper vessel, she could not possibly feed ten thousand people. She prayed desperately, "O Lord Krishna, Savior of the afflicted, I take refuge in You. Deliver me from this difficulty!"

Although he had been far away in Dwaraka, Krishna appeared instantly before Draupadi and said, "I am famished! Give me food right away!"

Draupadi said, "Lord Surya's copper vessel remains full only until I finish my meal. But I have already eaten, and now there is no more food!"

Krishna replied, "This is no time for jesting, Draupadi. Fetch the vessel!"

When Draupadi returned with the vessel, Krishna found one grain of rice and a tiny bit of vegetable sticking to its rim. He ate them and said, "May this satisfy Lord Vishnu." Then he said to Bhima, "The ascetics are at the river, bathing. Go there and invite them to dinner."

Bhima quickly departed while his brothers and Draupadi looked at each other in alarm. What could they do? Disaster was upon them!

But as Bhima approached the river to convey the invitation, the ascetics' stomachs suddenly became mysteriously full. They said to Durvasa, "Guruji, we cannot eat now. Our stomachs are full to bursting! What should we do?"

Durvasa answered, "We have spoiled the meal and wronged King Yudhisthira. The virtuous Pandavas will consume us with their anger as quickly as fire consumes a bale of cotton. All of you, run away before they see you!"

And run they did. Meanwhile, the Pandavas waited anxiously, fearing that Durvasa would return in the dead of night and demand food for himself and his disciples. But Krishna said, "Do not worry.

Durvasa told them to flee for fear of your ascetic powers. Permit me to return to Dwaraka."

The Pandavas and Draupadi bowed and said, "O Lord, we were drowning in distress, and you have rescued us. Go in peace, and may prosperity be yours."

Krishna vanished, and the Pandavas and Draupadi continued to pass their days in happiness.

· · · · ·

Before long, Krishna came for another visit — this time by chariot. One of his wives, Satyabhama, was with him.

Some days later, the men were engrossed in the wisdom and stories that one of the visiting rishis was sharing. Satyabhama and Draupadi decided to go for a walk in the relaxing quiet of the forest, away from all the activity.

Satyabhama said, "O Draupadi, I have been observing your interactions with your husbands. How is it that they are so obedient to you and never angry with you? Have you practiced severe vows or austerities to make that happen? Have you used special mantras or performed sacrifices? Have you put drugs in their food? Please tell me, as I wish to know how to make Krishna that obedient to me."

Draupadi was taken aback. "Why do you ask me about things that wicked women do? Such practices make a man fear and resent a woman. No, my way is to leave aside vanity, control my desires and anger, and serve my husbands with devotion. My heart belongs to them alone.

"I remain ever humble and devoted to virtue. My husbands always guide me. I never speak ill of my mother-in-law, and I humbly served her whenever we were together. I keep the home clean and organized. Day and night, I serve my husbands. I am the first to rise each morning and the last to retire at night. When we lived in Indraprastha, I alone monitored the income and expenses. I alone kept track of the wealth. All this, Satyabhama, has been the art of making my husbands obedient to me."

"Forgive me, O Princess," said Satyabhama. "As we are friends, I was jesting with you."

Draupadi continued, "I shall tell you how to attract Krishna's heart in a manner free of deceit. Always adore him with friendship.

When you give him the best of everything, he will be devoted to you, thinking, 'She truly loves me.' Then he will give you anything you desire. When he commands a maidservant to do a task, get up and do it yourself. And never reveal to others what he tells you in private, for he would become angry with you if they told him what you said.

"Serve those who are dear and devoted to him, but stay aloof from those who are deceitful or hostile toward him. Avoid excitement and carelessness in the presence of men; instead, observe silence when they are near. Form relationships with only those women who are high-minded and devoted to their husbands, and shun those with evil habits. Such behavior leads to prosperity and Heaven."

Satyabhama was deeply grateful to receive such inspiring guidance, and she immediately began to follow Draupadi's counsel. When she and Krishna were about to return to Dwaraka, she embraced Draupadi and said, "Do not worry. Soon, you and your husbands will surely regain what was lost. A woman with your disposition can never suffer misfortune for long. The wives of the Kauravas, who laughed at you as you entered this long exile, will soon be helpless and hopeless. And do not worry about your five sons. They are in excellent health and are much loved in Dwaraka. They have grown into fine young men and great warriors."

Satyabhama gave reverence to Draupadi by walking around her with palms joined at the heart. Then she bade farewell and joined Krishna in the chariot for the long journey back home to Dwaraka.

> Satyabhama may have been joking about wanting to control Krishna, but Draupadi was serious about serving her husbands — not to control them but to escape ego consciousness. As Swami Kriyananda said, "The best way to get out of ego is to serve others with love and sensitive attention to their needs." With the release of ego comes the rising of the Kundalini energy, which Draupadi symbolizes.

* * * * *

As the months passed, life followed a simple routine for Draupadi and her husbands. One day, a king named Jayadratha chanced upon their hermitage while traveling with his army en route to his wedding ceremony. The Pandavas were hunting elsewhere in the forest at that time, so Draupadi was alone with her maidservant.

Jayadratha saw Draupadi standing on the threshold of the hermitage, and her beauty immediately enthralled him. It shed a luster on the surrounding woods, like lightning illuminating a mass of dark clouds. He said to his companions, "Who is that beautiful creature? I do not need to marry if I can secure her. I shall rescue her from this primitive place and take her back to my kingdom."

> Jayadratha represents the inclination to be body-bound — in other words, the fear of death.

Draupadi received him graciously, as she would any guest, and they exchanged the usual pleasantries. He soon learned who she was and who her husbands were. Nevertheless, he said, "Come with me and be happy, beautiful one. Forget the miserable sons of Pandu, who have lost their kingdom forever. Become my wife and share my kingdom."

Draupadi became furious. "Do not say that! Are you not ashamed?" She was afraid of what he might do, so she began to speak at length, hoping to delay him until the Pandavas returned. She continued, "Out of childish folly, you are kicking a sleeping lion. If you lay your hands on me, you will be courting destruction!"

Jayadratha was unconcerned. "You cannot frighten me with these threats. The Pandavas are inferior men." He took hold of her upper garment and said, "Come with me and ask my forgiveness."

Draupadi pushed him so hard that he fell. She tried to run away, but he quickly got to his feet and caught her, then dragged her into his chariot and drove off, followed by his army.

The Pandavas were hunting some distance away when Yudhisthira suddenly sensed disharmonies in the forest. He also felt a severe pain in his heart. He said to his brothers, "Something is amiss. We must return to the hermitage immediately!"

When they arrived, Draupadi's maidservant told them what had happened. In a rage, they gathered their weapons and armor, mounted their chariots, and set out after Jayadratha. Very soon, they caught up to his army and began to decimate it. As Jayadratha saw his warriors scatter in all directions, he put Draupadi out of his chariot and sped away, desperate to save his life.

The Pandavas soon reached the place where Jayadratha had left

Draupadi. Yudhisthira and the twins took her back to the hermitage
while Bhima and Arjuna continued to pursue Jayadratha.

Before long, they caught up with him. Bhima leaped out of his
chariot and into Jayadratha's chariot. He caught hold of Jayadratha,
threw him out of the chariot onto the ground, and beat him severely.
Then he held him down while he shaved off all of Jayadratha's hair
except for five small patches.

"This," he declared, "is what comes from wronging the wife of the
five Pandavas!"

Bhima and Arjuna then returned to their hermitage, leaving
Jayadratha lying in the dirt—beaten, disfigured, and utterly humiliated. In outrage over this treatment, he began to practice severe austerities in the hope of receiving a boon from Lord Shiva. After a long
time and much tapasya, Shiva appeared to him and asked, "What is
the boon that you desire?"

Jayadratha said, "I want to defeat the five Pandavas in battle."

"That is not possible," replied Shiva. "You cannot defeat even
Arjuna, much less all five brothers. The most I can give you is the
boon of being able to hold the other four Pandavas at bay for one day."

"Then let it be so," said Jayadratha. "Someday, I will have the
opportunity. That shall be my revenge."

* * * * *

As the twelfth year waned, the Pandavas and Draupadi moved to
a new part of the forest. One day, a Brahmin rushed to their encampment, saying, "I need your help immediately! I was performing a sacred
ceremony when a huge buck caught my firesticks and churning staff
in his antlers, then ran away with them. Without them, I cannot proceed with my ceremony. I ask that you retrieve those articles for me."

Straightaway, all five brothers set out to find the buck. After
much searching, they spotted it and pursued it for quite some time.
But even though they shot many arrows at it, they could not bring it
down. Finally, the buck disappeared from view altogether.

The Pandavas were exhausted from the long, hot chase and dis-
concerted over their failure to bring down the buck. So they stopped
to rest under a tall tree. Yudhisthira said, "Nakula, all of us are extremely thirsty. Do climb this tree and see whether water is nearby."

Nakula began to climb, and as he neared the top of the tree, he said, "I see many trees of the sort that grow near water, and I hear the cries of cranes. A lake must be nearby."

Yudhisthira said, "Come down, then, and bring us some water from that lake."

"So be it," said Nakula. He climbed down, then set off toward where he thought the lake would be. He soon arrived at the shore of a beautiful crystalline lake where many cranes lived. As he bent down to slake his thirst, suddenly, a voice boomed from the sky: "This is my lake, and you may not drink until you have answered my questions, or you will die."

In his extreme thirst, however, Nakula ignored the warning and began to drink. Immediately, he dropped dead.

When Nakula did not return after some time, Yudhisthira asked Sahadeva to go and find out what had happened. Sahadeva set off, and he soon came upon Nakula's dead body on the lakeshore. His heart nearly burst from grief over the death of his twin brother.

In his extreme thirst, he bent down to drink from the lake. Again, the voice from the sky called out, "This is my lake, and you may not drink until you have answered my questions. Otherwise, you will die."

Nevertheless, Sahadeva drank—and he, too, fell to the ground, lifeless.

When Sahadeva did not return as expected, Yudhisthira became very concerned. He said, "Arjuna, it is strange that neither Nakula nor Sahadeva has returned. Do go and investigate."

Arjuna nodded, picked up his weapons, and departed. When he arrived at the lake and saw the lifeless bodies of the twins, he quickly took up his bow and scanned his surroundings. But he saw no one to fight. Meanwhile, his thirst drew him to the lake to drink. When the voice forbade him unless he answered its questions, Arjuna replied, "Do forbid me by appearing before me. When you find yourself badly wounded by my arrows, you will not speak this way again." He then shot arrows in all directions—even some that he had infused with the power of astras—but to no effect.

The voice said, "Why go to all this trouble? You need only answer my questions. Then you may drink as much as you like. But if you drink first, you too will die."

Ignoring the threat, Arjuna drank and fell dead.

After a time, Yudhisthira sent Bhima, who became distraught when he saw his three dead brothers. He thought, "I will surely have to fight someone. But first, I shall quench my thirst."

Again, the voice gave its warning, but Bhima ignored it and drank. He immediately collapsed in death.

Back at the tree, Yudhisthira was greatly concerned over his brothers' prolonged absence. He wondered, "Is this forest under some malign influence? Have they encountered some wicked beast? Or did they find no water nearby and decide to search farther afield?"

Yudhisthira set out to investigate. When he found all four of his beloved brothers lying dead on the shore of the lake, he was overwhelmed with grief. He thought, "Who could have done this? I see no wounds on their bodies, no signs of violence, no other footprints. Their faces have not lost color, so no one has poisoned the lake. Who else but Lord Yama could have killed these mighty warriors?"

Miserable as he was, however, he was also extremely thirsty. As he bent to drink, the voice again said, "This lake belongs to me. I have killed your brothers, as they chose to drink without first answering my questions. If you do the same, you will be the fifth corpse lying here. But if you answer my questions well, you may take as much water as you like."

Seeing his brothers lying dead, Yudhisthira decided to ignore his thirst. "Very well," he said. "Ask your questions."

The voice said, "I am a Yaksha." Immediately, that magical nature spirit materialized, perched on a nearby tree. Its massive body looked like a crane but appeared to be made of fire. It let out a great roar that shook the forest like thunder.

The Yaksha then posed a long series of challenging, abstruse questions. Yudhisthira's answers were so wise that perhaps only he or a great rishi could have given them. Among the last few questions was, "What is the most astonishing thing in the world?"

Yudhisthira replied, "Day after day, countless creatures leave this world and enter Lord Yama's world of the dead. Yet those that remain on Earth believe themselves to be immortal. What could be more astonishing?"

The Yaksha was pleased with that answer. After Yudhisthira had satisfactorily answered a few final questions, the Yaksha said, "You have truly answered all my questions. Name one of your brothers, and he shall live again."

Yudhisthira said, "Let Nakula live."

"Why him?" asked the Yaksha. "Why not Bhima or Arjuna, upon whose might you depend?"

"Non-injury is the highest virtue," replied Yudhisthira, "and I endeavor to practice it. My father had two wives, Kunti and Madri, who are equally dear to me. To choose Bhima or Arjuna would have hurt Madri, for she would then have no living son. I wish that both wives will have a child who lives."

The Yaksha said, "Because you value non-injury more than profit or pleasure, let *all* your brothers live." And the other four Pandavas immediately came back to life, neither thirsty nor tired.

Yudhisthira said, "As you can end and restore life, you cannot possibly be a Yaksha. You must be one of the celestials."

"Indeed, I am," said the Yaksha. "I am your father, Yama."

He changed his form from that of the fiery crane to his celestial self and then continued, "I came here to see you and test your merit. I am well-pleased with your wisdom and virtue. I wish to give you boons. What do you want, O King?"

Yudhisthira said, "I ask that the Brahmin's firesticks and churning staff, carried away by that buck, be returned to him so he can continue his ceremony."

"I was that buck," said Yama. "Those items shall be restored to him. Ask another boon."

Yudhisthira replied, "We have spent twelve years of poverty and deprivation in this exile. I ask that now, as we move to some inhabited region for the thirteenth year, we shall not be recognized, lest we have to spend twelve more years in exile."

"I grant you that boon," said Yama. "You should spend the thirteenth year in the realm of King Virata. No one shall recognize you. I have not yet been satisfied by granting boons to you. Ask another."

"O Father," said Yudhisthira, "it is enough that I have beheld you with my mortal eyes. But as you have not yet been satisfied, I shall ask one more boon: May I always conquer covetousness, folly, and anger. And may I ever be devoted to charity, truth, and austerities."

"My son," said Yama, "you already possess those qualities."

Then he vanished.

CHAPTER 15

Hiding in Plain Sight

Lord Yama had told the Pandavas and Draupadi to spend the thirteenth year in Matsya, the realm of King Virata. So that was where they would go.

Virata represents oneness, samadhi.

Yama had assured them they would not be recognized during that final year. Still, they needed to do their part by taking on new identities while in Matsya—identities that would enable them to support themselves while remaining inconspicuous.

Yudhisthira said, "I will represent myself as a Brahmin named Kanka, skilled in dice. I shall become one of Virata's courtiers and say that I was formerly a close friend of Yudhisthira."

His brothers looked at each other knowingly, for during the Pandavas' exile in the forest, Yudhisthira had once lamented to a visiting rishi how miserable his life had become. The rishi told him the story of an ancient king who had suffered an even worse fate than Yudhisthira, also because of losing at dice. The rishi then taught Yudhisthira the science of dice, so no one would ever be able to beat him again.

With a huge smile, Bhima said, "I will tell Virata I am a skilled cook. I shall say that I was formerly a wrestler and served as Yudhisthira's cook." He laughed loudly. "Finally, after twelve years in the wilderness, I will not have to hunt for food!"

Arjuna said, "When I was in Heaven, one of the Apsaras cursed me to become a eunuch. Lord Indra reduced the curse so it would apply only during this thirteenth year. So I will entertain the king and his family with stories. I will also teach singing and dance to the women and girls. My name will be Vrihannala, and I will say that I was Draupadi's attendant in Indraprastha."

Nakula said, "I will say that I was formerly in charge of Yudhisthira's stable, and I will find work caring for King Virata's horses."

Sahadeva added, "I shall become the keeper of Virata's cattle, having previously looked after Yudhisthira's livestock."

Yudhisthira turned to Draupadi. "And now, beloved wife, what disguise will you adopt?"

She answered, "I shall be the hairdresser of Sudeshna, King Virata's wife. My name will be the same as my occupation, Sairindhri. I will say that I served Draupadi in Indraprastha."

On the final day of the twelfth year, the Pandavas had servants take their horses and chariots to another kingdom. The brothers and Draupadi received a farewell blessing from the Brahmins who had been staying with them. Then, they set off on foot for Virata's kingdom.

Duryodhana's spies had been shadowing them under orders to discover their new location and send them into exile for twelve more years. However, Lord Yama's boon took effect as soon as they departed, and the spies could not find a trace of them.

After a long journey, the Pandavas and Draupadi arrived at the outskirts of Virata's capital city. The brothers needed a safe place to store their weapons—especially Arjuna's celestial bow, Gandiva, which was sure to attract attention. They wrapped the weapons in a large bundle and placed it high in a tree next to a cemetery, along with a corpse. They hoped that the stench of the decaying corpse would keep anyone from investigating.

Then, they entered the city and sought their desired positions. The brothers quickly succeeded, but Draupadi encountered an obstacle. Queen Sudeshna said to her, "I would retain you, but I fear that your beauty would tempt King Virata, and he would forsake me."

Fortunately, Draupadi had a solution. She told Sudeshna, "O Queen, neither Virata nor anyone else can have me, for I have five powerful Gandharva husbands. They will protect me from any man's advances."

That reassured Sudeshna, and she gave Draupadi a position.

The passing months were unremarkable, for the most part. Yudhisthira played dice with Virata and his sons, and his newfound knowledge of the game enabled him to win much wealth from the king. Virata was greatly pleased with the other four Pandavas' service, and he generously rewarded them. Bhima relished wrestling and cooking—and even more, eating! Arjuna enjoyed entertaining the royal ladies and teaching them the gentle arts. Nakula and Sahadeva cheerfully tended the king's horses and cattle. The five brothers lived in relative comfort, and all in all, they were happy.

Draupadi, however, was miserable. Although Queen Sudeshna treated her well, it was exceedingly painful for Draupadi to swallow her royal pride and toil as a lowly servant. Nevertheless, she endured while counting the days until the thirteenth year would come to an end.

. . . . .

Late in that year, circumstances changed when Kichaka, the king's general, happened to see Draupadi for the first time. He immediately felt driven to possess her. Kichaka was a big, brutish man whom even the king feared. He was also Queen Sudeshna's brother; they were of the Suta caste.

Time and again, with increasing fervor, Kichaka implored Draupadi to be with him. He would say, "I am the real lord of this kingdom. Why endure a life of servitude when you can have luxury, comfort, and everything you desire? No one can equal me in prowess, prosperity, or attractiveness. Come with me!"

Each time, Draupadi answered, "Do not throw away your life, O Sutaputra, for my five Gandharva husbands protect me. You wish for that which you can never have. If you persist in this foolishness, one of them will kill you."

Kichaka was undeterred. He even asked Queen Sudeshna to help him—and she agreed, partly out of pity for her brother's yearning and partly because she still worried that Draupadi's beauty might tempt her husband. So she sent Draupadi on an errand to Kichaka's apartment. Draupadi knew very well what would happen, and she whispered a desperate prayer to Lord Surya for protection. In answer, Surya assigned a Rakshasa to protect her while staying invisible.

The errand unfolded just as Draupadi had known it would. Kichaka made advances, which Draupadi once again rejected. But he was intoxicated with lust, and he grabbed her arm. Draupadi angrily shouted, "O wretch, I shall behold you dragged and lying powerless on the ground!"

She tried to break free and run away, but Kichaka seized her by her upper garment. In a burst of anger, she was able to break away and run off toward the royal court. Kichaka followed in hot pursuit.

Just as she entered the court, he caught up and seized her by the hair, then threw her down and kicked her in front of everyone.

King Virata and Yudhisthira had been absorbed in a dice game, and they looked up in alarm, as did Bhima, who had been serving food. The invisible Rakshasa immediately knocked Kichaka senseless while Yudhisthira and Bhima grew livid with anger.

Bhima clenched his fists and said quietly but forcefully, "I will kill that wretch!"

Yudhisthira whispered, "Wait, brother! Kichaka is extremely strong. Only one such as Bhima could slay him. Killing him now would reveal our true identity, and we would have to return to the forest for twelve more years."

Bhima relented, but only barely.

When her husbands did nothing to protect her, Draupadi became even angrier. "Alas, that Sutaputra has kicked the wife of five mighty Gandharva warriors capable of destroying the entire earth. Where are those warriors today, those great ones who have always protected anyone in need? Why do they, like eunuchs, quietly allow their wife to be insulted by an evil brute? And what can I do when King Virata, deficient as he is in virtue, allows such an outrage in his very court? This Kichaka is ignorant of duty and morality. Indeed, it seems that ignorance afflicts the entire kingdom of Matsya!"

Virata was intimidated by his general and did not wish to rebuke his brother-in-law, even though Kichaka was unconscious. He said, "What can I do? I did not see what caused this." But his courtiers applauded Draupadi's tirade.

Yudhisthira said to Draupadi, "No doubt, Sairindhri, your Gandharva husbands do not consider this a suitable occasion for expressing their anger. You do not know the timeliness of things, so you weep, shout like an actress, and interrupt the dice game in the king's court. Return now to the queen's apartments. The Gandharvas will surely take the life of him who has wronged you."

Draupadi's eyes blazed with fury. "My husbands, I think, are extremely kind. They are liable to be oppressed by all, for their eldest is addicted to dice!"

She turned and ran to the queen's apartments. When Sudeshna saw her disheveled hair and her eyes red with rage, she became very concerned and asked, "Sairindhri, what has happened?!"

After Draupadi explained, the queen shook her head and said, "My brother is mad with a lust that can never be satisfied. I shall have him slain if you wish."

Draupadi replied, "Those whom he has wronged will kill him," and went to her quarters. She knew who should kill Kichaka, and in the wee hours of the following morning, she went to Bhima's quarters. Seeing him fast asleep, she shook him.

"Get up! How can you lie there like a dead person? Surely anyone who is not dead will never sleep when a wicked wretch has disgraced his wife."

Bhima sat up and took her hands in his. "What is it? Tell me what you want, and I will do it."

She began to sob uncontrollably. "How can you even ask what I want? You know all my woes. How I have suffered with Yudhisthira as a husband! Dushasana shamed me at the game of dice! Jayadratha abducted me in the forest! Now that wicked Kichaka has assaulted me! And here I am, a serving woman with callouses on my hands, having to bear the shame of seeing the five mighty Pandavas subservient to those who are their inferiors. Anyone else in my position would wish to die. Great must have been my sins in past lives that I should be subjected to this."

Bhima said, "Fie on all of us that we have allowed you to suffer such a fate! The wicked Kichaka must die!"

Together, they devised a plan, and Draupadi ceased crying, although her eyes still blazed with anger. She returned to her quarters, confident that she would soon get satisfaction.

• • • • •

Later that same morning, Draupadi made it easy for Kichaka to find her. He boasted, "You saw that the king did nothing to stop me yesterday. I am the true ruler of Matsya. But I am your slave. Accept me!"

Draupadi replied, "I will do so only if no one knows about our union. I live in terror that my Gandharva husbands will find out and kill you."

Kichaka smiled broadly. "Then come to my private apartment."

Draupadi shook her head. "I fear that the Gandharvas would

find us there. Let us instead meet in the dancing hall at midnight. My husbands do not know that place."

Kichaka agreed, and at midnight, he entered the dark dancing hall to meet Draupadi. But it was a trap. Bhima leaped out of the shadows and attacked him. They fought like two mighty elephants fighting over a female in spring. It was a fearsome clash. Eventually, Bhima gained the advantage and began to pummel Kichaka mercilessly. Soon, Kichaka lost consciousness. Bhima then killed him, and dismembered and mutilated Kichaka's body.

Draupadi had been hiding nearby all the while. Upon seeing Kichaka's scattered remains, she felt the greatest delight. She called the palace guards to the gruesome scene, and they were horrified. They thought that only a Gandharva could have caused such destruction.

• • • • •

Word quickly spread through the capital that one of Draupadi's Gandharva husbands had killed Kichaka. Now, his fellow Sutas were enraged. Hundreds of them came after Draupadi, shouting and uttering threats. "Wicked woman, you are the cause of this! You shall burn atop Kichaka's funeral pyre!"

They ignored her piercing screams as they carried her away. Hearing the commotion, Bhima investigated and quickly discovered what was happening. He left the palace through a back door and raced to the cemetery, where the Sutas planned to burn Kichaka's body. With his tremendous strength augmented by rage, Bhima uprooted a tree. Soon, the mass of Sutas arrived, carrying Kichaka's body and shrieking, struggling Draupadi, both to be burned.

Swinging the tree like a gigantic mace, Bhima attacked the crowd of Sutas. In a matter of moments, he killed more than a hundred of them. The mayhem unfolded so quickly that no one recognized the massive being wielding the tree.

The survivors dropped Draupadi and the remains of Kichaka, fled the cemetery, and began to spread the word of a second Gandharva attack. Some went to Virata's court and told him, "O King, a Gandharva attacked us in the cemetery, and that Sairindhri was the cause of it!"

Meanwhile, Bhima quickly returned to the palace and slipped inside through the back door without being noticed. Draupadi slowly made her way back into the city, trembling after her close brush with death. Word of the attack had preceded her, and everyone who saw her either ran away or closed their eyes as if it were dangerous even to look at her.

She entered the palace, and when she saw Bhima, she bowed to him in gratitude. She passed the dancing hall while Arjuna was giving the king's daughters a dance class. The girls saw her, stopped their lesson, and clustered around her. They said, "By good luck, you have been delivered from your dangers! By good luck, your Gandharva husband saved you!"

Hearing this, Arjuna was puzzled. "What has happened, Sairindhri? Tell me."

Draupadi's eyes flashed with anger. "O Vrihannala, you always pass your days pleasantly in the girls' apartments. You do not concern yourself with my fate. You have no idea of the many griefs I have to bear."

Indeed, Arjuna knew nothing of the recent drama, and his reply was unsympathetic. "Vrihannala has unmatched sorrows of her own. She has become low as a brute, but you do not realize this. When you are afflicted, Sairindhri, everyone feels it. But you do not know anyone else's affliction. You do not know my heart."

Draupadi turned away, furious, and went to the queen's apartments, hoping for support and safety. But Sudeshna only gave her more bad news. "The king fears that, if you remain here, all of Matsya will meet with disaster at the hands of your Gandharva husbands. He orders that you quickly leave the kingdom."

Draupadi had been diligently marking the passage of time during the thirteenth year of exile, and she replied, "Please ask the king to let me stay for just thirteen more days. My Gandharva husbands will be highly grateful for this. Without doubt, the king and his friends will reap great benefits."

Virata feared what her Gandharva husbands might do if he forced her to leave, so he allowed Draupadi to stay for those additional days.

* * * * *

Meanwhile, in Hastinapura, Duryodhana was growing increasingly anxious. The thirteenth year was nearly at an end, and although his spies were everywhere, they had reported no sign of the Pandavas.

He assembled his supporters and several visiting allies to discuss what to do.

Karna said, "We should send out more spies, better spies, well disguised so they can search everywhere without attracting attention."

Dushasana said, "The Pandavas are so proud of their strength. Perhaps they became overconfident and were killed by animals or some freak accident."

Drona shook his head. "Yudhisthira is a man of high intelligence and virtue, and his brothers follow him faithfully. Such men will never perish. We should send virtuous ascetics to search for them. They will think like Yudhisthira, so they are more likely to understand where the Pandavas may be hiding."

"The preceptor is right," agreed Bhishma. "Wherever Yudhisthira lives, there will be both virtue and prosperity. We should search for the Pandavas in kingdoms that have recently become more virtuous and prosperous."

Kripa said, "I have no doubt that the Pandavas will soon emerge from hiding, and they will come out bursting with energy and prowess. If we build up our treasury and enlarge our army, perhaps when they see our strength, they will agree to a treaty that is advantageous to us."

Finally, King Susharma of Trigarta spoke. "It is too late to find the Pandavas, but another opportunity has arisen: We have heard that Kichaka is dead. He and the Matsya army have often decimated our kingdom. But without him, King Virata is greatly weakened. I propose that your army and ours attack Matsya and seize his cattle and wealth."

In the absence of any prospects for finding the Pandavas, Susharma's proposal met with general approval. The Trigarta army broke camp and marched off toward Virata's capital city. On a designated day, they would attack from the east. One day later, the Kuru army would attack from the west. When Virata's army marched east to counter the Trigartas, the cattle and capital city would be unprotected. Susharma's plan promised an easy victory.

CHAPTER 16

Reappearance

THE TRIGARTAS' INVASION OF MATSYA was a total surprise to King Virata, who was still in shock over the Gandharva incidents. In great haste, he mobilized his forces to defend his kingdom. Yudhisthira, Bhima, Nakula, and Sahadeva donned armor, took up weapons, and marched eastward with the troops to confront the Trigartas. Arjuna, of course, stayed in the palace with the women and children, for he was a eunuch.

The element of surprise greatly favored the Trigartas. Virata's warriors fought bravely, but they could not stem the enemy tide. It was not long before the foe captured King Virata himself. That spelled disaster for Matsya, and many of his warriors began to flee back toward the capital city.

Yudhisthira sought out Bhima, "We are indebted to Virata for sheltering us. We must rescue him."

Bhima pointed to a tall tree nearby and replied, "I will uproot this mighty tree and use it as my mace. Stand aside, brothers, while I rout the enemy!" (Remember, he had the strength of ten thousand elephants.)

"No, Bhima," said Yudhisthira. "If anyone sees such superhuman strength, they will know who you are. We must use ordinary weapons."

"Very well," said Bhima, so he took up a bow and began to shower the Trigartas with arrows. Then he rushed at the enemy with a mace. Yudhisthira and the twins joined the fighting, and the Trigarta warriors fell by the thousands. Seeing that, the Matsya warriors who had fled turned around and rejoined the fight.

The tide of battle was turning. Before long, Bhima was able to free Virata. Soon after that, he captured the Trigarta king, Susharma. Now, it was the Trigarta army's turn to flee.

Bhima brought his captive to Yudhisthira, who said, "I am freeing you, King Susharma. Never again do something like this. Now salute King Virata, then go home."

In great shame, Susharma bowed to Virata, then departed. The Trigarta invasion had ended in disaster.

Virata said to the four Pandavas, whom he knew only as mere courtiers and laborers, "Your prowess has saved my kingdom and myself. I will reward you with great wealth for your act of valor. Indeed, I shall give you my entire kingdom."

Yudhisthira graciously declined, saying, "We are well pleased with your words, O King. It is reward enough for us that you have been freed from your foes. May you be ever happy and righteous. Let messengers be sent back to the city to proclaim your victory."

The fight had been exhausting, and Virata's warriors spent the night on the battlefield, resting and savoring their victory.

* * * * *

The day after Virata's army marched eastward to confront the Trigarta invasion, the Kuru army invaded from the west and began stealing Virata's cattle. One of Virata's cowherds brought the news to the palace, causing a general panic because all the warriors had gone east to fight the Trigartas. It was bad enough to lose the cattle. Now, the city itself was defenseless.

King Virata's son, Prince Bhuminjaya, was too young to march with the Matsya army against the Trigartas. Still, he was the only remaining male close to fighting age. He boasted to the ladies of the palace, "Oh, if only I had a charioteer, I could crush the Kuru army all by myself. They are weak and unskilled. Like a second Indra, I would defeat them all and bring back the cattle. But, alas, all the charioteers have gone away with our army."

Amid the air of general hopelessness, Arjuna whispered to Draupadi, "Tell the prince that I drove Arjuna's chariot in many battles. I can be his charioteer."

Draupadi stepped forward. "O prince, Vrihannala has often been Arjuna's charioteer in battle. Truly, he has no equal as a driver. He will take you into battle so you can crush the Kuru army all by yourself."

The prince turned pale with fear. But having bragged to the ladies of his prowess, he could not decline. So Arjuna took the reins of Bhuminjaya's chariot and drove him out of the city to confront the attackers.

When the prince saw the massive Kuru army, led by Bhishma and Drona, he jumped out of the chariot and ran away. Arjuna stopped the chariot and ran after him. He quickly caught the prince, who cried, "Please release me, Vrihannala! I will give you gold and gems and an excellent chariot. Let me go!"

But Arjuna merely laughed and carried him back to the chariot. "If you will not fight, then you will be my charioteer, and I will fight the Kurus." Realizing he had no choice, Bhuminjaya agreed to drive the chariot.

Drona had observed that little drama from a distance, and he said to the other Kuru chariot warriors, "I have no doubt: That is Arjuna, and I see no one here who can withstand him. Disaster is upon us!"

Karna countered, "You always disparage us by speaking of Arjuna's prowess, but he is not equal to even one-sixteenth of myself or Duryodhana."

Duryodhana smiled, "If that *is* Arjuna, then all is well, for the Pandavas will have to go back into exile for twelve more years. And if that is not Arjuna, he will soon die."

Arjuna had Bhuminjaya drive the chariot to the tree where the Pandavas had hidden their weapons. He told the prince to climb the tree and retrieve his weapons, including the mighty celestial bow, Gandiva, and his conch and inexhaustible quivers. When the prince brought them down, he marveled at such glorious weapons, especially Gandiva. "These are magnificent. Who could they possibly belong to?"

"They belong to me, O prince," said Arjuna. "That bow is the famed Gandiva, and I, gentle Vrihannala, am Arjuna."

Bhuminjaya was stunned that this dance teacher, this eunuch, was the renowned Arjuna. But who else could such weapons belong to? He felt deeply honored to drive Arjuna's chariot, and his courage began to return.

Arjuna purified his body, then called to mind all his astras. They immediately said, "We are here, O illustrious one. We are your servants."

Arjuna bowed to them and said, "All of you, dwell in my memory."

He strung Gandiva and twanged it. It made a dreadful sound that caused violent winds to blow. A meteor struck the earth, and large trees fell. The Kurus now knew for certain that this was Arjuna.

Bhuminjaya drove the chariot to a promontory from which Arjuna could survey the Kuru army. He blew his conch so loudly that it threatened to tear apart the very universe. Hearing that enormous sound, the prince collapsed and clung to the chariot in fear. As the sound rumbled through the hills, Drona said, "That is Arjuna's conch. Ill winds are blowing, thunderclouds are rolling in, and all the omens foretell disaster for us!"

Karna shouted angrily to the other Kuru warriors, "Do not listen to the preceptor! Arjuna is his favorite, and everything is suddenly in confusion and disarray merely because he hears the neighing of Arjuna's horses. The wind always blows, and Indra always sends rain clouds. What has Arjuna to do with that? No doubt the Pandavas have sent Drona here to discourage us. We must disregard those who praise the foe. I can conquer even the gods. My arrows, like venomous snakes, will pierce Arjuna's body. Today, you shall behold his chariot broken, his horses killed, his valor gone, and himself slain!"

Kripa said, "Karna, your crooked heart always wants to fight. We all know Arjuna's many heroic deeds, yet you have done nothing. He defeated the Gandharva king after you fled the battlefield. Lord Indra himself could not defeat him. Anyone who wants to fight Arjuna in single combat is a fool who needs to take a sedative! Our only hope is that all of us together can be a match for him."

Aswatthama said, "O Karna, why do you boast? Men of true heroism speak not a word of their prowess. They fight. And Duryodhana, in what great combat have you defeated even one of the Pandavas? What Kshatriya would celebrate winning a kingdom through dice, and even that only through Shakuni's cheating? Now you presume to send them back to the forest because of a detail of the calendar? Fight, and let us see if Shakuni can protect you now. Gandiva does not cast dice; it shoots countless blood-drinking arrows."

Bhishma gestured for quiet. "We must indeed fight, but we must not fight one another. There is no greater calamity for an army than disunity among its leaders. Karna speaks as he does only to lift our courage. We must forgive one another, unite, and move forward."

He gazed at Arjuna standing majestically in the chariot up on the promontory, and he said, "By my reckoning, the thirteen years have passed, and these omens foretell great danger. Quickly, Duryodhana, take a quarter of our army and return to Hastinapura. Another quarter should protect the cattle. Let the remaining half of our troops form up to fight Arjuna."

Arjuna now directed the prince to drive the chariot down off the promontory and closer to the Kuru host. Then he had Bhuminjaya halt the chariot, and Arjuna shot four arrows at Drona: two landed at his guru's feet, and two whizzed past his ears. Drona smiled with pride in his disciple. "Arjuna has saluted me and whispered in my ears."

Arjuna ordered the prince to steer the chariot around the main Kuru army and pursue the departing Duryodhana. In the process, Arjuna scattered the Kuru warriors that had been protecting the cattle, then turned the cattle around and herded them back toward Virata's city.

Duryodhana had barely begun to move his troops when Arjuna attacked and single-handedly defeated Duryodhana, Drona, Aswatthama, and Kripa, prompting them to flee from combat. He also vanquished Karna twice, wounding him badly in the process.

Finally, the invincible Bhishma advanced upon Arjuna, and a duel ensued between grandfather and grandson. Each showered the other with countless deadly arrows. Then Arjuna pressed his attack so fiercely that Bhishma collapsed unconscious. Immediately, Bhishma's charioteer drove him away to safety.

Duryodhana then returned to the battle and attacked Arjuna, wounding him. Duryodhana's brother, Vikarna, joined the attack, fighting atop a giant elephant. But Arjuna quickly dispatched the elephant, forcing Vikarna to run away. He also seriously wounded Duryodhana, causing him and all the nearby Kuru warriors to flee.

Arjuna shouted, "Duryodhana, why do you turn your back on battle? Do not lose your honor. Behave like a king: Show me your face, and come fight! How ironic that your name means, 'he who is difficult to vanquish.' Fly away, then, and save your precious life from Pandu's son."

Duryodhana could not bear those insults. He turned back to fight, like a snake that had been stepped on. Karna joined him, as did Drona, Aswatthama, Kripa, Dushasana, and many others. A veritable ocean wave of chariots and mighty warriors roared toward Arjuna, surrounded him, and attacked with astras. But Arjuna repelled all those weapons with astras of his own.

He then invoked one of Indra's astras, called Sanmohana. It caused all the Kuru warriors to drop their weapons and fall asleep on their feet. Bhishma alone remained conscious, for he knew how to counter that astra. But he still felt disoriented after his collapse, so he did not attack. He could only watch as Arjuna ordered Bhuminjaya to gather the elegant robes of all the great Kuru warriors so he could give them as souvenirs to King Virata's daughters.

When Duryodhana awakened, Arjuna stood alone on the battlefield, glowing like Lord Indra. Duryodhana turned to Bhishma and demanded, "Grandfather, how is it that you have not killed Arjuna? You must attack and keep him from escaping!"

Bhishma replied, "Where was your prowess while you were sleeping, O King, having renounced your bow and arrows? The only reason we are still alive is that Arjuna will never betray his principles. Go home, O King, and let Arjuna return victorious to Virata, having routed us and reclaimed the cattle."

Duryodhana sighed deeply and became silent, no longer eager for battle. Realizing the wisdom of Bhishma's counsel, he ordered his army to return to Hastinapura.

As a parting gesture, Arjuna saluted Bhishma, Drona, Kripa, and Aswatthama by sending arrows into the earth at their feet. And with one final arrow, he shattered the jeweled crown upon Duryodhana's head. Once again, he filled the three worlds with the twang of Gandiva, then blew his conch mightily, piercing the hearts of all his foes.

He smiled and said to Bhuminjaya, "We have recovered the cattle, and our foes are leaving. Let us return to the city with cheerful hearts."

It was exceedingly wonderful.

* * * * *

King Virata and his army had barely arrived back in the city after their night on the battlefield when he learned of the Kuru invasion. But just as he was rallying his army to fight again, a runner arrived from the west, bearing news of the stunning victory.

Everyone assumed that Prince Bhuminjaya had singlehandedly defeated the Kurus. Virata was ecstatic over his son's heroism, and he proclaimed, "Let the roads be decorated with flags! Let the gods and goddesses be worshipped! Let warriors, musicians, beautiful women, and all the citizens go forth to give Prince Bhuminjaya a grand reception as he returns to the city!"

He said to Draupadi, "Sairindhri, fetch the dice." He turned to Yudhisthira and said, "Kanka, let us play!"

Yudhisthira replied, "Gambling is fraught with many evils, O King. Everyone should avoid it. You may have heard of Yudhisthira, who lost his kingdom and his brothers at dice. That is why I am opposed to gambling."

But the king insisted, so they began to play. All the while, Virata could not stop boasting of his son's greatness. Finally, Yudhisthira interrupted him and asked, "Why wouldn't your son triumph when he has such a charioteer as Vrihannala?"

King Virata angrily replied, "You wretch of a Brahmin! How dare you compare a eunuch with my son?! Only for friendship will I pardon you for this offense. But do not repeat it if you wish to live!"

Yet Yudhisthira persisted, "Only Vrihannala could conquer the entire Kuru army, led by Bhishma, Drona, Kripa, and other mighty warriors. With him as your son's ally, victory was certain."

Virata grew livid. "I told you to hold your tongue, and you did not!" He struck Yudhisthira in the face with one of the dice, and Yudhisthira began to bleed profusely. Draupadi quickly brought a vessel to catch the blood before it could fall upon the floor.

At that moment, an attendant entered the court and announced, "Sire, Prince Bhuminjaya and Vrihannala are at the palace gates."

"Bring them here," said the king. "I am eager to see them."

As the attendant turned to fetch them, Yudhisthira whispered to him, "Tell the prince to come alone. Vrihannala has taken a vow that whoever wounds me shall not live. He would kill the king and destroy his entire army."

The attendant nodded, and soon Bhuminjaya entered alone. He noticed Yudhisthira bleeding and asked, "Father, who has done this?"

The king answered, "I struck this crooked Brahmin, and he deserves worse than that. While I was praising you, he praised that eunuch."

The prince said, "You have acted improperly, Father. Quickly, you must apologize to him, else the virulent poison of a Brahmin's curse will consume you to your roots!"

The king realized his son was right. He began to soothe Yudhisthira and ask for forgiveness.

Yudhisthira replied, "I have already forgiven you, O King. Your entire kingdom would have been destroyed had my blood reached the floor. But I do not blame you. Those who are powerful tend to act with unreasoning severity."

When the bleeding stopped, Virata asked that Arjuna enter the chamber. After saluting the king and Yudhisthira, Arjuna stood silent as the king again began to praise Bhuminjaya unreservedly. He asked, "Tell me, my son, how were you able to defeat Bhishma and Drona and all the others?"

The prince replied, "Father, the great warrior who brought us victory was the son of a Deva. It was not I."

"Where is he?" asked the king.

"He disappeared immediately after the fighting ended, Father. But I think he will show himself soon."

The king was satisfied, and the joyful victory celebration resumed.

• • • • •

The Pandavas and Draupadi maintained their disguises for two more days while the entire kingdom celebrated the twin victories. On the morning of the third day, the brothers donned elegant white robes adorned with many ornaments. Then, along with Draupadi, they entered the council hall, shining like five suns. They sat upon five thrones customarily reserved for visiting kings and waited for Virata.

When the king arrived and saw lowly servants and a courtier sitting upon thrones, he became furious. He began to rail at Yudhisthira, "Kanka, you are nothing but a courtier, a mere dice player! How dare you sit upon a throne dressed in such handsome robes and ornaments?!"

Arjuna smiled. "O King, this man deserves to occupy the same throne as Indra himself. He is the seat of all knowledge and virtue. He is the great King Yudhisthira."

Virata was stunned. He asked, "How can that be? Then who are Bhima, Arjuna, Nakula, and Sahadeva? And where is the celebrated Draupadi?"

Arjuna pointed out the other Pandavas and then gestured to Draupadi. "This lady with eyes like lotus petals, of slender waist and sweet smiles, your wife's Sairindhri, is Draupadi. It was for her sake that Bhima killed Kichaka."

Bhuminjaya then explained that Vrihannala was actually Arjuna, and it was he who had singlehandedly overpowered the Kurus.

Virata now realized that it was the mighty Pandavas who had saved his kingdom, his life, and his son's life. Fearing their anger, he quickly sought to appease them: "I offer you my throne, my treasury, my city, everything. And let Arjuna accept my daughter, Princess Uttara, as his wife."

Arjuna answered, "Such an alliance between us is highly desirable. But it would not be proper for me to marry your daughter after spending a year in a close relationship as her dance teacher. I will instead accept her as my daughter-in-law and marry her to my son, Abhimanyu."

"So be it," said King Virata.

Virata invited the Pandavas to reside in Matsya. They, in turn, invited Krishna, King Drupada, and many other kings to join them there for the wedding of Abhimanyu and Uttara. It was a grand celebration, and Abhimanyu and Uttara received many lavish gifts. The Pandavas, too, were given great wealth, most of which Yudhisthira gave to the Brahmins.

For all the nuptial festivities, however, it was as much a gathering for war as for a wedding. The Pandavas' allies were beginning to come together.

CHAPTER 17

Lengthening Shadows

AFTER THE WEDDING OF ABHIMANYU and Princess Uttara, it was time for the Pandavas to ask Duryodhana to return their kingdom. They met with King Drupada and several other friendly kings to formulate a strategy for conveying firmness without starting a war. After much discussion, they decided to send Drupada's Brahmin priest to Hastinapura to deliver the request.

No one expected that Duryodhana would return the Pandavas' kingdom. So, as soon as the priest departed, Yudhisthira sent emissaries to many kings, seeking to form military alliances to support the Pandavas' cause. When Duryodhana's spies sent word of this effort, he, too, began to recruit allies.

Krishna was the most formidable ally anyone could have. Almost no one could perceive that Krishna was the Lord Narayana. However, nearly everyone knew he controlled vast wealth and a massive army—and he was widely regarded as the greatest warrior in the world.

So Yudhisthira sent Arjuna to Dwaraka to solicit Krishna's aid. When Duryodhana's spies sent word of Arjuna's mission, Duryodhana hastily set out for Dwaraka, intent on arriving before Arjuna and gaining Krishna as an ally.

Duryodhana's haste paid off, for he arrived at Krishna's palace only minutes before Arjuna. Krishna was sleeping, but Duryodhana barged past the attendants into Krishna's bedroom. He sat down haughtily in a chair next to the head of the bed, impatient for Krishna to awaken. Shortly after that, Arjuna quietly entered the bedroom and stood reverently at the foot of the bed, palms together.

When Krishna awakened, he opened his eyes and saw Arjuna gazing at him with love. He said, "Arjuna, what brings you here?"

Duryodhana all but shouted, "I came here first!"

Startled, Krishna turned toward him. "Duryodhana! Welcome, both of you. Tell me, what can I do for you?"

Duryodhana said, "Krishna, it behooves you to fight for me in the coming war. Right-minded persons always help those who come to them first. *That* is the ancient custom." Ingratiatingly, he added, "And you, O Krishna, are the foremost of all right-minded persons in the world."

Krishna replied, "I do not doubt you arrived first, Duryodhana, but I saw Arjuna first." He pondered momentarily, then said, "Therefore, I must help both of you. Yes, one of you may have my army of tens of thousands of fierce warriors. The other may have myself, unarmed and vowed not to fight. The younger person should have the first choice; *that* is the ancient custom. Arjuna, you are the younger. Choose what seems best to you."

Duryodhana flushed with anger over Arjuna getting the first choice. But his upset turned to delight when Arjuna quickly said, "I choose *you*, Krishna!" Duryodhana thought Arjuna had lost his mind. He smiled broadly and, without a word, promptly left the palace to make arrangements for bringing Krishna's army to Hastinapura.

Krishna turned to Arjuna and asked, "Why did you choose me when I have vowed not to fight?"

Arjuna answered, "You are very great, Krishna, and your greatness will accompany you on the battlefield, even if you do not fight. It has long been my cherished wish that you will drive my chariot in the coming war. Surrounded by your greatness, perhaps I too will become great."

Krishna replied, "Let your wish be fulfilled."

He and Arjuna immediately set out to rejoin the other Pandavas in Matsya. Krishna's dear friend and kinsman, Satyaki, accompanied them.

Satyaki represents devotion.

＊　＊　＊　＊　＊

Many other kings had accepted requests for an alliance with Yudhisthira or Duryodhana, and their armies soon began to converge on Matsya and Hastinapura.

One of those kings was Salya. He was Madri's brother and, therefore, the Pandavas' uncle. He and his army were marching toward Matsya to fight for the Pandavas.

Salya represents material pride.

When spies informed Duryodhana of Salya's intentions, Duryodhana ordered elegant pleasure pavilions to be built all along Salya's route, filled with excellent comforts and entertainments. Salya assumed Yudhisthira had provided those enjoyments, and he made full use of them.

At one point, Salya asked the servants, "Where are Yudhisthira's people, who have prepared all this for me? I must grant them a boon."

Duryodhana had been hiding nearby, and as soon as he heard that, he stepped into view with a broad smile. Salya was mortified when he realized that he had promised to reward Duryodhana. Nevertheless, as was proper, he asked, "What can I give you?"

Duryodhana replied, "I ask that you be the commander of my army."

"So be it," said Salya without hesitation. "But first, I must go to Matsya and greet my nephews, the Pandavas. I will send my army directly to Hastinapura, and I will soon join you there."

As Salya stood to leave, Duryodhana said with a smile, "Remember your boon, O King."

When Salya arrived in Matsya, he was ashamed to tell Yudhisthira what had transpired. But Yudhisthira said, "It was right and proper that you thanked the source of your enjoyment. I have only one request: When the great duel between Arjuna and Karna comes, as I know it will, I am sure you will be Karna's charioteer, for he considers you as good a driver as Krishna. I ask that you protect Arjuna and find ways to discourage Karna, so Arjuna may triumph. I know this is improper, but you must do it."

"And I will do it," said Salya, "as well as anything else that will support your cause. Destiny is all-powerful in this world, O King, and even the greatest of high-minded persons must endure miseries, as you have done. But you shall prevail."

• • • • •

As Drupada's Brahmin priest approached Hastinapura, he saw that ten other armies—including Krishna's—had been sent to support the Kuru army. So Duryodhana had eleven armies, and their camps spread over the surrounding countryside as far as the eye could see. The hills bristled with power and menace. It was an awe-inspiring sight.

The Brahmin received a cordial welcome at the Kuru court. When Dhritarashtra invited him to speak, the priest came straight to the point: "The Pandavas have endured mistreatment and treachery at the hands of the sons of Dhritarashtra. Still, they wish for peace and ask only for the rightful return of Indraprastha. I have seen that the Kauravas have assembled eleven armies, whereas the Pandavas have only seven. But the Pandavas have Arjuna, and he can defeat all eleven armies by himself. Who would dare stand against him? The Kurus cannot hope to win a war against the Pandavas. Morality, prudence, and the terms of the game of dice dictate that Indraprastha must be returned."

Bhishma said, "Your words are very sharp, O Brahmin, but no doubt they are true. The Pandavas deserve their kingdom. And the gods themselves could not defeat Arjuna …"

Karna interrupted, "Everyone knows what has happened. We recognized Arjuna before the end of the thirteenth year, so the Pandavas must return to the forest for twelve more years. Those were the terms of the dice game, O Brahmin. After those twelve years, they can live as dependents of Duryodhana. But if they abandon dharma and make war, they will regret it!"

Bhishma gave him an angry look. "That is nonsense, Karna! Have you forgotten that Arjuna defeated all of us when we attacked Matsya? And he defeated you twice! He will slay us all in battle if we do not act as this Brahmin asks."

Dhritarashtra waved his hands. "No more arguing. What Bhishma has said is best for everyone. But return to Matsya now, O Brahmin. I shall consider what has been said here and send my response."

The priest bowed and departed.

∙ ∙ ∙ ∙ ∙

It wasn't long before Sanjaya, Dhritarashtra's advisor and charioteer, arrived in Matsya to convey the blind king's response. He was given an audience with the Pandavas, and after the proper courtesies were exchanged, he said to Yudhisthira, "O King, I bring King Dhritarashtra's reply to the message that the Brahmin brought to

Hastinapura. The king said, 'Why do you speak of war, Yudhisthira? Fighting against your relatives would ruin your good name. Virtuous as you are, surely you would never commit such a sin. Even if you win, your lives would be like death for killing your own kin. And you may not win, for Bhishma, Drona, and Karna are great warriors.'"

Yudhisthira interrupted. "What need is there of war? Just give me Indraprastha, as was agreed upon, and there will be no war."

Sanjaya drew a breath and continued, "King Dhritarashtra also said, 'Yudhisthira, it is beneath you to covet wealth and king-dom — you who always seek to follow dharma. Do not let greed rob you of your fame and virtue. Do not forsake the path of dharma, the only route to Heaven. Renounce this sinful desire. Give up your an-ger. Let there be peace.'"

Arjuna and Bhima fumed with rage over this response. Yudhisthira signaled them to stay calm, then gave Sanjaya a brief reply. "Tell the king this: If Duryodhana will give us even five villages, there will be peace. But we are equally ready for war."

Arjuna added, "Tell Duryodhana, and also that foul and wicked Sutaputra, of stupid mind and numbered days, that if our kingdom is returned, then and only then will the sons of Dhritarashtra live. Otherwise, Duryodhana will commit a great folly, fighting against those who could not be defeated even by the Devas. As a blazing fire consumes a forest in summer, so will my astras leave behind no rem-nant of those who oppose me."

• • • • •

Sanjaya returned to Hastinapura and gave Yudhisthira's re-ply to Dhritarashtra, the Kuru elders, and Duryodhana and his al-lies. He also conveyed Arjuna's threat. The elders were certain that Duryodhana would never give back the Pandavas' *entire* kingdom, so they saw Yudhisthira's offer as a welcome way to avoid war.

Drona said, "Five villages, Duryodhana — such a small price to pay for peace. Accept their offer."

Karna said, "No, it is time for the war to end all wars."

Bhishma thundered, "You want a war, do you, O foul Sutaputra? Well, you shall have one! Rishi Narada has said that Arjuna and Krishna are the two ancient rishis, Nara and Narayana. They are born whenever destructive wars are necessary. Their *mission* is to fight! And you think you can defeat them? You are utterly deluded!

"Duryodhana, I do not blame you for this. You have been led astray by the evil counsel of Shakuni, Dushasana, and that lowborn Sutaputra. Turn away from them before they destroy you and cause the slaughter of many men!"

Karna shot back, "I will slay all the Pandavas in battle! A wise man never makes peace with those whom he has injured."

Bhishma said to Dhritarashtra, "O King, this Sutaputra always boasts that he will slay the Pandavas, yet he is not equal to a sixteenth part of them. When Arjuna rescued Duryodhana and many other Kurus from the Gandharvas, did he not defeat the same enemy that had defeated Karna, who now bellows like a bull? And in Matsya, when Arjuna vanquished all the Kurus and took away their robes, did he not defeat Karna twice? Ever beautiful and never virtuous, these are the many false words he utters. O King, this wretched Sutaputra is the cause of the great calamity that is about to overtake your wicked sons!"

Drona added, "O King, listen to Bhishma. Do not follow the counsel of those who covet wealth. What Arjuna has vowed, he will accomplish, for there is no archer to compare with him in all the three worlds!"

Duryodhana waved those words aside. "Do not worry, Father. We can defeat the Pandavas. Long ago, Grandfather and our famed preceptor Dronaji promised to vanquish them if they ever attacked us. And we all know that Grandfather is invincible; he cannot die until he chooses to die. Besides, the Pandavas' offer to accept just five villages shows weakness. No, I will not give them so much land as can be covered by the point of a needle!"

And so it is with us: When we first come onto the spiritual path, there seems to be plenty of room for both the material side of our nature and the spiritual side. But as Paramhansa Yogananda pointed out, when we grow serious about the path, the material side begins to feel threatened — and rightly so, because spiritual progress will eventually eliminate our material inclinations. That is why Duryodhana, who represents the material side of our nature, refused to take any chances: He would not give the Pandavas (representing our spiritual side) any land at all.

Dhritarashtra pleaded, "My dear Duryodhana, the Pandavas are sons of gods! If you do not make peace, the gods themselves will help their children!"

Duryodhana dismissed that thought with a wave of his hand. "Pah! If the gods were going to help, they would have done so long ago. Even then, I could defeat them all. They could not stop me from exiling the Pandavas, and they cannot stop me now. My intelligence is superior! My prowess is superior! And my resources are *far* superior!"

Karna added, "And I have the Brahma weapon. I will slay the Pandavas and all their allies in the blink of an eye!"

Bhishma scoffed, "O lowborn fool of a Sutaputra, your mind is clouded at the approach of your hour. The Pandavas will destroy you *and* all your astras! And you certainly can never slay Arjuna, protected as he is by the Lord Himself. You are but a cowardly braggart with no prowess to back up your empty boasts!"

Karna's eyes blazed with anger. "Let the grandfather see the effect of his abusive speech: I hereby lay down my weapons! I shall not fight until he has fallen in battle. *Then* the world will know my prowess!"

And he stormed out of the court.

* * * * *

When the Pandavas received word that Duryodhana had rejected their compromise offer, war seemed inevitable. Yudhisthira was worried, for he valued peace second only to Truth itself. In a council of all his allies, he asked Krishna, "How can we regain the kingdom that is rightfully ours without violating dharma by killing?"

Krishna said, "I understand your concern, O King. I will go to the Kurus and try to find a peaceful solution without sacrificing your interests. If I succeed, I will earn much good karma and save many lives."

"But they are treacherous and dangerous," said Yudhisthira. "I cannot bear the thought of you being harmed."

"I am well aware of Duryodhana's evil nature," Krishna replied. "Do not worry. If the Kauravas try to harm me, I will destroy them all."

Bhima said, "Go with peaceful words, Krishna. Do not threaten war. We must not annihilate the entire Kshatriya caste."

Krishna burst out laughing. "Bhima, you have been wanting to fight more than anyone else. How is it that you now speak like a eunuch?"

"You insult me, Krishna," said Bhima. "I spoke only out of compassion. I will trample the Kauravas underfoot if need be!"

Sahadeva added, "O Krishna, do whatever it takes to provoke a war. I can never rest until we have avenged the mistreatment of Draupadi!"

Those words brought a roar of approval from everyone present. Draupadi's eyes blazed as she said, "O Krishna, everyone knows the persecution we have suffered, and how my husbands said nothing while I was humiliated at the dice game. Now Bhima speaks of making peace!" She began to sob, spilling hot tears over the floor. "For thirteen long years, I have hidden my anger in my heart like a smoldering fire, waiting for the evil Kauravas to receive what they deserve. I will not rest until justice and dharma have been served and all the evil Kauravas have been slain!"

Krishna answered, "Soon, Draupadi, the Kaurava wives will weep as you weep, for the sons of Dhritarashtra will lie in the dirt as morsels for dogs and jackals. The Earth might split into a hundred pieces, and the stars might fall from the sky, but I will accomplish this! Dry your tears. I swear that the Pandavas will be crowned with prosperity!"

Krishna left the assembly and prepared to travel with Satyaki to Hastinapura. As he mounted his chariot, Arjuna approached him and declared, "If they return our kingdom, Krishna, I will be greatly pleased. But if Duryodhana acts otherwise, I will annihilate the entire Kshatriya caste!"

Krishna nodded his approval of those words. Then, with cheerful hearts, he and Satyaki departed for Hastinapura.

· · · · ·

Kaurava spies immediately sent word that Krishna and Satyaki were coming to Hastinapura in quest of peace. Dhritarashtra called a council to decide what to do. He suggested, "We could give Krishna lavish and bountiful gifts to separate him from the Pandavas."

Duryodhana scoffed. "That will not work! He is devoted to them. Besides, if we give him gifts, he will think we are honoring him out of fear. No, when war has been decided upon, it must not be put off by hospitality. We should imprison him!"

Dhritarashtra was alarmed. He said, "My son, never say that! Krishna is coming as an ambassador. And he is our dear, dear cousin. Imprisonment would be very wrong!"

Bhishma rose in fury. "O Dhritarashtra, your wicked son walks a thorny path, and you are following him! If he tries to capture Krishna, he will be destroyed in an instant. I dare not listen to that sinful wretch!"

With that, the grandfather stormed out of the council hall.

In the end, Duryodhana decided to try to buy Krishna's favor in the same way that he had bought Salya's favor: He ordered that workers erect luxurious pleasure pavilions all along Krishna's route. They were to be elegantly furnished, decorated with precious gems of every kind, and filled with beautiful women and excellent drinks. Duryodhana hoped that would win Krishna over to his side.

The Kuru workers quickly completed the task, but Krishna passed by those pavilions without even glancing at them. Upon arriving in Hastinapura, he refused a dinner invitation from Duryodhana. Instead, he arranged to stay overnight with Vidura and his wife.

After dinner, Vidura said, "O Krishna, I fear there is no chance for peace. Duryodhana will never return the Pandavas' kingdom. You should not have come. You have exposed yourself to danger."

Krishna replied, "I know Duryodhana's evil nature, but great will be my merit if I can save the earth from the meshes of death. That person is a wretch who does not try to dissuade a friend from sin. I am trying to bring about the good of all concerned. If Duryodhana misjudges my intentions, still I shall have the satisfaction of my conscience. Let no one say that Krishna did not try to avert a great slaughter. And if the Kurus seek to injure me, I tell you that all the kings of the earth, united together, are no match for me!"

And with that, Krishna lay down to sleep.

CHAPTER 18

Final Efforts for Peace

K RISHNA WALKED INTO KING DHRITARASHTRA's council hall, arm in arm with Vidura and Satyaki. The Kuru elders and the Kauravas were there. So also were Karna, many rishis, and all the kings who had agreed to fight for Duryodhana. Even the celestial rishi, Narada, had come.

With his deep blue skin and yellow robes, Krishna looked like a sapphire mounted in gold. When he took his seat, perfect silence reigned in the hall.

After a time, Krishna turned to Dhritarashtra and broke the silence, saying, "O King, I have come that peace might be established between the Kurus and the Pandavas. The Kurus are the greatest of all royal dynasties. Yet Duryodhana and your other wicked sons have brought the world to the brink of war. Deprived of their senses by greed, they have abandoned virtue and are behaving most unrighteously toward their cousins. If you allow this to continue, it will produce a universal slaughter.

"It is not too late, O King. If you unite with the Pandavas, you will rule the world. If you oppose them, the world will be destroyed. Do not lose your virtue and prosperity, O King. Save the lives of all these kings who have assembled their armies for war. The Pandavas have abided by the terms of the game of dice. Now you must, also. I say this for your good as well as theirs. Peace—or destruction—is in your hands."

In their hearts, the other kings applauded Krishna's words. But no one spoke for fear of Duryodhana, who was frowning darkly and breathing heavily.

Then Duryodhana looked at Karna and laughed. He said, "I am precisely what the Creator has made me. What has been ordained for me must happen; I cannot act otherwise. Why, therefore, must this discussion continue?"

Dhritarashtra said, "O Krishna, your words are indeed beneficial and virtuous. But as you have seen, my foolish and wicked son never obeys me or the other elders, though we all seek his good. O Best of Men, do persuade Duryodhana to make peace."

Krishna turned toward Duryodhana and said, "Duryodhana, I speak for your good. You are well-educated, yet your conduct is ignorant and sinful. It will lead you directly to death. If you make peace, the whole world will benefit, as will you. All your allies, even the Devas themselves, cannot defeat Arjuna. He vanquished all of you single-handed in Matsya. And I was not his charioteer in *that* battle," he added.

Krishna gestured toward the other Kauravas. "Look at your brothers. Must they perish on your account? Do not become the exterminator of the Kuru people. The Pandavas ask only for their half of the kingdom. If you give it back, you will obtain great prosperity and happiness."

The Kuru elders agreed with Krishna, and with strong words, they chastised Duryodhana, who became indignant and said, "You all criticize me, but I do not find the slightest flaw in myself. The Pandavas accepted the challenge to the game of dice. Is it my fault they lost? And now they make threats! What have we ever done to harm them? Well, we are not frightened. A Kshatriya *never* bows down to an enemy to save his own life. We will fight! The gods themselves cannot defeat us, let alone the sons of Pandu. Know this, O Krishna: The kingdom that was given away to the Pandavas when I was but a child shall not be given away again!"

Krishna said, "You wish for the hero's bed of arrows—and you shall have it soon enough, along with your followers. How can you say you have done no wrong? Everyone knows you have persecuted your cousins for many years. All your life, you have tried to kill them. And now you scorn the wise counsel of your elders. Duryodhana, you do not know what is best for you. What you intend to do is sinful and shameful!"

Without another word, Duryodhana rose from his seat and stalked out of the hall, followed by Karna and Dushasana.

Dhritarashtra said, "Vidura, bring Gandhari here. If she can talk sense into that wicked wretch, we may yet be able to follow the counsel of our friend, Krishna."

As Vidura left, Bhishma shook his head and said, "O Krishna, I see that the hour of Duryodhana and all his followers has come. That fool has abandoned both virtue and profit, possessed as he is by anger and greed."

Krishna stood, and his expression hardened as he gazed one by one at Bhishma, then Drona, Kripa, and finally, Dhritarashtra. "O elders of the Kuru people, you have allowed this injustice to occur! You should have bound the wicked Duryodhana long ago! Even now, it is not too late. Bind him fast and make peace with the Pandavas! Do not let the entire Kshatriya caste be slaughtered on your account!"

The elders gazed at the floor without responding to Krishna's words. The hall was silent until Vidura returned with Gandhari and announced her. As always, she was wearing a blindfold.

Dhritarashtra said, "O Gandhari, your wicked son is about to lose both his sovereignty and his life. Disregarding his superiors and well-wishers, he has rudely left the court."

Gandhari said, "Vidura, bring my sick, kingdom-coveting son to the council hall." Vidura departed, and Gandhari continued, "He does not deserve to rule a kingdom, yet for all that, he has obtained one. O Dhritarashtra, you are too fond of your son; you are to blame for this. Knowing well his sinfulness, you have still followed his counsel. Now, he is ruled completely by anger and greed. With his wicked counselors, he is beyond your control. You are reaping the fruit of having given the kingdom to an ignorant, wicked-souled fool."

Vidura returned with a petulant Duryodhana and announced, "Your son, O Queen."

Gandhari said, "My dear Duryodhana, listen to me. He who cannot control his passions may *win* a kingdom, but he cannot keep it. Anger and greed will steal it from him. Ruin soon comes to the person who seeks to conquer others without first conquering himself.

"O Son, there is no virtue in battle, no profit. How, then, can it bring happiness? You will lose your prosperity if you fight the Pandavas. They have conquered their passions. Krishna and Arjuna are invincible. You are no match for them, nor is Karna or Dushasana. And do not rely on Bhishma and Drona. They will fight for you because they have lived off the Kuru wealth for all these years. But they will not fight with all their might, for their affection toward the Pandavas and yourselves is equal. If you wish to enjoy even half the kingdom, give the Pandavas what is theirs — then you will win great fame. Do not let the world be destroyed for your sake.

Give up your greed, my son. Make peace. Remember: where there is dharma, there is victory."

Without saying a word, Duryodhana turned and stormed out of the council hall, followed by Karna, Shakuni, Dushasana, and a number of his other brothers. He gathered them around him and said, "Krishna and our elders want to seize us. But we will seize him first! Then the Pandavas will lose heart and be unable to oppose us, like snakes whose fangs have been broken."

Satyaki had followed them to eavesdrop. He quickly returned to the council hall and said to Dhritarashtra: "O King, your foolish son and his followers seek to do a highly sinful act. They plan to seize Krishna." He laughed. "They are like idiots who think to seize a blazing fire by means of their own garments!"

Vidura said, "Such an act would be infamous and unrighteous—also impossible! They will perish like insects in a blazing fire."

Krishna turned to Dhritarashtra. "If your sons wish to use violence against me, let them do it. I will not harm them."

Dhritarashtra sighed. "Vidura, bring him back. I shall try one last time to lead him to dharma."

Vidura soon returned, along with Duryodhana and his followers.

Dhritarashtra said to Duryodhana, "O wicked wretch, you seek to do a sinful deed. Like a child wishing to have the moon, you wish to do what the gods themselves could not do. Like the wind, which no one can seize with his hands, Krishna cannot be seized by force."

Duryodhana made no reply as he and his followers spread out and surrounded Krishna, then began to close in on him.

Krishna smiled as Duryodhana approached him. He said, "You think me to be alone, O ignorant one, and therefore you seek to capture me." He spread his arms and lifted his gaze. "But here are the Devas, Brahma, Shiva, and all the great rishis!"

Krishna burst into laughter, and those and a host of other celestial beings emerged from his body, clothed in fire and brandishing terrible weapons. Fierce flames leaped from his eyes and every part of his body, which grew to tremendous size. Celestial drums began to beat, and flowers rained from Heaven. The Earth shuddered, and the oceans churned. Duryodhana and his followers closed their eyes, fell to the floor, and curled up in sheer terror.

Then Krishna withdrew that divine form, and the hall fell into a powerful stillness. He let the silence build for a time, then stood and began to walk out. The only sounds were the echoes of his footsteps.

Dhritarashtra rose from his throne. "Wait, O Krishna! You heard what I said to Duryodhana. You have seen what little power I wield over my sons. I have no sinful feelings toward the Pandavas. And everyone knows that I have made every effort to ensure peace."

Krishna stopped and swept his fierce gaze through the entire hall. "Indeed, all of you have seen what has happened here, and how *King* Dhritarashtra describes himself as powerless." He turned to Dhritarashtra. "With your permission, O King, I shall return to Yudhisthira!"

Without waiting for a reply, he walked out of the council hall, followed by Satyaki.

* * * * *

Before leaving Hastinapura, Krishna made one more attempt to secure peace. He sought out Karna and took him in his chariot to a quiet place outside the city. They stepped out of the chariot and began to walk arm in arm.

Krishna said, "Karna, you are a great soul. All your life, you have sought to learn Truth. You are well-versed in the subtle conclusions of the scriptures. You know that the Vedas say that he who is born of a maiden is the son of the man she later marries. Karna, *you* were born of a maiden: the maiden Kunti. Therefore, you are the son of Pandu. *You are the eldest* Pandava, the rightful king.

"Come with me to Yudhisthira. Let your brothers and their allies bow at your feet. They and I will install you as the lord of the entire earth. People will sing your praises in chants and hymns beyond number. Let the Pandavas proclaim, "Jai Karna! Victory to Karna!" Surrounded by your brothers like the moon by the stars, rule the kingdom."

Karna was stunned. "I ... am the son of Kunti? The Pandavas ... my mortal enemies ... are my brothers? How can that be? But since you say it, Krishna, I know it is true. And I know you say it for my benefit, out of love for me."

He sighed, shaking his head. "So, I am the son of Pandu." He remained silent for a time as the truth sank in. Then he continued, "But Kunti abandoned me at birth, and I was raised as a Suta. Neither wealth nor kingdom could tempt me to betray those who lovingly raised me as their son. Nor can I betray Duryodhana, who has been loyal to me all these years — not even for the sake of preventing a war or living longer.

"Please, do not reveal this conversation to anyone. If Yudhisthira learns that I am his elder brother, he will give me the kingdom — and I will certainly give it to Duryodhana. No, let the virtuous Yudhisthira become king forever. With you as his counselor and his four mighty brothers at his side, he is fit to rule the world.

"O Krishna, the world's Kshatriyas have gathered to meet their glory. Do not let them die miserably of old age. Accomplish your purpose so the entire Kshatriya caste may attain Heaven. As long as the hills and rivers will last, so long will the fame of their achievements in this battle endure. That fame is the wealth of Kshatriyas! All I ask is that you bring Arjuna to me for battle, and *I beg of you*, keep this conversation a secret!"

Krishna said, "Karna, I am offering you the entire world. It is yours to rule. Do you truly not wish to have it?"

Karna shook his head. "O Krishna, you already know what will happen. Why must you try to beguile me? The destruction of the world is at hand, and its cause is Shakuni, myself, Dushasana, and Duryodhana."

Krishna sighed. "Then I have no doubt. The victory of the Pandavas is certain. Arjuna's banner of triumph seems already to be waving proudly in the breeze. Go back, then, and tell Drona, Bhishma, and Kripa that the time has come. It is a delightful season of the year. The weather is mild, the roads are free of mire, food and fuel are abundant, and the rivers run pure. Seven days hence is the day of the new moon. Let the battle commence then, for that is the day ruled by Indra. Tell all Duryodhana's allies that I will fully accomplish their cherished desire: They will die in battle and attain Heaven."

Karna said, "I know that where there is dharma, there is victory. You will ensure the Pandavas' victory, and I ... will be slain by Arjuna."

"Indeed, Karna," said Krishna, "the destruction of the entire world is at hand when your heart does not accept my words. As destruction approaches, wrong seems to be right."

Karna said softly, "O Krishna, if we survive this battle, then may we meet again. Otherwise, we shall certainly meet in Heaven."

They embraced. Then Karna turned and slowly walked away. Krishna went back into the city, where Satyaki was waiting. Together, they departed Hastinapura to rejoin the Pandavas in Matsya.

*   *   *   *   *

Throughout the Pandavas' exile, Kunti had lived in Hastinapura with Vidura and his wife. Now, she was in extreme torment over the tragedy of the coming war. She knew that her sons had to fight—she *wanted* them to fight—lest their lives be nothing but poverty and humiliation. Yet fighting would mean killing their own relatives.

She was sure that Bhishma and Drona would gladly make peace, for they loved the Pandavas. It was only Karna who hated her sons and willingly followed the wicked Duryodhana. Ever since seeing Karna at the exhibition where the newly trained Kuru princes had displayed their skills, she had known that he was her firstborn son. But for fear of scandal, she had told no one.

Now, not knowing of Krishna's talk with Karna, she resolved to tell Karna the truth of his birth, hoping to turn his heart toward his brothers. She found him at the River Ganga, facing the rising sun with upraised arms, chanting Vedic hymns. She stood patiently, waiting for him.

When he finished his worship, he stepped out of the river and said to her, "I am Karna, the Sutaputra. What may I do for you?"

Kunti could not restrain herself. "You are *not* a Sutaputra! You are my son! You are a Kshatriya—more than a Kshatriya, for your father is Lord Surya!

"O Son, it is wrong for you to serve that wicked Duryodhana. Make him give back Yudhisthira's kingdom. Stop this war. Unite with your brothers. Let the evil Kauravas bow down before you. Claim your Kshatriya heritage. *You are my eldest son!*"

A voice from the heavens resounded through the skies: "Karna, it is I, your father. Your mother's words are true. Follow her wishes, O tiger among men, and great good will come to you."

Karna narrowed his eyes and gazed at her fiercely. "O lady, you abandoned me at birth. And now you tell me to claim my Kshatriya heritage? It was you who deprived me of it! No *enemy* could have done me greater harm! You ask me to prevent this war. It is you and your secrecy that have caused it! You have never cared about me as a mother should. You care only for yourself!

"What warrior would not fear Arjuna, with Krishna as his char-ioteer? If I go to the Pandavas now, everyone will think I am afraid. And I cannot betray Duryodhana, who has always supported and depended upon me. *He* has always been loyal to me. Now he thinks I will win this war for him. Well, *I* will not be disloyal!

"No, I shall fight your sons with all my might! Yet you have asked of me a favor, so by my vow, I must grant you one. Very well. I promise not to kill your other four sons, but I will fight to the death with Arjuna. O great lady, when this battle has ended, you will still have five sons — either with me and not Arjuna, or with Arjuna and not myself."

Kunti began to weep. "Then the Kauravas will certainly be exter-minated. Destiny is all-powerful." Impulsively, she stepped forward and embraced him. But he stiffened and pulled away. She wiped her eyes. "When the battle comes, O Karna, remember your pledge to grant safety to four of your brothers. Blessings to you, my son."

"So be it," said Karna, his words cold and remote. Then he turned and strode quickly away. Kunti watched him go, having just spoken with her firstborn son for the only time in her life.

Every effort had been made to bring about peace. Every effort had failed. There was nothing left to do but prepare for The Great War.

CHAPTER 19

The Bhagavad Gita

WITH ALL HOPE OF PEACE now dashed, Duryodhana and Yudhisthira mobilized their massive armies to fight for the kingdom. Duryodhana was confident of a quick victory, for his army was far larger, and it boasted many great warriors—above all, the invincible Bhishma, the preceptor Drona, Aswatthama (Drona's son), and the mighty Karna.

On a clear, bright morning, Duryodhana and his warriors arose and purified themselves by bathing. All of them had great strength, bravery, and combat skill. Clad in white robes and decked with garlands, they poured libations on the sacred fire and received blessings from the Brahmins. Then they took up their weapons, raised their banners, and set out for the battlefield called Kurukshetra, eager to attain the highest regions of Heaven through battle.

Yudhisthira also arose and, after performing his worship and honoring his allies, commanded his army to depart for Kurukshetra. With their handsome armor and golden earrings, those heroic warriors looked as resplendent as the planets on a moonless night. There were hundreds of thousands of foot soldiers, horses, chariots, and elephants, and support workers beyond number. As they marched in a long column, they looked like the irresistible current of the Holy Ganga.

When the opposing armies reached Kurukshetra, they set up their encampments on opposite sides of the field and made final preparations for war. Duryodhana chose Grandfather Bhishma as his commander, while Yudhisthira chose Dhrishtadyumna, the fire-born son of King Drupada. Though he was born to kill Drona, Dhrishtadyumna had become his disciple some years after the Pandavas and Kauravas completed their training. Now he would be fighting against his guru, as would the Pandavas.

On the evening before the battle was to begin, the two commanders, together with the Pandavas, Duryodhana, and Drona, met to agree upon the rules of engagement. Combat would take place only between sunrise and sunset. Warriors were to fight only with equals: chariot warriors with other chariot warriors, elephant warriors with other elephant warriors, and foot soldiers with other foot soldiers. Even then, one should fight only with a worthy opponent. No one was to assault another who was unprepared, panic-stricken, asking mercy, retreating, or without armor or weapons. Charioteers and horses were *never* to be attacked.

As darkness fell, those mighty warriors retired to their tents to rest.

* * * * *

Before dawn the following day, in the Hastinapura palace, Dhritarashtra was pacing back and forth in great agitation over the imminent prospect of his sons being killed in battle. The rishi Vyasa perceived his anguish and came to him, saying, "O King, the hour of your sons and the other kings has come. They will all perish. I will grant you divine vision if you wish to see the battle."

The blind king shook his head. "I could not bear to see the slaughter of my sons."

Vyasa said, "Then I will give divine sight to your councilor, Sanjaya. He will see and hear all that happens in the war—the fighting, the conversations among the warriors, even their thoughts. He will report everything to you. Do not grieve, O King. It is all destiny. Where there is dharma, there is victory."

* * * * *

Meanwhile, the opposing commanders arrayed their forces for combat. The armies stretched across Kurukshetra like two vast, agitated oceans. The sounds of elephants, horses, chariots, drums, conches, and shouting soldiers filled the air. Violent winds began to blow, thunder sounded, and rain fell from the cloudless sky. Meteors flashed toward the eastern horizon, and the entire Earth trembled.

At the forefront of the Kuru army was its commander, Bhishma. Cased in shining white armor and standing tall in a magnificent chariot, he looked like the full moon rising. Beholding him, the Pandava soldiers cowered in fear, like small animals before a mighty lion.

Seeing this, Yudhisthira lamented to Arjuna, "How can we ever defeat this mighty army led by our invincible grandfather?"

Arjuna replied, "Fear not, O King, for victory is not won by superior numbers and might so much as by truth, compassion, righteousness, and energy. Know this: our triumph is certain, for Krishna is with us. Rishi Narada has told us, 'Where Krishna is, there is victory.' I see no cause for despair when the Lord of the Universe is on our side."

Then, after worshipping the Brahmins and invoking the blessings of the gods, the Pandavas mounted their chariots, ready at last for The Great War.

 . . . . .

In the Hastinapura palace, Dhritarashtra asked Sanjaya, "My sons and the sons of Pandu—tell me, what have they done?"

> Dhritarashtra's question marks the beginning of The Bhagavad Gita, "The Song of the Lord." He asked it as though the war had already begun, and he wanted to know what had happened. Allegorically, this suggests introspection, the faculty that Sanjaya represents: We examine our actions *after* performing them. Then only can we see who "won" — our positive tendencies (the Pandavas) or our negative tendencies (the Kauravas).

Sanjaya answered him, using his divine sight to convey the Gita as well as the details of all eighteen bloodstained days of battle. What follows is his account.

 . . . . .

As dawn approached, the battlefield fell silent. Duryodhana said to Drona, "Our army far outnumbers theirs. We must, at all costs, protect Bhishma." Bhishma overheard that, and he immediately blew his great conch to bolster Duryodhana's spirits.

> Why would Bhishma (ego) need protection? After all, he had the boon of invincibility. Yes, but the Kurukshetra War symbolizes the inner struggle that can arise as the devotee goes into meditation. Upon entering the inner silence, breath and mind become calm, and energy begins to withdraw from the senses. That weakens the

egoic feeling of separateness and limitation, and thereby endangers desire, which has its roots in ego consciousness. Duryodhana (material desire) began to fear for his very existence. Fear agitates the ego, so the breath resumes, symbolized by Bhishma blowing his conch. With the ego re-energized, Duryodhana felt comforted.

Inspired by their commander, the rest of the Kuru army sounded a great cacophony of conches, drums, and trumpets. Far across the battlefield, the Pandava army responded in kind.

The sounds made by the Kuru army symbolize the chaos and tumult of sensory engagement. The Pandava army's response signifies the subtle, uplifting sounds of the chakras, which grow louder as our consciousness becomes interiorized.

When silence finally returned to the field, Arjuna said to his charioteer, "O Krishna, take me between the two armies. Let me see who I will have to fight."

Krishna drove Arjuna's chariot to a point midway between the two armies, where Arjuna surveyed the opposing forces.

In the Gita, Arjuna no longer represents the specific quality of self-control. He represents the devotee — us — sitting in meditation, with the mind still enough to see our inner tendencies: those that support our quest for true happiness as well as those that oppose it. Krishna represents God or the guru, speaking to us through our soul intuition. He will guide us in the spiritual battle between our positive and negative tendencies. At stake is the kingdom of happiness.

I will offer only a few of Paramhansa Yogananda's and Swami Kriyananda's many penetrating insights into the Gita, which deserve a thorough exploration. For that, I highly recommend Kriyananda's book, *The Essence of the Bhagavad Gita: Explained by Paramhansa Yogananda.*

Arjuna gazed across the battlefield, savoring the prospect of avenging the many years of persecution and humiliation at the hands of Duryodhana. Among the enemy army, he saw his cousins, nephews, and uncles; his dear grandfather, Bhishma; and his beloved guru, Drona.

Arjuna's resolve began to falter, and he said, "O Krishna, seeing

my relatives ready for battle, my limbs are failing me, my skin is burning, and my mouth is parched. My bow slips from my hand. I see no
benefit in slaying my kinsmen. Of what use is kingdom or wealth if
we must kill our relatives? It would be a great sin. Better they should
kill me!"

He dropped his weapons and sat down in the chariot.

> Allegorically, Arjuna is lamenting the imminent death of his negative
> qualities and his enjoyment of sense pleasures, as if saying: "I know
> they are not good for me, but they are part of me, and they have
> given me some happiness, however fleeting! Destroying them would
> be the end of both pleasure and parts of my very self. I would be less
> than I am now, and certainly less happy."
>
> Paramhansa Yogananda said of such thinking, "When the mind feels
> sympathy for sense pleasures, picture that your very dear, sensitive,
> pleasure-loving body eventually will have to be dumped into the grave
> or cast into the hungry crematory flames, and make a stronger effort
> to contact God through deep meditation, and get acquainted with
> the forgotten, deathless, indestructible, real Soul, which is hidden
> behind the false, pleasure-infested, perishable, pretending-to-be-
> your-own body."
>
> Strong words!

Krishna was appalled by Arjuna's sudden change of attitude. "In
such a critical moment as this, Arjuna, how has this come over you?
It is disgraceful and detrimental to the attainment of Heaven. Forsake
this faint-heartedness! Arise!"

"O Krishna, how can I fight with my grandfather and preceptor?
I should worship them, not fight them!"

> Bhishma and Drona represent ego and habit, which have been the
> architects of our human existence. They made us everything that
> we mistakenly believe we are. Naturally, then, they are dear to us.
> Killing them would feel like killing ourselves.

Arjuna continued, "I feel sympathy for those dear ones and am
bewildered about my dharma. I am your disciple. Tell me what I
should do."

He paused and considered for a moment, then shook his head and
said, "Still, I see nothing that can justify fighting—not a kingdom,

not wealth, not even sovereignty over the gods." He paused again, then exclaimed, *"I shall not fight!"*

Krishna smiled. "Arjuna, do not grieve for those who will die in battle. The Lord, Who pervades all things, can never perish. The body is transitory, but the Self is eternal. Arrows cannot harm it. Fire cannot burn it. Wind cannot wither it. One who knows the Self would never believe he could kill anyone. Why, then, do you lament?

> Taken literally, that is a flimsy justification for killing: "Don't worry, they will reincarnate!" But Krishna was speaking allegorically, saying that our inner tendencies — positive and negative — are merely patterns of energy, life force, within us. When we overcome a negative tendency, we break the pattern, but we do not kill the energy that animates it. Instead, we free that energy; we will then have even more strength for the next battle.

Krishna continued, "You are a Kshatriya, and for a Kshatriya, there is nothing higher than righteous battle. It is your good fortune that such a battle has come to you. It would be sinful and dishonorable not to fight. All the other great warriors will say you were afraid. Your allies will be ashamed of you, and your enemies will have contempt for you. What could be more painful?"

> Our inner tendencies are like muscles: Whatever we use grows stronger, and whatever we don't use atrophies. If we allow our negative tendencies to run our lives, they will grow stronger. And our positive tendencies — the qualities that could help lift us out of delusion toward soul freedom — will weaken through disuse. Indeed, what could be more painful?

"Arjuna," said Krishna, "if you die in battle, you will gain Heaven. And if you are victorious, you will enjoy earthly glory. Therefore, arise and fight the battle of life. Be even-minded during both triumph and failure, joy and sorrow. Such is the wisdom of Shankhya."

> Here, the Gita shifts from allegory to the overt spiritual teachings that constitute the remainder of the Gita. Shankhya is one of the three central teachings of India's spiritual tradition. It explains the nature of this world and human existence, and why we will never find true, lasting happiness outside the Self, outside soul consciousness. The second teaching is Yoga, which shows us

how to find that lasting happiness. Vedanta is the third teaching, and it describes the nature of that happiness: *Satchidananda*, which Yogananda translated as "ever-existing, ever-conscious, ever-new bliss."

Krishna continued, "Now hear the wisdom of Yoga, through which you will master your mind and break the shackles of karma. Even a little practice of this inward science will save you from dire fears and colossal sufferings.

"Be nonattached and even-minded during both pleasure and pain, success and failure. That is the way of the wise, the way to freedom from all sorrow."

"O Krishna," said Arjuna, "tell me about the person of wisdom."

Krishna replied, "Like a tortoise withdrawing its head and limbs into its shell, the wise person withdraws the five senses from the objects they perceive, releases all desires and attachments, and is totally contented in the Self.

"But all too easily, the eager, excitable senses seize the mind of even a wise spiritual seeker. One who dwells on sense objects becomes attached to them. Attachment leads to craving, and from unfulfilled craving springs anger. Anger gives rise to delusion, which makes one forget the soul. With the soul forgotten, one cannot discriminate correctly, and all right understanding is lost."

> The ego might rebel when told to give up even the *thought* of sense-pleasure. Yogananda offered a highly practical response: "When rebellion sets in, relax and don't be too strict in disciplining the unconvinced mind. Overcome rebellion by concentrating upon the peace born of renunciation and allowing moderate indulgences in wholesome sense pleasures."

Krishna continued, "The person of self-control, who has conquered the senses and has no likes or dislikes, attains inner calmness. But the undisciplined person has neither discrimination nor meditation. Without meditation, one cannot find peace. And without peace, how is happiness possible?

"Therefore, control the senses and give up desire. In this way, you will become secure in Spirit and never again fall into delusion."

Krishna then shared with Arjuna the timeless teachings of Yoga: the workings of the ego, mind, and emotions—and how they can lead us astray. He explained the essential attitudes and practices that will take us toward true happiness, toward God. Those include even-mindedness, nonattachment, seeing God as the Doer of all actions, the sacred practice of *yagya* (offering to God all our thoughts, emotions, and actions), and above all, wholehearted devotion to God.

He described the illusory nature of this world and how it confines most people in feelings of separateness and limitation, binding them to *samsara*, the wheel of reincarnation. Krishna explained the hidden workings of creation, and how to see through the illusion and align ourselves with the subtle universal forces that can help us find freedom.

"Meditation," he said, "will take you to the state of Yoga, union with God. It is the state of complete mental tranquility, sense-transcendent bliss, immunity to every sorrow, freedom from all pain and rebirth. It is the treasure beyond all treasures."

Arjuna protested, "I meditate, but I do not experience those high states. My mind is restless, tumultuous, obstinate! It is as difficult to master as the wind!"

"No doubt, Arjuna, the mind *is* fickle and unruly. But through dispassion and yoga practice, you can master it and achieve union with God."

"But what if I fail?" asked Arjuna. "What if I can never keep my mind from running away? Will I be doomed?"

Krishna answered, "One who performs right actions is *never* lost. Even if you do not find freedom in this life, your yoga practice will carry you forward in your next life. As you regain the discrimination you developed in your former lives, you will strive even harder for spiritual success. Diligently following your path for many lifetimes if necessary, you will finally unite with God."

Arjuna had long known that Krishna was a highly advanced soul. Now, more clearly than ever, he realized that Krishna was one with God, and he addressed him accordingly: "My Lord, please tell me about Yourself—Your countless manifestations, qualities, and powers."

In reply, Krishna described—as well as human language can convey—the nature of God and His limitless expressions within creation. He told Arjuna how Spirit pervades and sustains the entire universe, yet is also beyond it. He explained how all beings and all qualities arise from God—and much more.

Arjuna said, "My Lord, You have blessed me greatly by revealing the secret wisdom of the soul. Still, I long for one more thing: to see Your infinite form. If I am worthy, please show It to me."

Krishna replied, "O Arjuna, you cannot see Me with mortal eyes, but I shall give you divine sight. Then you can gaze upon My myriad celestial forms, the entire universe resting within My Cosmic Body, and whatever else you desire to see. Behold My supreme power of Yoga!"

Krishna touched him, and the battlefield scene dissolved before Arjuna's eyes. In its place, he saw the Lord of Creation in countless forms, shining like a thousand suns, his mouths and eyes everywhere. Resting in the center of that divine vision was the entire universe.

Arjuna bowed in awe. "Lord, I see You as everything, everyone, everywhere, blazing with a splendor that is difficult even to look at. Your infinite forms with gaping mouths, sharp fangs, and fiery eyes make the three worlds tremble in fear. And I am terrified!

"And there," he said, pointing, "I see the Kauravas, Bhishma, Drona, Karna, the Kuru army—also our army—all rushing headlong into Your mouths like moths rushing to the flame. You are devouring everything! O Lord, who *are* You? I want to know You and Your divine plan."

A voice resounded from everywhere—and from nowhere: "I am endless Time, the destroyer of all. Even if you do not fight, all those warriors will perish. I have already slain them, but be My instrument, Arjuna. Arise and fight! You *shall* prevail."

Arjuna bowed even lower. "Truly, You are eternal, omniscient, omnipresent, the All-in-All. Please forgive me for ever having treated You as a mere human friend. O Lord, I rejoice to have seen You, but I am petrified with fear. Please return to Your form as Krishna."

The voice replied, "Fear not, Arjuna. Behold once again, My familiar form."

The cosmic vision condensed into Krishna's body, and Arjuna breathed a deep sigh of relief. "Now my mind is quieted, and I feel my normal self again."

Krishna said, "It is extremely difficult to see My Cosmic Form, Arjuna. Even the Devas yearn for it, but rituals, charity, austerities, intellectual knowledge, following the scriptures—those are not enough. The only way to know Me is through unswerving devotion.

Whoever works for Me alone, makes Me the Goal, is devoted to Me and not attached to My creation, bears ill will toward no one — that devotee comes to Me!

"Arjuna, only by following your inborn dharma can you attain the highest success. And as a Kshatriya, *your* dharma is to fight. Even if you say, 'I will not fight,' your very nature will compel you to fight. You cannot avoid it."

Why can we not avoid the battle? It is because our true nature is eternal bliss, and we will never be satisfied until we are living in that bliss. This is why everyone in the world is seeking happiness.

Most people seek it through sense pleasures, human love, wealth, importance, power, fame — the list goes on. How could those bring us the unceasing bliss that we seek? After all, we may not attain them. Even if we attain them, they rarely last for long, in which case our happiness will end. Even if we succeed and they endure, our enjoyment of them will sooner or later fade. And even if we attain them, and they last, and our enjoyment lasts, *we* do not last! Not as human beings, anyway.

The game of life is rigged. There is only one route to true happiness. We try all the outward possibilities because they look easier, but they all disappoint us in the end. It is inevitable: Every soul eventually turns within and seeks the divine Self, the only source of lasting happiness.

As Swami Kriyananda often said, "You're going to live in the right way sooner or later. Why waste time?"

Krishna continued, "Therefore act, but dedicate all your actions to Me. Leave the fruits of your actions in My hands. Absorb your heart's feelings in Me. Forsake all other dharmas and remember Me alone. I will free you from all sin. You are dear to Me, Arjuna, so do I promise: By My grace, you shall overcome every impediment and attain Me."

Arjuna rose to his feet and once again gazed across the battlefield at the Kuru army, his eyes now blazing with fierce determination.

Krishna said, "Arjuna, have you listened to this wisdom with a concentrated heart? Has your delusion been destroyed?"

Arjuna replied, "My delusion has been destroyed, O Krishna.

Through your grace, I have regained the knowledge of my soul. My doubts have vanished, and I will fight."

Krishna then drove Arjuna's chariot back to rejoin the Pandava army.

So ends the Bhagavad Gita.

CHAPTER 20

Bhishma's Glory

W HEN KRISHNA AND ARJUNA REACHED the Pandava lines again, they turned to face the enemy army, ready for battle.

Suddenly, however, Yudhisthira laid down his weapons, stripped off his armor, stepped out of his chariot, and began walking across the battlefield toward the Kuru army. The Kuru warriors jeered at him, thinking he was a coward and would surrender without a fight.

Arjuna worried that Yudhisthira might indeed do that. He asked Krishna, "What is our eldest doing? Has he lost his senses?"

Krishna answered, "Do not worry, Arjuna. It is said that he who honors his preceptors and kinsmen before fighting with them will surely be victorious. That is what Yudhisthira is going to do."

And so it was. Upon reaching the Kuru army, Yudhisthira knelt and touched Bhishma's feet. "O Grandfather, give us permission to fight with you—and give us your blessing."

Bhishma smiled as he raised Yudhisthira upright, saying, "I am pleased with you, O King. Do battle and obtain victory. I cannot fight for you, but I will give you counsel if you wish."

Yudhisthira then asked the uncomfortable question that he knew he must ask: "Tell me, O Invincible One, how we can kill you?"

Bhishma gazed across the field at the Pandava army and said, "I do not see the man who can slay me. The time of my death has not yet come."

Yudhisthira bowed in farewell. Then he went to Drona, knelt, and touched his preceptor's feet.

He said, "Guruji, give us permission to fight with you—and your blessing."

Drona lifted him and replied, "You have my permission, O King. May you be victorious. Ask of me a boon."

Yudhisthira replied, "Pray for my victory, Guruji, and counsel me about what is for my good."

"I will pray, O King," said Drona, "but with Krishna as your counselor, your victory is certain. For where there is dharma, there is Krishna. And where Krishna is, there is victory."

Yudhisthira said, "Guruji, how can we vanquish you in battle?"

"As long as I fight," Drona replied, "you cannot win. And I do not see the man who can defeat me. The only way you can prevail is to induce me to lay down my weapons. And I will do that if I hear distressing news from a truthful person."

Yudhisthira bowed to Drona and walked away.

> Those two encounters hold significant inner meanings. Bhishma knew that dharma (righteousness) was with the Pandavas. However, his lifelong commitment to the Kuru throne compelled him to fight for Duryodhana. In the same way, although the ego eventually comes to understand that soul qualities are the only path to true happiness, deeply ingrained identification with body and personality ensures that the ego ultimately will side with material consciousness.

> Drona's (habit's) role in the kingdom was less lofty than Bhishma's (ego's). So it is in our lives: habit is more a matter of momentum than self-identity. Drona, too, knew that dharma was with the Pandavas. Still, he felt obligated to fight for Duryodhana because he had lived off Kuru wealth for many years — and because, after the dice game, he had promised to protect Duryodhana. It was all about the momentum of the past. Such is the way of habit.

> It may seem odd that Bhishma and Drona saw no man who could defeat them. Allegorically, that means that human qualities alone cannot overcome ego and habit. Superconscious awareness is required. But as we will see, even that needs help from some human qualities.

Yudhisthira proceeded to Kripa and his uncle, King Salya, whom Duryodhana had tricked into becoming his ally. Both gave Yudhisthira permission to fight—and their blessings.

Yudhisthira next addressed the entire Kuru army, saying, "We welcome anyone who will fight for us."

Only one Kuru warrior wanted to defect: Yuyutsu, Dhritarashtra's son by his Vaishya wife. He said, "I will fight for you, O King, if you will accept me."

Yudhisthira said, "We accept you. Come and fight against your foolish brothers, whom we will exterminate. It seems that the continuation of Dhritarashtra's line rests on you alone."

Recall that Yuyutsu represents the desire to give psychological battle.

Together, they walked across the battlefield to the Pandava lines. Yudhisthira climbed back into his chariot, donned his armor, and picked up his weapons.

Then began The Great War.

The graphic "Warriors at Kurukshetra" will help you follow the fighting.

Warriors at Kurukshetra

Below are the main warriors mentioned in the storytelling.
The qualities they represent are in italics.

Kaurava Side	Pandava Side
Duryodhana *Material desire*	Yudhisthira *Calmness in psychological battle*
Dushasana *Anger*	Bhima *Vitality*
98 Kaurava Brothers *Other negative qualities*	Arjua *Fiery self-control*
Bhishma *Ego*	Nakula *Niyama*
Drona *Habit*	Sahadeva *Yama*
Aswatthama *Attraction*	Krishna *God/Guru*
Karna *Attachment*	Satyaki *Devotion*
Shakuni *Material attachment*	Dhrishtadyumna *Calm inner light*
Kripa *Delusion*	Yuyutsu *Desire to give psychological battle*
Salya *Material pride*	Shikhandin *Self-transcendence*
Jayadratha *Fear of death*	Abhimanyu *Self-mastery*
Kritavarma	Ghatotkacha
Sanjaya *Introspection*	

* * * * *

The noise of the battle was deafening: the shouting of soldiers, the crash of weapons upon armor, the thunder of horses' hooves, the roar of chariot wheels, and the piercing trumpet calls of the war elephants.

Those elephants were terrifying—fully armored and trained to trample anything in their path, with a skillful warrior fighting from atop each one.

Even more fearsome were the Rakshasas, huge demons with green bodies, red necks, and blue heads. Their mouths reached from ear to ear and were filled with sharply pointed teeth. They were mighty warriors with extraordinary powers, including the ability to change their size and shape. They had superhuman strength—and at night, they grew even stronger.

Most Rakshasas fought for Duryodhana, but Bhima's son, Ghatotkacha, fought for the Pandavas. As he had promised many years before, he had come when his father needed him.

But more fearsome still was Grandfather Bhishma, who was indeed like his name, which means "terrible." Day after day, he devastated the Pandava army. Bhima, Arjuna, and Ghatotkacha were also formidable, causing heavy losses among the Kurus.

Upon waking on each morning of the war, Bhishma, Drona, and Kripa exclaimed, "Victory to the sons of Pandu!" Nevertheless, they fought for Duryodhana.

> Ego, habit, and our deluded mind (Bhishma, Drona, and Kripa) all know where true happiness lies. But that knowledge is distorted by false understandings and contrary habits and inclinations, reinforced by the power of maya.

By sunset on the eighth day of battle, both armies had suffered heavy losses, and the outcome remained uncertain.

Duryodhana was frustrated that his much larger army had not yet triumphed, and he confronted Bhishma. "Grandfather, you promised to slay our enemies, but you have not. If you are sparing the Pandavas out of affection for them or hatred for me, then I ask that you retire from battle. Then Karna will no longer be bound by his vow to stay off the battlefield so long as you fight."

Bhishma replied, "Duryodhana, your mind is clouded by your folly. Do you not realize that the Pandavas are invincible? Have you forgotten how Arjuna defeated all of us when we invaded Matsya? And can you not see that the Lord of the Universe is protecting him? Still, I will strive to the utmost to achieve victory for you. Tomorrow, I will fight such a fierce battle that men will recount it for as long as the world endures."

The next day, Bhishma scorched the Pandava army like a wildfire burning through dry grass. Krishna urged Arjuna to attack him, and Arjuna did so. But out of respect and affection for his grandfather, Arjuna could not bring himself to fight fiercely. Krishna repeatedly pressed Arjuna to fight harder, yet Arjuna still did not try his best. And the wildfire that was Bhishma burned on.

Finally, Krishna would bear it no longer. He stopped the chariot and jumped down, intending to slay Bhishma with his bare hands. He gave a ferocious roar as he strode toward Bhishma with his charioteer's whip in hand, shaking the earth with every step. Clothed in yellow silk, his skin the color of lapis lazuli, Krishna looked like a dark cloud charged with flashes of lightning.

All the other Kuru warriors were sure that Krishna would slay the grandfather. Bhishma nocked an arrow on his bowstring, drew the bow, and aimed at Krishna, but he whispered, "O God of gods, I bow to Thee. Slay me today in this mighty battle, and I will be greatly blessed."

Arjuna jumped out of his chariot and ran after Krishna. He threw his arms around him and pleaded, "Stop, Krishna! Do not break your vow by fighting!"

But Krishna continued to stride powerfully toward Bhishma, dragging Arjuna along with him. Finally, Arjuna caught Krishna around the legs and, with great difficulty, halted him.

"This very day, I will slay the grandfather," cried Arjuna. "I swear by my weapons, by Truth, and by my good deeds."

Without a word, Krishna turned and angrily stormed back to the chariot, followed by Arjuna.

> Despite its martial setting, this passage conveys sweetness: God (Krishna) is willing — even wants — to break His law of karma ("break his vow") by sending His grace to help us (Arjuna) overcome ego (Bhishma).

Why did Arjuna refuse Krishna's help? Was it only so Krishna could keep his vow? Or did Arjuna feel honor-bound to be the one to kill Bhishma? Or does his refusal symbolize the devotee's fear of leaving behind what is known — ego consciousness — and venturing into the unknown realm of soul consciousness?

Swami Kriyananda likened this third possibility to a bird that has lived in a cage all its life and is afraid to fly out of an open cage door into its natural habitat: the wide world. Eventually, the call of freedom will grow stronger than that fear, and he will exit the cage. It is the same with us: Someday, our desire for inner freedom will become stronger than our fear of the unknown, and we will do our utmost to return to our natural habitat: soul consciousness.

But when?

Paramhansa Yogananda often praised the spirit he found in America, which he characterized as: "Eventually? Eventually? Why not now?!" That is the attitude that the devotee needs. Yogananda said, "Most people don't advance spiritually because they lack a sense of spiritual adventuresomeness. We should think: 'I lack spiritual imagination and spiritual experience, and that is why I think that the present sense-happiness is the only happiness. Let me believe in the scriptures and my guru.'"

Yogananda further said, "Don't take my word for it. Test the teachings!" He often emphasized that spiritual understanding and growth come from personal experience, not mere belief.

Krishna and Arjuna mounted the chariot, and Krishna immediately drove Arjuna into combat with Bhishma. Arjuna fought harder than before, but he still could not extinguish the wildfire that was Bhishma, who continued to devastate the Pandava army.

By the end of that ninth day, the Pandavas' situation was desperate. They *had* to stop Bhishma lest their entire army be exterminated. But how? No one but Krishna could kill him. Krishna offered to do so, but Yudhisthira insisted that he abide by his vow not to fight.

However, Yudhisthira recalled Bhishma's offer to give counsel. So that night, the Pandavas and Krishna left behind their armor and weapons, and walked across the battlefield to the Kuru camp.

They entered Bhishma's tent and offered him reverence. The grandfather greeted them affectionately. "Welcome, my children!

How may I enhance your joy? Tell me now. Even if it is exceedingly difficult, still I shall accomplish it."

Yudhisthira said, "Grandfather, you are crushing my army like an elephant crushing a forest of reeds. You are invincible. Rushing against you, we are like moths rushing to the flame." He lowered his gaze. "Tell us, Grandfather, how can we kill you?"

"It is well that you have realized my invincibility," said Bhishma, "else many lives would have been wasted. Here is what you must do. Among your warriors is Draupadi's brother, Shikhandin. However, Shikhandin was born a female, and only later, through the powers of a sorcerer, was she changed into a male. Because his true nature is female, it would be unrighteous of me to fight him. Therefore, the way to defeat me is for Arjuna to use Shikhandin as a shield and attack me."

The Pandavas looked at each other, eyes wide with wonder. A female changed into a male?!

Bhishma explained, "I am sure you have heard the family lore of how I once abducted three princesses as brides for your grandfather, King Vichitravirya. My plan did not work out for one of them — her name was Amva. She felt I had ruined her life, and she began practicing extreme austerities in hopes Lord Shiva would help her get revenge. After many years, Shiva granted Amva the boon of killing me in her next life. Shikhandin *is* her next life."

> Yogananda said that Shikhandin represents self-transcendence and the will to perform uplifting actions.

The Pandavas decided to ignore the question of how Bhishma could know all that, and follow the grandfather's counsel. On the next day, they would focus all their efforts on getting Arjuna and Shikhandin close enough to Bhishma to attack him. When Duryodhana's spies told him of that plan, he decided to surround and protect Bhishma with ring upon ring of warriors.

As the sun rose on the tenth day, the Pandavas began fighting through those rings. Hour after hour, they attacked fiercely while the Kurus desperately tried to block their progress. Just before sunset, the Pandavas broke through the innermost ring of protection. Arjuna then attacked Bhishma, shooting arrow after arrow while using Shikhandin as a shield so Bhishma would not fight back. All the while, Shikhandin, too, shot arrows at the grandfather. Soon, they had pierced him with so many arrows that two fingers could not fit between them anywhere on his body.

Bhishma, who had control over his own time of passing, decided to take a step toward that moment: He toppled out of his chariot onto the ground.

The Pandava army shouted and blew their conches in triumph. The invincible Bhishma had fallen! The Kuru warriors were stunned with grief. Both armies ceased fighting as they realized the indomitable grandfather would not rise again.

Silence and gloom settled over the battlefield. All the mighty chariot warriors on both sides laid down their weapons, removed their armor, and came to pay their respects.

Bhishma's body was so riddled with arrows that it did not touch the ground. But he chose not to die, for it was not yet an auspicious time of year for him to die. He simply lay on his bed of arrows, facing upward and fully conscious.

He said to the assembled warriors, "My head is hanging down. Give me a pillow."

They quickly fetched many excellent pillows that were soft and made of delicate fabrics. But Bhishma said, "Those pillows are not suitable for a warrior's bed. Arjuna, give me a pillow fit for a hero!"

Arjuna quickly retrieved his celestial bow, Gandiva, pulled three arrows from his quiver, and inspired them with special mantras. One after the other, he placed them on Gandiva and shot them into the earth under Bhishma's head. The grandfather rested his head on the tails of those arrows and was gratified.

Surgeons then arrived to extract the arrows from Bhishma's body, but he said, "What need have I now of physicians? Send them away with due respect. I have won the highest goal of a Kshatriya: a bed of arrows. My body should be burned with these arrows still in it."

The other warriors saluted Bhishma, then walked around him three times in reverence before returning to their camps. Only the Pandavas and Kauravas remained.

"My children," Bhishma cried, "I am burning with pain. Give me water."

Several of them quickly brought him vessels of cool water, but

Bhishma waved them away. "I am beyond human enjoyments. I wish to see Arjuna."

Arjuna stepped forward and saluted Bhishma. "I am here, Grandfather. What may I do for you?"

"Arjuna, my body is burning with agony. My mouth is parched. Give me water!"

Arjuna placed a blazing arrow on Gandiva and infused it with the power of the Parjanya astra, then shot it into the earth next to Bhishma. Immediately, an auspicious fountain of pure, cool water gushed forth. It was of celestial scent and taste, resembling the divine nectar of amrita itself.

Bhishma drank and was gratified. "Arjuna," he said, "you are the greatest of all bowmen. With Krishna as your ally, you will achieve feats that the Lord Indra would not even attempt. Drona, Vidura, and I warned Duryodhana that he could never triumph. But like a senseless idiot, he ignored our warnings. Soon, he will lie down forever, overwhelmed by the might of Bhima."

Bhishma turned to Duryodhana and said, "You saw Arjuna create this celestial fountain. No one else but Krishna could achieve such a feat. No one else possesses all the astras. Can you not see that he is invincible? The Devas and the Asuras together could not defeat him. Stop this folly! Let this battle end with my death. Let your army live. Give back the Pandavas' kingdom. Make peace!"

But Duryodhana rejected that counsel, like a dying man refusing medicine. He turned away and sadly walked back to his encampment. The other warriors bade farewell to the grandfather and returned to their tents.

> Bhishma's invincibility reflects our inability to kill the ego; it must voluntarily give up its existence. So it was that Bhishma took his first voluntary steps toward death by telling the Pandavas how to overcome him, then by allowing Arjuna (self-control) and Shikhandin (self-transcendence) to pierce him with countless arrows. Until then, he had fought ferociously for the Kurus despite knowing what the war's outcome would be. So also does our ego cling ferociously to its pleasures, despite knowing that, sooner or later, ego itself must go!

* * * * *

As darkness descended on the battlefield, Karna came alone to Bhishma and said, "O Sire, I am Karna, whom you have always hated."

Bhishma lifted his head, turned toward Karna, and embraced him with one arm. He said, "My son, I bear you no malice. You are a great giver and a mighty warrior, full of courage, the equal of Arjuna. But through pride and through keeping the company of lowly persons, you have abandoned dharma. I spoke against you only to curb your pride and prevent this war. Even now, it is not too late. Do not take up your weapons and enter the battle. You are not a Sutaputra. Vyasa has told me: You are the son of Kunti and Surya. You are the eldest Pandava, the rightful king of the Kurus. Unite with your brothers and save the world from this great peril."

Karna answered, "O best of Kurus, your words are undoubtedly true. But Kunti abandoned me, and I was raised as a Suta. I have been Duryodhana's friend and ally all these years. I cannot forsake him now, nor can I cast off my hatred for the Pandavas. This war will run its course, and all omens foretell victory for the Pandavas. With a cheerful heart, I will follow the dharma of all Kshatriyas, and I will fight Arjuna. Please forgive me for speaking harshly against you, and give me your blessing."

Bhishma sighed and laid his head again upon his pillow of arrows. "I have tried to bring about peace, and I have failed. Fight then, O Karna, with courage and righteousness. May you find in righteous battle that which you seek. You have my blessing."

CHAPTER 21

Solitary Heroes

The loss of Bhishma left the Kuru army in despair. However, Duryodhana's council of kings took heart when they realized that, with Bhishma's absence, Karna's vow would no longer prevent him from fighting.

They began to chant, "Karna! Karna will save us!" They eagerly set about making plans for Karna to kill Arjuna with Indra's infallible spear—or, better still, to kill Krishna.

Duryodhana was exceedingly cheered by this, and he asked Karna, "Who should command our army now?"

Karna thought briefly, then said, "Many great kings are fighting for you. If you select one of them, you will elevate him over the others. They will feel insulted and might not fight hard for you. However, they all greatly respect Drona. Moreover, he is your guru. If you appoint him commander, everyone will be satisfied."

So it was that Drona became the second commander of the Kuru army.

> Even when the ego (Bhishma) is no longer active, the inner war has not yet been won. The momentum of past habits (Drona) can still energize and guide the forces of material desire. And another powerful force also remains on the Kuru side: attachment (Karna).

Duryodhana ordered Drona to win the war by capturing Yudhisthira. As dawn broke on the eleventh day, Drona arrayed his forces in a formidable attack formation and began driving them through the Pandava defenses toward Yudhisthira.

Arjuna led the Pandava army in a defensive thrust that stopped the Kuru advance just short of capturing Yudhisthira. Drona then regrouped his formation and ordered a second attack, but Arjuna also halted that. Drona attacked repeatedly, yet each time, Arjuna kept the Kurus from capturing Yudhisthira.

Throughout the day's fighting, Karna eagerly sought to kill

Arjuna with Indra's celestial spear. But all day long, and on the days that followed, Krishna either did not bring Arjuna's chariot close enough to Karna for combat, or he made Karna forget to use the magical spear.

Finally, sunset brought an end to Drona's assaults.

At the Kuru council of kings that night, Drona said, "We cannot capture Yudhisthira so long as Arjuna protects him. Some brave warrior must challenge Arjuna to combat and draw him far away. Then I will be able to capture Yudhisthira."

Susharma, the king of Trigarta, stood and declared, "We Trigartas vow to challenge him, take him far away, and then slay him!"

So, on the twelfth day, Susharma lured Arjuna to a distant part of the battlefield to fight the Trigarta host. Drona then led another assault on Yudhisthira, but this time, the other Pandava brothers thwarted the attack while Arjuna vanquished the Trigartas.

That night at the council of kings, Duryodhana angrily said to Drona, "Guruji, you vowed to capture Yudhisthira, yet you did not do it! What have you to say for yourself?!"

Drona calmly replied, "I have a new strategy, O King. I will form our army into an impenetrable circular array. If King Susharma again challenges Arjuna and lures him far away, I will advance on Yudhisthira and capture him."

So it was that, on the thirteenth day of the war, Susharma challenged Arjuna and led him to a distant part of Kurukshetra. As soon as Arjuna departed, Drona formed his troops into the circular array, positioned himself in the vanguard, and commanded his forces to move forward. They quickly began to cut a swath through the Pandava forces that protected Yudhisthira.

Dhrishtadyumna, the Pandava commander, sent legions of warriors against that array. But Drona and his forces repulsed them like a mountain pushing back the surging ocean.

It was impossible to stop that fearsome circle of death by attacking it from the outside. The only way to thwart it was to break through its outermost ring and destroy it from within. Otherwise, Drona would certainly capture Yudhisthira.

Yudhisthira knew that only two warriors in the entire Pandava army could penetrate the circular array: Arjuna and his teenage son, Abhimanyu.

Arjuna was far away, fighting the Trigartas, so Yudhisthira approached Abhimanyu and said, "O child, only you know how to break into that array. Take up your arms and attack!"

Abhimanyu said, "I shall do so, O King. My father taught me how to penetrate that array and devastate it. However, I am not sure I will be able to come out again."

"Fear not," Yudhisthira replied. "My brothers and I, along with the rest of our army, will follow you into the array and protect you."

Abhimanyu ordered his charioteer, "Quickly, take me toward the Kuru array!"

Recall that Abhimanyu represents the quality of self-mastery.

Abhimanyu soon broke into the circular formation and was immediately attacked by legions of Kuru warriors. Following close behind him, Bhima, Nakula, and Sahadeva led the Pandava forces in a charge toward the opening he had made, intending to enter the array and devastate it from within.

One of Duryodhana's allies, King Jayadratha, quickly rushed to prevent the Pandava warriors from entering. Lord Shiva had given him the boon of holding off the Pandavas for one day, provided Arjuna was not present. That boon enabled him to keep anyone else from entering Drona's array for the entire day. Young Abhimanyu would have to fight alone inside the formation.

And fight he did! He began to devastate the Kuru ranks, dispatching thousands of warriors to the realm of Yama. One after another, he vanquished Dushasana, Duryodhana, Karna, and many others, causing them to flee from combat. He also killed Duryodhana's beloved son, which caused the enraged Duryodhana to scream to his allies, "Slay that one!"

Six mighty Kuru warriors responded to Duryodhana's call: Drona, Kripa, Karna, Aswatthama, Dushasana's son, and Kritavarma (the leader of Krishna's army) all came to fight Abhimanyu. But one by one, Abhimanyu overpowered them all, and they fled from combat rather than lose their lives. He also pierced Shakuni with an arrow, causing him to shout, "All of you together, grind this one into the earth, or else he will slay us all."

So the six warriors returned to the fight and surrounded Abhimanyu. In flagrant disregard of the rules of engagement, all six attacked simultaneously. Still, hour after hour, Abhimanyu held his own against those great warriors.

Finally, the six Kuru warriors changed tactics: In addition to attacking Abhimanyu directly, they began to destroy his equipment and weapons. While Abhimanyu dueled with one, another slew his horses and charioteer. A third cut his bow. A fourth destroyed his chariot. Yet another broke his sword. Abhimanyu picked up his broken chariot wheel to continue fighting, whirling it like Krishna's chakra. The Kurus broke that weapon also. All the while, they were piercing Abhimanyu's body with countless arrows.

Though deeply wounded, Abhimanyu picked up a mace and counterattacked. Just before sunset, however, exhaustion and his wounds caught up with him, and Dushasana's son was able to kill him. The six mighty Kuru warriors had managed to slay a young boy. But his courageous fighting had wreaked havoc on Drona's array and kept Yudhisthira from being captured. The mighty Pandava warriors who had failed to penetrate the array and protect Abhimanyu returned to their camp in despair.

By day's end, Arjuna had once again defeated the Trigartas. When he returned to the Pandava camp, he found it silent and mournful. No one would speak to him or even look at him. He realized that something was very wrong. When Abhimanyu did not come out to congratulate him on the day's victories, as he had done on the previous days, Arjuna guessed what had happened. He began questioning the others, and as they related the details, his breath came in deep gulps, and his eyes filled with tears. He glanced about like a madman, exclaiming, "My son! My beloved son!"

After a time, he calmed down somewhat, yet his eyes blazed with rage. He proclaimed, "So the cause of this is that wretch, Jayadratha! Truly, I swear that by sunset tomorrow, I will slay him unless he forsakes Duryodhana or begs for our protection. If I fail to kill him, I will enter the fire."

To underscore his vow, Arjuna blew a mighty blast with his conch, and Krishna blew his conch to encourage him. The Pandava army shouted their support, and the mingled sounds shook the battlefield.

Duryodhana's spies quickly brought news of Arjuna's oath to the Kuru council of kings. Jayadratha began to tremble, stupefied by fear.

He lamented, "Arjuna intends to send me to the abode of Yama tomorrow. I shall go home now, for I wish to live."

> Recall that Jayadratha represents attachment to the body — fear of death.

Jayadratha rose to leave the council, but Duryodhana gently restrained him and said, "Fear not, O King. You are a powerful warrior, and we have other great warriors who will protect you."

Drona assured him, "I will surround you with an impenetrable array of warriors. The gods themselves cannot slay him who is under my protection."

Jayadratha was much comforted by this, and he agreed to stay.

In the Pandava camp, Krishna scolded Arjuna, "You made a very rash vow, and you did so without first consulting me."

Arjuna answered, "Do not think lightly of me, Krishna. My prowess in battle is irresistible. I can achieve anything through my might and your grace."

Krishna nodded and said, "If you do not succeed, I will slay Jayadratha."

Arjuna slept fitfully that night. In a dream, Krishna came to him and said, "Do not grieve over your son's death. Grief is an impediment to action. It gladdens the foe and saddens one's friends. Do what needs to be done. That is all."

Fully aware while dreaming, Arjuna replied, "I know I made a grave vow. I know also that Duryodhana will give Jayadratha all possible protection. And in this season of the year, the sun sets early. How can I succeed?"

Krishna said, "Worship Lord Shiva and ask for the blessing of success — and remember that he has given you his great Pasupata weapon. With it, you cannot possibly fail to accomplish your vow."

In his dream, Arjuna immediately began to worship Lord Shiva, who appeared and blessed him.

· · · · ·

As dawn approached on the fourteenth day of the war, Drona sent Jayadratha twelve miles to the rear of the Kuru army and surrounded him with Karna, Aswatthama, Kripa, and many other formidable chariot warriors. He also placed legions of foot soldiers between Jayadratha and the Pandava forces.

As soon as the sun rose, Arjuna began cutting through those defenses. Early on, he encountered Drona and engaged him in a fierce duel. It was a memorable battle, guru versus disciple. Both called upon the full extent of their combat skills, but neither could gain an advantage. After a long while, Krishna said to Arjuna, "Time is passing. We have more important work to do. Let us push forward."

Arjuna consented, and when Drona saw Arjuna's chariot pulling away, he called out, "Arjuna, where are you going? A noble warrior does not stop fighting until he has vanquished his foe!"

Arjuna called back, "You are my guru, not my foe. A disciple is like the guru's son. Besides, no one in the world can defeat you." Arjuna then resumed cutting through the Kuru army. As the hours passed, he came ever closer to Jayadratha.

Duryodhana confronted Drona. "How is it that you allow Arjuna to destroy my army? You are always devoted to the Pandavas' welfare, not to ours, even though you live off our wealth. I was a fool to expect that you would protect Jayadratha."

Drona replied, "I cannot catch Arjuna, so I will go after Yudhisthira while you go after Arjuna. I will give you a suit of impenetrable armor so Arjuna cannot kill you."

Duryodhana donned the armor and departed in his chariot to confront Arjuna. At the same time, Drona set off toward Yudhisthira and began devastating the rank and file of the Pandava army along the way. Meanwhile, Dhrishtadyumna, the Pandava commander, was crushing elements of the Kuru army.

·   ·   ·   ·   ·

It was well past midday when Jayadratha came within sight. Arjuna and Krishna were keen to press the attack, but their horses were exhausted and wounded. Arjuna asked Krishna to stop and unyoke them so they could rest and drink while he removed the many arrows lodged in them. During that delay, Duryodhana caught up and stationed himself between them and Jayadratha.

Krishna said, "Now is your chance, Arjuna. Kill that wicked wretch."

Arjuna narrowed his eyes and said, "I will cut off his head and avenge the insult to Draupadi."

They yoked the horses and set out toward Duryodhana, who shouted, "Arjuna, I have never seen you do anything that deserved applause. Show me some prowess now!"

In the fierce duel that followed, Duryodhana's sharp arrows pierced not only Arjuna but also his horses—and even Krishna. Arjuna countered with a fearsome barrage of arrows, but he was stunned to see that they dropped harmlessly to the ground. He quickly realized that Duryodhana was wearing impenetrable armor, so he changed tactics. He slew Duryodhana's horses and charioteer, then began to cut up his chariot. He cut Duryodhana's bow so his foe could not fight back. And when a horde of Kuru warriors came to rescue Duryodhana, Arjuna began slaughtering them.

But the afternoon shadows were lengthening as the sun sank lower in the west. Krishna blew mightily on his conch to strengthen Arjuna's resolve. Then he and Arjuna left the powerless Duryodhana behind and sped toward Jayadratha.

Across the battlefield, Yudhisthira heard the blast from Krishna's conch and feared it was a distress call. He decided to sacrifice his own protection by sending Bhima to help Arjuna. With his great mace, Bhima ferociously smashed through the Kuru army. Soon, much to Duryodhana's frustration, Bhima, too, was nearing Jayadratha.

Duryodhana confronted Drona and said, "Guruji, how is it that Bhima has gotten past you? Our warriors are speaking ill of you for this. We must save Jayadratha. How can we do it?"

Drona replied, "You should go and help protect him. The Pandava army is charging in this direction. I will stay here and stave them off."

As Bhima fought his way across the field, he killed many sons of Dhritarashtra. He also engaged in a ferocious duel with Karna and forced him to flee from further combat. Karna soon returned to fight, but Bhima quickly made him retreat again. They fought two more duels, and each time, Karna had to flee.

Between those duels, Bhima killed more sons of Dhritarashtra, including Vikarna. Bhima regretted that because Vikarna had protested the winning of Draupadi in the dice game. Nevertheless, anyone who fought for Duryodhana had to die.

When Karna attacked Bhima a fifth time, Bhima overpowered him yet again. He was about to kill Karna when he remembered that Arjuna had vowed to do that. So he spared Karna's life and let down his guard.

Yet Karna kept fighting and soon had Bhima at his mercy. He did not kill Bhima, for he had promised Kunti that he would kill only Arjuna, not the other four brothers. Instead, he rapped Bhima on the head with the end of his bow and taunted him. "Unskilled as you are, child, do not fight with me! You are nothing but a eunuch, an ignorant, gluttonous fool. You belong where there is much food and drink—but never in battle. You are suited only to live in the forest, eating roots and flowers. Go to Krishna and Arjuna; they will protect you. Or go home, child. You have no business in battle!"

Bhima laughed loudly. "O wicked Sutaputra, I have repeatedly vanquished you. How, then, can you indulge in such idle boasts? Come wrestle with me!"

Wisely, Karna declined. Just then, Arjuna came to Bhima's rescue and drove Karna away with a barrage of arrows.

With Bhima now safe, Krishna said, "Arjuna, the sun is about to set. You do not have time to fight your way past the six mighty warriors who are protecting Jayadratha. I must bring him out from behind his protection."

Krishna used his divine powers to shroud the sun, and darkness descended upon the battlefield. The Kuru warriors began celebrating the sunset, for Arjuna now had to enter the fire.

Krishna said, "Arjuna, this is the moment. Use the Pasupata." Arjuna nodded, for he was skilled at shooting in the dark. He took up an arrow, infused it with the mantra of Lord Shiva's Pasupata weapon, and aimed it where he intuitively felt Jayadratha was, behind a protective screen of great warriors.

As he was about to shoot, Krishna said, "Wait, Arjuna! There is something more you must do. At Jayadratha's birth, it was foretold that his head would be cut off in battle. So his father invoked a curse, saying, 'Whoever shall cause my son's head to fall on the earth, his own head will shatter into a hundred pieces.' So when you cut off Jayadratha's head, you must transport it onto his father's lap."

Arjuna nodded and loosed that mighty weapon at Jayadratha, who was celebrating his survival. The arrow severed Jayadratha's head and carried it away like an eagle snatching a small bird from a tree. Arjuna then shot a series of arrows that, one after the other, carried Jayadratha's head ever farther away. Finally, the last arrow deposited it, unnoticed, on the lap of Jayadratha's father as he was finishing his evening meditation. When he stood, his son's head fell to the ground. Immediately, his own head shattered into one hundred pieces.

Krishna then unshrouded the sun. Everyone was astonished to see that the sun had not set after all. The Kurus were devastated that Arjuna had fulfilled his vow. Krishna and Arjuna blew their conches in celebration. Arjuna then resumed devastating the Kuru army, while Bhima slew many more sons of Dhritarashtra.

Finally, the sun set on the fourteenth day of the war. That should have ended all fighting, but it did not. The two armies were so angry and bitter that the battle continued into the night.

CHAPTER 22

The One Lie

As combat continued into the fourteenth night, Duryodhana was greatly distressed. The war was not going well for his army. He called a meeting of the Kuru council of kings and confronted Drona. "Guruji, I say again, you are not keeping your promise to win this war for me. Arjuna is annihilating our army. You have always favored him, so you are not fighting fiercely against him."

Drona sighed. "O King, I have told you many times. The Pandavas cannot be defeated — not even by the Devas themselves."

Karna said, "Do not blame Drona. He is old and slow. The Pandavas are not succeeding due to superior prowess or intelligence. It is all a matter of Fate, even for the mightiest men. Ever intent on its purposes, Fate is awake when all else sleeps.

"But do not worry, O King. I can defeat Arjuna, for I still have Indra's infallible spear. When I kill Arjuna with that mighty weapon, his brothers will either surrender to you or return to exile in the forest. And I will give you the entire world."

Kripa said, "Karna, if words alone could win this war, then you would provide Duryodhana with the amplest measure of protection. But the Pandavas have defeated you in every encounter. Kshatriyas show their prowess by their deeds; you merely build castles in the air."

Karna replied angrily, "When a person resolves to bear a burden, Destiny aids him. That is why I spoke as I did. You are old, decrepit, and unskilled in battle. If you speak to me this way again, I will draw my scimitar and cut out your tongue."

That threat infuriated Kripa's nephew, Aswatthama. He drew his scimitar and rushed toward Karna. But Duryodhana restrained him, saying, "Have peace, O great warrior. Do not be angry with Karna. A mighty burden rests upon you and him, as well as on Drona and Kripa. We must all work together and focus on our common goal: defeating the Pandavas."

Kripa grudgingly said, "O wicked-hearted Sutaputra, I forgive you. Arjuna will soon quell your pride."

Karna went off in search of Arjuna, intent on killing him. But when he found him and they fought, Arjuna quickly gained the upper hand and made him flee. Karna then fought Sahadeva and caused him to run away. Karna pursued and soon caught him, but remembering his promise to Kunti, he did not kill Sahadeva. Instead, he rapped him on the head with the end of his bow and taunted him, "Do not fight with your superiors, child. Fight only with equals. Go to Arjuna; he will protect you. Or go home."

Then Karna began to wreak havoc among the Pandava troops. Yudhisthira lamented to Arjuna, "Karna is scorching our army like the blazing sun. We must find a way to stop him."

Arjuna said to Krishna, "Take me to the Sutaputra. Either I will kill him, or he will slay me."

Krishna replied, "Truly, no one can stand against him except you and Bhima's son, Ghatotkacha. But the time has not yet come for you to fight Karna. He has a celestial spear that will always slay its target. He is saving it to slay you, Arjuna. Tonight, let Ghatotkacha fight him."

So they summoned Ghatotkacha and charged him with confronting Karna. It was nighttime, so the Rakshasa's magical powers were at their strongest. He grew his body to gigantic proportions and began to crush the Kuru army beneath his enormous feet. No one could stand against him. The Kuru soldiers implored Karna, "Use your celestial spear. Kill the Rakshasa before he kills us all!"

Karna shouted, "No! I am saving the spear for Arjuna!"

They protested, "If you do not use it now, he will annihilate us! Throw the spear!"

Finally, Karna relented and hurled Indra's spear at Ghatotkacha. It found its target and killed Bhima's beloved son. When he fell, his massive body crushed thousands of Kuru warriors. The surviving Kuru warriors shouted for joy over their deliverance as Karna grimly watched the spear fly back to Indra in Heaven.

The Pandavas grieved deeply over the loss of their nephew. Ghatotkacha had been so dear to them. But Krishna was transported with delight. He embraced Arjuna again and again, shouting triumphantly all the while.

Arjuna was shocked. "Krishna, do you not understand? Bhima's son, our beloved nephew, is dead! This is a time to grieve, not to rejoice."

Krishna grasped him by the shoulders and gazed sternly into his eyes. "Arjuna, it is you who do not understand. I have been so worried about you that I have been unable to sleep. No one, not you, the gods, or even myself, could have withstood Karna so long as he had his natural armor and earrings, and Indra's spear. But, by good luck, his armor and earrings have been taken away. By good luck, his infallible spear is now gone. You have been rescued from the jaws of death. Even now, you are the only one who can slay him. You will get just one chance. When his chariot wheel sinks into the mud, you must kill him. I will give you a sign, and you must act."

*   *   *   *   *

The battle raged all night and into the fifteenth day. No warrior on either side had slept. Now, Drona began devastating the Pandava army more than ever. As he shot his deadly arrows left and right, his bow was incessantly drawn into a circle, like a terrible ring of fire.

Arjuna rushed to stop Drona, and they fought with such skill as had never been seen before. All the other warriors stopped fighting to watch the magnificent duel between preceptor and disciple. Drona launched many fierce weapons at Arjuna, but Arjuna destroyed them with arrows. Drona destroyed Arjuna's weapons in the same way. Seeing Arjuna's skill, Drona was very proud of his disciple.

Then, Drona invoked the Brahma weapon. That mighty astra caused the entire earth to tremble. Fierce winds blew, and the oceans churned. Every creature was filled with dread. But Arjuna countered that astra with a Brahma weapon of his own, and all nature quickly became calm once again.

Finally, each realized he could not defeat the other, so they broke off their duel. Then the Pandava commander, Dhrishtadyumna, who had been born to kill Drona, attacked the preceptor. They fought a long and fierce battle, but neither could kill the other. After a time, they too disengaged.

The two armies resumed fighting, and once again, Drona began to decimate the Pandava army like a raging fire consuming a heap of straw. Fear entered the Pandavas' hearts, and they lost all hope of victory.

Seeing their faint-heartedness, Krishna said to them, "Listen to me. The gods themselves could not defeat Drona. Therefore, we must cast aside virtue and use deception, or he will slay us all. He told Yudhisthira that he would lay down his weapons if he heard distressing news from a truthful person. The death of his son, Aswatthama, would be distressing, I think. Let us tell him that Aswatthama has been slain in battle."

Arjuna and Yudhisthira were aghast at this suggestion, for it would be a lie. Aswatthama was hale and hearty, and he was devastating the Pandava army elsewhere on the field.

Bhima, however, felt no qualms about Krishna's idea. He immediately went to where one of the Pandavas' war elephants stood—an elephant named Aswatthama. With one mighty blow from his mace, he killed the elephant.

He then approached Drona, who was continuing to decimate the Pandava army. Keeping the truth within his mind, he said what was untrue: "Guruji! Aswatthama has been slain!"

Drona did not believe him. He knew that Aswatthama was invincible in battle.

> Indeed, Aswatthama was immortal, just as the quality he represents — attraction — is immortal. It will be with us always. As Yogananda often said, our job is to transmute the attraction we feel to ego pleasures into attraction to soul pleasures.

Still, Drona wondered, "Could it be that my beloved son is dead?" Doubt clouded his mind, and his judgment grew faulty. He again invoked the mighty Brahma weapon, this time to slay a host of foot soldiers—ordinary troops unfamiliar with celestial weapons.

The great rishis instantly appeared to him, saying, "You are fighting unrighteously. Such a sinful act does not become you, who are well versed in the Vedas and devoted to Truth. Lay aside your weapons. The hour of your death is at hand."

Drona stood in silence for some moments as those words sank in. Then he approached Yudhisthira and said, "O King, I am certain you would not lie, even if it meant you could rule the three worlds. I must know the truth: Is my son dead or not?"

Indeed, Yudhisthira had never lied in his entire life. He was so truthful that his chariot floated four fingers' breadth above the ground. He could not bring himself to say that Drona's son was dead.

Seeing his hesitation, Krishna assured him, "If Drona continues to fight, he will annihilate your army within a half-day. In such circumstances, falsehood is better than truth. O King, telling a lie to save lives is not a sin."

Bhima pressed Yudhisthira, "Accept Krishna's advice if you want to win this war. Throughout the three worlds, you are known to be truthful. If you tell Drona that his son is dead, he will surely cease to fight."

Still, Yudhisthira hesitated. Finally, he reluctantly turned toward Drona and called out. "Guruji, Aswatthama is dead!" Then he whispered, "Aswatthama, the elephant."

Yudhisthira's chariot immediately fell to the ground. Drona believed him and could not fight as fiercely as before. Still, he was formidable, and he continued slaughtering the Pandava forces.

Bhima again approached him. "Guruji! Non-injury is said to be the highest of virtues, and Brahmins are said to be the root of all virtue. What, then, can be said of yourself, except that you are a hypocrite? Wretch that you are, you have lost your Brahmin nature, fighting as a Kshatriya. Your son, Aswatthama, the light of your life, is dead, even as Yudhisthira has told you. Do not doubt it!"

At last, Drona believed that Aswatthama had been slain. He stopped fighting and called out, "O Karna! Kripa! Duryodhana! Be careful! Do not let the Pandavas injure you! I am laying down my weapons!"

He dropped his bow and sat in his chariot, intent on leaving his body. He shut out the noise and violence of the conflict raging around him, focused his mind, and quickly went deep into inner stillness.

Dhrishtadyumna saw his opportunity. He dropped his bow, drew his sword, and rushed to Drona's chariot. He stepped up and stood over the preceptor, sword in hand, savoring the imminent fulfillment of his life's purpose.

Seeing what Dhrishtadyumna was about to do, Arjuna shouted, "Do not kill the preceptor! Capture him and bring him here!"

Other warriors were shocked that anyone would slay the meditating Drona, and they cried, "Fie! Fie!"

Suddenly, Drona's soul rose from his body and ascended to the highest regions of Heaven. Only a few people, including Arjuna and Krishna, had the inner sight to perceive the soul's exit.

Dhrishtadyumna was not one of them. Thinking that the guru still lived in that body, he grasped Drona's hair and, with one mighty swing of his sword, lopped off the guru's head. In celebration, he whirled his sword overhead, shouting with glee. Then he threw Drona's head at the horrified Kuru soldiers, who fled in all directions.

> Just as no one could defeat Drona until he believed Aswatthama was dead, we cannot truly overcome a habit so long as the attraction that gave rise to it persists. Swami Kriyananda often emphasized that the ultimate way to overcome such attraction is to commune with the calm inner light of Spirit (Dhrishtadyumna). That will implant in us a higher attraction.
>
> In the Gita, Krishna puts it this way: "The man who abstains from sense enjoyments may forget them for a time, but the taste for them will linger. That person, however, who beholds the Supreme Spirit loses the taste for anything but the Infinite." (Gita 2:59)
>
> Fortunately, we can overcome a sense attraction long before we behold the Supreme Spirit. We only need to cultivate a stronger attraction to something more beneficial, such as a healthier diet, harmonious companions, or inner peace. Yogananda often put this in down-to-earth terms: "Once you taste good cheese, the stale kind you've enjoyed will lose all attraction for you."

· · · · ·

The Kuru soldiers were so distraught over Drona's death that they began to flee the battlefield. Even the mightiest chariot warriors fled — Karna, Duryodhana, Dushasana, Salya, Kripa, and others.

Only Aswatthama continued to fight. Like a huge crocodile rising against the current of a river, he rushed against his foes and killed many Pandava soldiers. He could not understand why the other Kuru warriors were fleeing.

Then, Kripa told him how Drona had died, and he became angry as a snake that had been stepped on. He ground his teeth, and his tear-filled eyes turned blood-red as he vowed, "Today I will destroy the entire army of that evil, lying Yudhisthira, who assumes only the outward garb of virtue. And I will slay the wicked Dhrishtadyumna, who desecrated the body of my father. He defiled his own guru! Indeed, I shall eradicate all of them, for I have the Narayana weapon, the most powerful astra of all. I will grind them down to nothing!"

Greatly cheered by this statement, many Kuru warriors rejoined the fighting with renewed energy. Aswatthama attacked Dhrishtadyumna, and they engaged in a long, fierce battle. When neither could gain the advantage, Aswatthama broke off the combat and invoked the Narayana weapon. That mighty astra blackened the sky with countless weapons: arrows with mouths like snakes, iron balls, razor-sharp discs, and many other armaments that rained death on the Pandava army. Those who survived the bombardment — warriors, horses, elephants — began to flee the battlefield in terror.

As Yudhisthira saw that, he became afraid and called out to his allies, "Fly away! Fight no longer! Save your lives! I and my brothers will ascend the funeral pyre. Let Duryodhana be crowned with success today, for I have caused the death of the preceptor."

But Krishna shouted, "No, do not flee! Remain here, but lay down your weapons. If you stand weaponless on the earth and do not think about fighting, this weapon will not slay you. Otherwise, even if you imagine fighting, it will follow you wherever you go and destroy you."

Bhima cried, "No, do not lay down your weapons! With my mighty mace, I shall destroy that blazing astral weapon. Let everyone witness my prowess!"

Bhima then launched a salvo of arrows at Aswatthama. As a result, the Narayana weapon flared even brighter, like a wildfire fanned by the wind. It took the form of a gigantic ball of flame and descended quickly upon Bhima, engulfing him and his chariot.

Seeing that, the Pandava warriors believed Krishna's warning. They threw down their weapons and stood completely still. Only Arjuna still held a weapon: his celestial bow, Gandiva. But the Narayana weapon did not attack him because he thought only of protecting, not fighting. He nocked an arrow and invoked the Varuna weapon, infusing the arrow with the power of water. He shot the arrow, and that astra enveloped Bhima in a cocoon of water, protecting him from the fiery Narayana weapon.

Arjuna then laid aside Gandiva; together, he and Krishna dove into the fireball that enveloped Bhima. The Narayana weapon did not harm them because of their peaceful intent, the strength of the Varuna weapon, and their own power. They grasped Bhima and began to drag him off his chariot, away from his weapons.

Bhima roared in protest. "Leave me to fight! That weapon cannot hurt the mighty Bhima! I shall pulverize it with my mace!"

Krishna scolded him, "Can you not see that you are near being incinerated? Your comrades are safe because they laid down their weapons. Drop your weapons! Come with us and save your life!"

Sighing like a snake, eyes red with rage, Bhima reluctantly relinquished his weapons and allowed Arjuna and Krishna to escort him from his chariot. With that, the Narayana weapon became pacified and disappeared. The sky grew clear, and sweet breezes began to blow. The warriors became cheerful, as did the horses and elephants. The surviving remnant of the Pandava army picked up their weapons again and prepared to fight the Kurus.

Duryodhana shouted to Aswatthama, "Quickly, invoke that weapon again!"

Aswatthama replied, "No one can use that weapon twice. If I bring it back, it will slay me."

Duryodhana insisted, "Then use some other astra! Now! Kill them all!"

So Aswatthama launched the fiery Agneya astra. Immediately, a dense shower of flaming arrows erupted from it and rained death upon the Pandava army. Meteors flashed down from the sky, and heat scorched the very universe. A thick gloom enveloped the Pandava host, and thousands perished from the heat. The Kaurava warriors shouted in triumph.

Then, from within the darkness, Arjuna invoked the Brahma weapon. It dispelled the darkness in moments, and cool winds began to blow. Arjuna and Krishna burst out of the gloom uninjured, blowing mighty blasts on their conches. The mingled sounds filled the Pandava warriors with joy and the Kaurava warriors with dismay.

Seeing this, Aswatthama became exceedingly cheerless. He could not understand how his astra had not killed Arjuna and Krishna. He cried, "O fie, fie! Everything is untrue!" Then he laid aside his bow, jumped out of his chariot, and ran away from the fighting.

Finally, the sun set on the fifteenth day of the war, and all conflict ceased. Warriors on both sides were exhausted from two full days of nonstop fighting, and they gladly returned to their camps to rest.

That night, Vyasa paid a visit to the Pandava camp. Arjuna said to him, "All day yesterday, while I was slaying the Kuru warriors who blocked my path to Jayadratha, I saw a blazing form before me. Wherever that being led us, the enemy warriors broke before him. Everyone thought it was I who broke them, but it was he. His feet never touched the earth, nor did he hurl his lance even once, yet thousands of lances issued from it. Who was that?"

Vyasa answered, "It was the great Lord Shiva Himself, wielding his mighty Pasupata weapon. He is with you, Arjuna. Fight on! You shall be victorious."

CHAPTER 23

The Long-Awaited Duel

AFTER DRONA'S PASSING, DURYODHANA made Karna his new commander.

> The leadership of the forces of material desire has passed from one formidable warrior to another: from ego (Bhishma) to habit (Drona) and now to attachment (Karna).

As battle resumed on the sixteenth day of the war, Nakula began to fight more fiercely than ever, wreaking havoc on the Kuru army. Karna hurried to stop him.

Upon seeing Karna, Nakula shouted, "You are the cause of all this, wretched Sutaputra. I will at last dispel the fever of my heart by slaying you."

Karna replied with contempt, "Strike me, then! Show me your manliness."

A tremendous battle began. Nakula fought valiantly, and for a long time, neither warrior could prevail. Eventually, however, Karna was able to kill Nakula's horses and charioteer. Then he cut Nakula's chariot to pieces and sliced his bow in half. Having neither a chariot nor a weapon, Nakula had to flee from the field.

But Karna gave chase and caught him around the neck with his bow, shouting, "What do you say now, O great hero? Do not fight with your superiors. Take shelter in Arjuna and Krishna. Or go home, child." Karna then honored his promise to Kunti by releasing the thoroughly humiliated Nakula.

Meanwhile, Yudhisthira and Duryodhana fought an intense duel. Yudhisthira managed to gain the advantage and was about to kill Duryodhana when Bhima intervened, saying, "Wait, brother. Let him live so I may fulfill my vow to kill him." Only thus was Duryodhana's life spared.

Soon afterward, the sun set, and the day's battle ended.

At Duryodhana's council of kings that night, Karna said to him,

"Tomorrow, O King, I shall at last slay Arjuna, for I am far superior to him in every way. I lack only a driver who is the equal of Krishna. But if King Salya will drive my chariot, victory will be ours."

Duryodhana turned to Salya. "O King, I ask that you drive Karna's chariot tomorrow. The gods themselves could not stand against the two of you, let alone Arjuna and Krishna."

But Salya took offense. "I am a far greater warrior than that Sutaputra. I will not stoop to being his driver. I shall return home." He stood and began to walk out of the council.

Recall that Salya represents material pride.

Duryodhana sweetly replied, "Wait, O King. We all know you are a great warrior. But to ensure his victory, Karna will need a charioteer who is superior to Krishna. You alone are that person."

Salya stopped and turned back toward Duryodhana. He said, "Since you say I am superior to Krishna, I am gratified. I will drive Karna's chariot on one condition: I must be able to say to him whatever I like."

Duryodhana replied, "So be it." Karna, too, agreed to that unusual condition. Salya nodded and returned to his seat.

* * * * *

As dawn broke on the seventeenth day of the war, Karna joined Salya in his chariot and said, "Let us proceed so I can slay not only Arjuna, but the other four Pandavas as well. Then Duryodhana will be victorious."

Salya immediately began to fulfill his pledge to try to discourage Karna. He said, "Why do you think so little of the Pandavas? They are invincible. They could inspire fear in Lord Indra himself! You will not speak like this when you hear the twang of Gandiva, which resembles the peal of thunder."

Karna ignored his words and grimly ordered, "Proceed."

As Salya drove Karna toward battle, fierce winds began to blow, and a frightful shower of bones fell from the sky. Karna's horses stumbled and fell, and many other dark omens also appeared. But Karna only sneered. "I am not frightened. Today I will slay Arjuna. The gods themselves could not stop me!"

Salya laughed. "Do not brag so, Karna! Arjuna defeated Indra himself in battle. He defeated the mighty Gandharvas after you fled the field. In Matsya, he overpowered you and all the other great Kuru warriors. If you are superior to him, why did you not defeat him then? You are like a foolish young deer challenging a raging lion. If you do not flee, he will slay you!"

Karna became irate. "O Salya, you have no merit yourself, so you are unfit to judge the merits of others. You are merely an evil fool with no prowess whatsoever. I have in my quiver a poisonous blood-drinking arrow that I have worshipped for years in preparation for this moment. With it, I shall kill both Arjuna and Krishna!"

Salya dismissed these words with a wave of his hand. "You boast that you will kill Krishna and Arjuna, yet they are the sun and moon, whereas you are a mere firefly!"

Karna's rage began to boil over. "The only reason you are alive is that I agreed you could say whatever you wish. But after this battle, I will crush your head with my mace!"

Duryodhana had overheard their exchange, and he intervened. "O great warriors, cease this animosity. Focus on your task: You must kill Arjuna!"

Despite Salya's insults, Karna kept him as his charioteer, and they grudgingly turned their attention from bickering to the confrontation with Arjuna.

As the day unfolded, all the great chariot warriors fought numerous fierce duels, but without conclusive results. Each time one of them was on the verge of being killed, he withdrew from combat and returned later.

Finally, Karna wounded Yudhisthira so severely that Yudhisthira ordered his driver to take him back to the Pandava camp. But instead of allowing Yudhisthira to withdraw peacefully, Karna continued to attack and wounded Yudhisthira even more severely. Nakula and Sahadeva tried to protect Yudhisthira from further harm, yet they could not repel Karna.

Salya saw Yudhisthira's peril and cautioned Karna, "You are to fight Arjuna. Why do you battle with Yudhisthira? If you continue, you will use up your weapons and exhaust your horses. You will be wounded, and Arjuna will kill you.

"And look over there!" he said, pointing in another direction.

"Bhima is on the verge of killing Duryodhana. You must go and save your king!"

Karna looked where Salya indicated and saw that Duryodhana was indeed in trouble. He ordered Salya to rush to Duryodhana's rescue. Karna fiercely attacked Bhima and quickly forced him to flee. But the distraction had spared Yudhisthira's life.

When Arjuna learned of Yudhisthira's injuries, he was furious. "O Krishna, take me to Karna for battle. Today, I will certainly kill him!"

Krishna replied, "You are a mighty warrior, Arjuna, capable of destroying the gods themselves. But do not disregard Karna. Wicked-souled though he is, I regard him as your equal in battle, perhaps even your superior. He is a great hero, as powerful as the god Agni and as swift as the wind. When angry, he is like Shiva himself. No one, not even the gods, could defeat him — except for you. Slay him, therefore, as a lion slays an elephant."

Arjuna asked, "What if Karna kills me?"

Krishna shook his head. "Arjuna, the sun may fall from the sky. The Earth may shatter into a thousand pieces. Fire itself may become cold. Still, Karna will not be able to slay you. Yet if he does, I will slay him with my bare hands — and then I will destroy the entire universe. May prosperity be yours, O great warrior, and may you obtain victory."

Arjuna said, "Your blessing ensures my victory, O Krishna." He took a deep breath. "The terrible battle is now at hand. For as long as the world lasts, people will speak of it. Let us mount the chariot, for time is passing."

Krishna immediately began driving the chariot toward Arjuna's lifelong enemy. When Karna spied them from a distance, he said to Salya, "Arjuna is the greatest warrior ever born. Seeing him desirous of battle with me, with the Lord Himself as his charioteer, fear enters my heart, along with courage. My long-cherished desire for combat with Arjuna will soon be fulfilled. Either I will slay them both, or they will slay me."

Karna called to the other Kuru warriors. "Quickly! Surround Arjuna and Krishna, and attack them! Tire them out and wound them deeply so I may easily slay them!"

Roused by Karna's call, those warriors attacked relentlessly from all sides, showering Arjuna and Krishna with countless arrows. But

Arjuna, smiling all the while, calmly destroyed those arrows with his own. He was so brilliant that looking at him was like gazing at the sun. And he continued relentlessly moving toward Karna.

Elsewhere on the battlefield, Bhima was busily slaying even more sons of Dhritarashtra. At last, he came upon Dushasana, the brute who had humiliated Draupadi at the dice game. For thirteen years, all five Pandavas had ached to avenge that evil deed, Bhima most of all. Nothing would stop him now.

In a ferocious duel, Bhima broke Dushasana's weapons, knocked him to the ground, and stood over him, eyes crazed with bloodlust. Then Bhima fulfilled his long-ago vow: With a single mighty thrust, he drove his spear through Dushasana's armor and into his chest. He ripped out Dushasana's heart and brought it to his own lips. With great satisfaction, Bhima contemplated his triumph. Then he laughed softly, "What more can I do to you, dear cousin? Death has rescued you from my hands."

Seeing this gruesome display, the nearby Kuru warriors screamed with terror, "That one is a Rakshasa! Run for your lives!" And they fled.

Meanwhile, as Arjuna and Krishna drew ever nearer to Karna, all the creatures of Heaven and Earth gathered to witness the momentous duel. They began to take sides: The earth, rivers, trees, and mountains sided with Arjuna; the sky and stars favored Karna. Wolves, deer, and all kinds of auspicious animals and birds took the side of Arjuna. Ravens, dogs, jackals, and sea monsters sided with Karna. Brahmins and Kshatriyas supported Arjuna, while the lower castes wanted Karna to win. The Devas, rishis, Gandharvas, and other celestials favored Arjuna, except for Surya, the sun god, who supported his son, Karna, as did the Asuras and Rakshasas.

At one point, Duryodhana, Shakuni, Kripa, and several other great warriors attacked Arjuna together. But he easily swept their weapons from the sky with his arrows, killed their horses, and destroyed their chariots, forcing them to flee.

Aswatthama was profoundly distressed by the carnage. He approached Duryodhana and said, "Fie on war! Bhishma and my father are gone. No one can defeat the Pandavas. Make peace, O King, and share the kingdom with them. They will agree to that arrangement. I say this as a friend. If you choose peace, I will dissuade Karna from fighting."

Duryodhana reflected momentarily, breathing deeply with a heavy heart, then said, "I can never forgive Bhima for what he did to Dushasana, and the Pandavas will never forgive me for all I have done to them. Besides, we cannot ask Karna not to fight with Arjuna. He has waited many long years for this final encounter. Arjuna is tired, and I am sure Karna will soon kill him."

The Kuru warriors continued to attack Arjuna, but they could not stop him or even slow his progress. Soon, he arrived near Karna, and Krishna halted the chariot. All the other warriors stopped fighting to watch the great duel. The Pandava troops blew their conches and shouted encouragement: "Be quick, O Arjuna! Cut off his head, and with it, Duryodhana's desire for the kingdom!" The Kuru warriors shouted, "O Karna, slay him with your sharp arrows! Let the sons of Kunti return to the forest in exile—forever!"

Arjuna and Karna faced each other, their eyes and hearts filled with mutual loathing. Standing in their magnificent chariots, drawn by white horses, they looked nearly identical. Both were tremendously strong and rivaled the very gods in their beauty. They were fully armored, with excellent bows and quivers, and swords strapped to their belts. Multitudes of other weapons were close to hand in their chariots.

Arjuna shouted, "O proud fool, you are the cause of this war. Today, I shall certainly slay you."

Karna replied—not with words, but with arrows. He quickly pierced Arjuna with ten sharp arrows, and Arjuna responded in kind. Their duel was fierce and skillful, and all who were watching applauded their prowess.

Each warrior launched countless weapons against the other—and against the other's charioteer. Some found their mark, but the foe destroyed most of them before they could reach their target. Neither hero could gain the advantage with ordinary weapons, so they resorted to astras.

Arjuna placed a mighty arrow on his bow, infused it with the power of the fiery Agneya astra, and launched it. That weapon covered Heaven and Earth with its brilliance and set the other warriors' robes ablaze, causing them to run away. But Karna quickly invoked the water-born Varuna astra, which extinguished that fire.

So the battle continued as each countered the other's weapons.

Then, Karna took up the weapon he had mentioned to Salya: the mighty, blood-drinking arrow that he had long worshipped for the sake of Arjuna's destruction. It was an extraordinary weapon, exceedingly sharp, with a mouth like a snake. Its very presence caused meteors and thunderbolts to strike the earth all around.

Salya said, "O Karna, you can never cut off Arjuna's head with this arrow. Use a different one." But Karna ignored him and infused the arrow with its specific mantra. He drew his bow, aimed carefully, and launched the astra, shouting, "You are dead, Arjuna!"

Beholding that mighty arrow coursing toward Arjuna to cut off his head, Krishna pressed down with his feet, causing the chariot to sink a full cubit into the earth. That fearsome arrow then merely shattered the precious diadem that had been adorning Arjuna's head.

As Krishna raised the chariot from the earth, Karna's hour came near. The long-ago curse of the Brahmin, whose cow he had accidentally killed, caused his left chariot wheel to become stuck in the mud created by so many days of bloodshed. Karna then tried to invoke the Brahma weapon, but Parashurama's curse made him forget the mantra for invoking it.

In frustration, Karna began to rail against dharma, shouting, "The wise say that dharma protects those who follow it. I have always tried to follow dharma, but it is not protecting me now!"

Still, he continued to fight, piercing Arjuna and Krishna with many arrows, while Arjuna wounded Karna in return.

After they exchanged several more volleys of arrows, Karna realized that it would be fatal to remain a stationary target. He had to free his wheel from the mud, so he jumped out of his chariot. Amid tears of rage, he raised a hand and said, "Wait, Arjuna, while I free my wheel. Virtuous warriors never shoot at those who have turned from battle. Only a coward would shoot at me now. You are virtuous and well-acquainted with the rules of combat. Do not shoot at me while I am exposed and weaponless, here on the ground."

Krishna's eyes blazed with anger. "By good luck it is, O Sutraputa, that you now remember virtue! Tell me, when you applauded Shakuni's dishonest victory in the dice game, where was this virtue? When you laughed as Draupadi was humiliated before the assembly, where was this virtue? When the Pandavas' exile ended, and you continued to support Duryodhana's greed for their kingdom, where was this virtue? And when young Abhimanyu penetrated your array, and six of you—six vile cowards—attacked him all at once, where was this virtue? If virtue was nowhere to be found on those occasions, why parch your palate by uttering that word now? It is too late, Karna. You shall not escape with your life!"

Enraged and ashamed, Karna leaped back into his chariot to resume fighting. He took up a terrible arrow that blazed like fire. Its presence caused the entire earth to tremble and violent winds to blow, enveloping the battlefield with dust. The Devas began to wail in grief, thinking Arjuna would surely be slain. Karna placed that mighty arrow on his bowstring, recited its mantra, drew the bow to full circle, and shot the arrow. It cut through Arjuna's armor and pierced his chest. Arjuna reeled, dropped his bow, and collapsed in his chariot.

Karna again jumped down to try to free his chariot wheel. He pushed and pulled and lifted, but strong though he was, he could not free it. Meanwhile, Arjuna began to recover. As he slowly got back on his feet, Krishna said, "Now, Arjuna! Kill him before he gets back into his chariot!"

Arjuna placed another fearsome arrow on his bowstring. With special mantras, he transformed the arrow into an astra as mighty as Indra's thunderbolt, as irresistible as the Rakshasas at night, and as brilliant as the sun. He drew Gandiva to full circle, lifted his gaze to the heavens, and said, "If ever I have practiced austerities, gratified my superiors, and listened to the advice of well-wishers, let this arrow, worshipped by me and possessed of great power, slay my enemy, Karna."

As he unleashed that mighty weapon, it caused all points of the compass to blaze with light. In a heartbeat, it reached Karna and severed his head from his body, which collapsed lifeless onto the blood-soaked earth. A light emerged from that body, rose into the sky, and disappeared into the sun.

In celebration, Arjuna and Krishna blew tremendous blasts on their conches. The sound pierced the hearts of the Kuru warriors, who cried out in despair and began to flee in every direction.

Arjuna, Bhima, Dhrishtadyumna, and the other Pandava warriors pursued the fleeing Kuru troops and began to slay them as they ran.

Duryodhana called out to his army, "Of what use is running away? The Pandavas will find you and kill you. Their army is small, and Krishna and Arjuna are badly injured. If we stay and fight, victory will surely be ours. It is a sin for a Kshatriya to run from combat. Your duty is to fight. That is the way to eternal bliss."

A few of the warriors halted and turned to rejoin the battle. But most continued to flee, unable or unwilling to fight anymore.

Salya approached Duryodhana and said, "Your troops have fought bravely for you, but many are badly wounded, and the sun is about to set. Let them stop fighting for today. Return to your camp. Remember, O King: You are the cause of all this."

But Duryodhana could barely hear Salya's words as grief began to deprive him of his senses. His eyes filled with tears, and he could only lament, over and over, "Oh, Karna! Oh, Karna!"

Aswatthama and the other Kuru chariot warriors came to comfort him. As they led the weeping king back to his camp, they often turned to look at the banner waving atop Arjuna's chariot. It was ablaze with his fame.

> Thus did Karna perish. He is the central tragic figure of the Mahabharata, a good quality gone bad. Attachment to inner joy, to our soul nature, is our ticket to freedom. However, Karna was attached to worldly fame and respect, and human friendship. His loyalty to Duryodhana might seem dharmic, but it set him against a higher dharma by putting him on the side of jealousy, hatred, greed, and oppression.
>
> Similarly, attachment sometimes compels us to prefer a lower action over a higher one. However, a sincere *desire* to choose the higher can save us, for as Yogananda often said, "God reads the heart." He once encouraged a disciple: "I don't ask you to overcome delusion. All I ask is that you resist it." To resist delusion is to turn toward God, and that is when God can help us.

CHAPTER 24

A Vow Fulfilled

IN THE AFTERMATH OF KARNA'S death and the Kuru soldiers' flight from battle, the Kuru camp was quiet and gloomy.

Kripa addressed the council of kings, saying, "No doubt a Kshatriya's dharma is to fight, and death in battle has great merit, whereas fleeing from the field is a terrible sin. But Bhishma, Drona, Karna, and many other great warriors have fallen. Even if they were still fighting, Arjuna could never be defeated, for Krishna protects him. We cannot prevail."

Kripa turned to Duryodhana. "You must save yourself, O King. Give back the Pandavas' kingdom. You will still have your kingdom. I say this as a friend. Make peace."

Duryodhana shook his head, "You have fought valiantly for me, but I cannot do as you ask. The Pandavas would never trust a peace treaty with me. Also, they want revenge for all I have done to them and Draupadi. All of that is a fire that no one can extinguish.

"Besides, how could I enjoy a kingdom that remained mine only because of the Pandavas' generosity? No, having lived on the mountain's peak, I could never live at its base—especially not in the shadow of Yudhisthira.

"And with so many great heroes having died for me, how could I now seek to save my own life? No, I shall acquire Heaven by fair fight."

The other kings found his words so inspiring that they forgot the day's defeat and became enthusiastic to fight again.

Duryodhana asked, "Who should command my army now?"

Aswatthama answered, "King Salya is superior to all others in prowess, energy, fame, and every other accomplishment, and he still has a large army of his own. You should make him the commander."

The other kings cheered this suggestion. Salya stood and declared, "Krishna and Arjuna together are not equal to me in prowess. I can conquer the whole world of Devas, Asuras, and men. Tomorrow, I will form such an array that our enemies will be helpless against it. There is no doubt in this."

Duryodhana promptly invested Salya as his commander by anointing him with sacred water. As word spread through the Kuru camp that Salya was their new commander, all the warriors cheered loudly and blew their conches, confident that victory would be theirs. Then they lay down for the night, determined to fight even more heroically on the morrow.

· · · · ·

As dawn approached on the eighteenth day of the war, the Pandava and Kuru soldiers prepared for yet another day of gruesome battle. Despite their many prior defeats, the surviving Kuru army was still three times as large as the Pandava army. They also had a powerful new commander, and their confidence had fully returned.

When the sun rose, the two armies charged forth into fierce combat. The five Pandavas, Dhrishtadyumna, and Shikhandin fought so ferociously that the Kuru warriors soon began to flee the field. Seeing this, Salya attacked the entire Pandava army by himself. He lived up to his boasts by singlehandedly stopping the Pandava advance, which inspired the other Kuru warriors to return to battle with renewed determination.

Many fierce duels followed among the great chariot warriors. For a long time, there were no decisive outcomes. Each time a warrior was on the verge of defeat, he turned away from combat before his adversary could slay him.

Finally, however, Yudhisthira slew Salya, and the tide of battle turned in the Pandavas' favor. Bhima killed the last of Duryodhana's brothers. Arjuna killed Susharma, the Trigarta king who had lured him away on the day Abhimanyu was slain. And Sahadeva had the deep satisfaction of slaying the wicked Shakuni.

Those triumphs inspired the Pandava army to fight even more fiercely. Before long, all the Kuru soldiers either had been killed or had fled the field. Only four great Kuru chariot warriors remained alive: Duryodhana, Aswatthama, Kripa, and Kritavarma, the leader of Krishna's army.

But Duryodhana was seriously wounded. With his army devastated and all his brothers slain—and unaware that the other three chariot warriors still lived—he lost any hope of victory. He fled the battlefield with his mace, seeking a place to rest and recover.

He chose a nearby lake as his sanctuary. As he approached it, he encountered Sanjaya and said, "You are our only surviving warrior. Go tell the blind king Dhritarashtra I am still alive, though exceedingly wounded, and am resting in the depths of this lake."

"So be it," said Sanjaya, and he departed.

Duryodhana used his powers of illusion to create a space for himself in the lake, then jumped in and solidified the waters overhead. He remained there for hours, grieving deeply over his army's defeat.

In the chaos of battle, no one had seen where Duryodhana went when he fled the field. With the fighting now ended, Pandava soldiers began to search for him. They could not find him, however, so the Pandavas eventually called off the search and returned to their camp to rest.

Later, Sanjaya encountered Aswatthama, Kripa, and Kritavarma; all three were severely wounded. They said to him, "By good luck, you are still alive! Do you know what happened to King Duryodhana? Is he still alive?"

Sanjaya told them of his encounter with Duryodhana, and they set off for the lake. Upon arriving on the shore, Aswatthama called to Duryodhana, "O King, we are Kripa, Kritavarma, and Aswatthama. Arise and fight beside us! Either be victorious or gain Heaven through death in battle. You have slain almost all of the Pandava warriors, and the remainder are exceedingly mangled. They will not be able to resist your prowess. Arise, O mighty warrior!"

Duryodhana replied from deep within the lake, "By good luck, you three have survived. Your hearts are noble, and I am grateful for your devotion to me, but this is not yet the time for fighting. We shall go forth and conquer our enemies after we have rested and regained our strength."

The three allies kept trying to convince Duryodhana to return to battle, but he insisted on resting.

Some hunters overheard the conversation. They knew the Pandavas had been searching for Duryodhana, and they reasoned that the brothers would handsomely reward them for knowledge of Duryodhana's whereabouts. So they set out for the Pandava camp.

. . . . .

News of the destruction of the Kuru army and Duryodhana's flight from the battlefield quickly reached the Kuru camp. It caused widespread panic among the thousands of servants, cooks, guards, physicians, and others who had served the Kuru army throughout the war. Everyone feared that the Pandava army would now destroy the camp and everyone in it. So they hastily fled toward Hastinapura, taking with them only the necessities.

The Kaurava wives had been staying in the camp during the battle. Upon learning of the deaths of their husbands and the defeat of the Kuru army, they broke down in tears and great distress. Their attendants hurriedly helped them join the exodus bound for the Kuru capital.

Soon, the vast Kuru encampment was deserted.

. . . . .

When the hunters reached the Pandava camp and gave the news of Duryodhana's whereabouts, they received a generous reward. The Pandavas and Krishna joyfully set out for that lake, followed by legions of cheering, shouting soldiers. When Aswatthama, Kripa, and Kritavarma heard the boisterous crowd approaching the lake, they stopped trying to persuade Duryodhana to come out and fight. Instead, they quickly left the area.

Upon arriving at the lakeshore, Yudhisthira called out, "Duryodhana! You have sent so many to their deaths. Why do you now hide, trying to save your own life? A Kshatriya's dharma is to fight. Fleeing from battle is sinful; it does not lead to Heaven. You are a coward, not a hero!"

Duryodhana's voice came from the depths of the lake. "All my warriors were dead, and I was alone on the battlefield. I did not come here out of fear or grief. I came here only to rest. You, too, should rest. Then I will fight all of you."

Yudhisthira shook his head and replied, "We have rested sufficiently. Come out now and fight!"

Duryodhana answered, "Take the kingdom. I do not want it, for all my allies and brothers are dead. I will retire to the forest."

Yudhisthira's eyes blazed with anger as he said, "No true king would give away his kingdom when assailed by foes. Anyway, I do not want the *gift* of the kingdom. I want to *take* it from you in battle! Besides, it is no longer yours to give. You have been bereft of righteousness for many years, pursuing your evil schemes. Now, we will make you bereft of life as well. Come fight!"

Duryodhana protested, "It would be unfair to fight all of you at the same time. I have no armor or troops, and I am wounded."

Yudhisthira replied, "I will give you armor, and you may choose your weapon."

Duryodhana reflected for a few moments and then said, "Very well. I choose the mace. I will fight you, one at a time."

Yudhisthira offered even better terms: "If you slay *any* of us, you will still be king. Choose your adversary."

Krishna was shocked. He said to Yudhisthira, "What rash words you have spoken, O King! What if he chooses anyone but Bhima? Even Bhima is not so skilled with the mace. Duryodhana has long been preparing for this moment: He has practiced on an iron statue of Bhima for thirteen years. Bhima has tremendous strength, but Duryodhana has great skill—and in a match between might and skill, skill always prevails!"

Krishna began to pace fretfully along the shore. "You are once again playing a wretched game of chance, even as you did in the dice game. Who in all the world would gamble like this—with sovereignty within his grasp, after having conquered all but one of his foes, and that one plunged in difficulties? Truly, the sons of Pandu are destined not to rule, but to live in exile in the forest!"

Indeed, what could have possessed Yudhisthira to risk disaster when he was so close to victory? His gamble is further allegory for the fact that even highly advanced souls can fall spiritually.

Swami Kriyananda warned that we are not safe from delusion until we have transcended all sense of an existence separate from God. Even in the high state of *sabikalpa samadhi*, conscious oneness with all creation, the sense of "I" (ego) remains and can cause a fall, back into delusion. Only in the higher state of *nirbikalpa samadhi* are we free from "I" and all delusion.

Suddenly, Duryodhana emerged from deep in the lake and appeared standing on the shore. He said, "I will fight whomever you wish."

Bhima eagerly stepped forward, his eyes blazing with hatred. "I will fight you, Duryodhana!"

Krishna was relieved. Duryodhana was given armor, and the duel began. Again and again, the two great warriors rushed at each other to deliver their blows. Sparks flew from their great iron maces like fireflies. After each furious encounter, they stepped back to recover before the next assault.

For a long time, the match was even — Bhima's strength balanced against Duryodhana's skill. But as the battle wore on, Duryodhana was able to deliver many telling blows. One broke Bhima's armor and knocked him to the ground, leaving him barely conscious. After some moments, he slowly struggled to his feet, his eyes rolling and unfocused as he tried to clear his mind. Only with great effort was he able to steady himself.

Krishna said to Arjuna, "If Bhima fights fairly, he will never win. Through Yudhisthira's folly, danger has once more overtaken us. Duryodhana was defeated, all his troops killed, and he faced nothing but a life of exile in the forest. Now, he has hope once again, a desperate man with no fear of death. We are in peril.

"But I tell you this: As the Devas vanquished the Asuras through deceit, let Bhima also use deceit. You told me that, during the dice game, Bhima vowed to break Duryodhana's thigh in battle. Let him now fulfill that vow."

Arjuna nodded. He waited until the two combatants had separated and were gathering their strength for the next assault. He then caught Bhima's attention and slapped his own thigh resoundingly to remind Bhima of his vow.

Bhima nodded and backed farther away. He took several deep breaths, summoned all that remained of his enormous strength, and charged at his foe with an upraised mace. Duryodhana skillfully dodged the expected blow, but Bhima did the unexpected: Against all rules of fair fight, he struck his foe below the navel. Duryodhana roared with pain and outrage as he crumpled to the ground in agony. Bhima's blow had broken both his thighs.

Bhima stood over him and smiled with spite and satisfaction. Then he kicked Duryodhana's head with his left foot. "You have deceived us." He kicked him again. "You have humiliated us." He kicked him once more. "Now I do the same to you." After one last kick, he placed his foot on Duryodhana's head.

Yudhisthira quickly intervened. "This is wrong, Bhima. Duryodhana is a king and your kinsman. His army has been exterminated. His friends and counselors, brothers and sons, have been slain, and he has been struck down in battle. You have repaid him for his evil. Now leave him alone."

Bhima reluctantly took his foot off Duryodhana's head. Then he saluted Yudhisthira, "Today, the entire world is yours, O King. The wicked wretch who caused this war has been defeated, as have all his supporters."

The Pandavas and their allies cheered loudly and denounced Duryodhana's wickedness. But Krishna raised a hand to quiet them and said, "It is wrong to slay with cruel words one who is already dead. This sinful wretch brought disaster upon himself, and he is no longer fit to be regarded as either friend or foe. Do not waste your breath on one who is now nothing but a piece of wood! Let us leave this place."

Despite his injury and agony, Duryodhana was so enraged that he was able to push his upper body up and support himself with his arms. His eyes bulged with pain and fury, and his chest was heaving. "Krishna, do you think I did not see you suggest this unrighteous act by Bhima? You have caused many warriors to die by unfair means. Do you feel no shame? Think of how Bhishma fell through that trickery with Shikhandin. You caused Ghatotkacha to intercept Indra's spear, which Karna had saved for Arjuna. You had Yudhisthira lie to cause Drona's death. You caused Karna to be slain while he was defenseless, trying to free his chariot wheel. Who is more sinful than you? If you had fought fairly, you never would have won!"

Krishna replied, "O proud fool, you and all your followers have been slain by your own evil deeds. I gave you every chance for peace, but you would not listen to wise counsel. You were never righteous, never humble. You were forever persecuting the Pandavas. You poisoned them. You tried to burn them alive, along with their mother. You humiliated their queen before the assembly. You stole their kingdom, then refused to abide by the terms you had set. Enslaved by jealousy and greed, you have perpetrated many unrighteous acts. Bear now the consequences!"

Duryodhana lifted his gaze to the sky and smiled fiercely through his pain. "I have ruled the world, stood over the heads of my foes, enjoyed comforts worthy of the gods, and now I shall die gloriously from battle. Who is so fortunate as myself? I am going to Heaven!" He turned his gaze toward Krishna. "As for you, torn by grief and with your purposes unachieved, do enjoy this unhappy world!"

At those words, a thick shower of fragrant flowers fell from the heavens. Gandharvas played their instruments, and Apsaras sang, "All praise to King Duryodhana!" Invisible voices cried out, "Bhishma, Drona, and Karna were indeed slain by unrighteous means."

Hearing this, Duryodhana smiled as he slowly, agonizingly, lowered himself back onto the earth. The Pandavas hung their heads in shame.

Krishna said to them, "Listen to me! Bhishma, Drona, Karna, and Duryodhana were great warriors. Even with all your prowess, you never could have defeated them in a fair fight. Had I not used my powers of illusion and caused their death in battle, victory would never have been yours, nor kingdom or wealth!

"Do not feel bad about this. One who is greatly outnumbered by foes must triumph by any means possible. The Devas walked that path when they defeated the Asuras; therefore, all may walk it. We have fought hard, and success is ours. Now let us rest."

· · · · ·

The Pandava army joyously returned to their camp, shouting and singing in celebration of their victory. The five Pandavas, Krishna, and Satyaki proceeded to the Kuru camp, which they found deserted and in total disarray.

Krishna said, "Arjuna, dismount the chariot. Take with you Gandiva and your inexhaustible quivers."

Krishna dismounted after Arjuna. The moment his feet touched the earth, the chariot burst into flames and was reduced to ashes in moments. The Pandavas' eyes went wide with wonder.

Arjuna said, "O Krishna, why has this happened?"

Krishna replied, "Your enemies launched many astras at this chariot, and I have been holding them at bay. Now that you have won the war, I allowed them to fulfill their purpose."

Krishna embraced Yudhisthira and said, with a little pride, "By good luck, O King, your foes have been slain, and all of you have escaped with your lives."

Yudhisthira replied, "Who else but you, O Krishna, could have withstood the astras of Drona and Karna? Who else but you could have brought us this victory? All that has happened has been through your grace. Before the war began, Drona told me, 'Where there is dharma, there is Krishna. And where Krishna is, there is victory.' And it is so!"

Yes, Vyasa's account does say that Krishna felt "a little pride" over what he had accomplished. His use of divine powers to ensure the Pandava victory symbolizes divine grace, which can seem unfair because it is not limited by the laws that govern this physical world. It operates by higher laws.

The Indian scriptures declare that when a dharma conflicts with a higher dharma, it ceases to be a dharma. That is why Krishna made Karna forget to use Indra's magical spear, helped Arjuna kill Jayadratha, and urged Yudhisthira to lie to Drona: his actions saved many lives. In those ways and others, Krishna used his divine powers to ensure the Pandavas' victory because that was a higher dharma. The world would have suffered greatly under Duryodhana's rule — just as we suffer when ruled by material desire.

Krishna's statement that the Pandavas could not have won had he not used his divine powers has further meaning. Maya, delusion, aided by our ingrained habits and desires, is a mighty adversary. We cannot overcome it through our efforts alone. But our efforts, plus soul receptivity, can attract the divine grace that will take us to victory.

CHAPTER 25

Terror at Midnight

THE GREAT WAR HAD FINALLY come to an end. While their army celebrated, the Pandavas, Krishna, and Satyaki were exploring the deserted Kuru camp. They entered Duryodhana's tent and found a bounty of gold, gems, and other wealth. The brothers took possession of it, as plentiful riches would be necessary for ruling the newly reunited Kuru kingdom.

But Yudhisthira had a lingering worry. He said, "O Krishna, I know that Dhritarashtra and Gandhari will be devastated by the loss of their one hundred sons — and they will surely be exceedingly angry. I also know that Gandhari has tremendous inner power. I am concerned that she might use it to curse us. Will you go to Hastinapura and appease her?"

"I will do that, O King," replied Krishna. "As for you, it would be auspicious if you and your brothers do not sleep in our camp tonight. Find a quiet place, far from your army's celebrations, and stay there."

As the sun was setting, Krishna and Satyaki set out for Hastinapura. The Pandavas decided to spend the night on the banks of a stream some distance away.

* * * * *

Back on the lakeshore, Duryodhana lay in unceasing agony and covered with blood and dust, his eyes still burning with rage. Jackals, dogs, and crows surrounded him, eagerly anticipating his demise.

Now that the Pandavas and their army had departed the lake, Duryodhana's three surviving allies — Aswatthama, Kripa, and Kritavarma — returned and found him lying in the dirt. Aswatthama looked at Duryodhana in dismay and lamented, "Truly, nothing is forever. You ruled the entire world, yet here you lie, alone and in great agony."

Duryodhana wiped the angry tears from his eyes and replied, "Death comes to all beings. But by good luck, I have always been courageous and persevering. By good luck, I shall have died from battle, along with my friends and kinsmen. By good luck, you are safe and sound. Do not grieve for me, you who have always supported me. I am going to Heaven."

Aswatthama said, "The wretched Pandavas killed my father by evil means, and I seek revenge. I ask your permission to send them and all their allies to the abode of Yama."

Duryodhana was eager to oblige. He installed Aswatthama as the commander of this three-person army of heroes. Aswatthama bent down and embraced Duryodhana, then stood and let out a fierce roar of anger and determination that resounded through all points of the compass.

The three allies departed from the lakeshore and found a resting spot in the forest, where they spent the rest of the day pondering how to exact revenge on the Pandava army.

As night descended, they let their sorrow and anger over the war's devastation sink in. Eventually, Kripa and Kritavarma fell asleep, but Aswatthama lay awake, consumed by rage and breathing like an angry snake. As he gazed about him, he noticed a large banyan tree where hundreds of crows were roosting for the night, sleeping easily. Suddenly, a large owl flew swiftly into their midst and slaughtered many of them.

That gave Aswatthama an idea. He awakened Kripa and Kritavarma, then said, "The Pandava warriors are all celebrating their victory. I heard them shouting for joy as they marched back to their camp. Let us enter their camp tonight while they are asleep and kill them all."

"That would be most unrighteous," said Kripa. "We should instead ask King Dhritarashtra, Gandhari, and Vidura to tell us what to do."

"Righteousness!" spat Aswatthama, his eyes red with anger and bitterness. "The Pandavas have already broken the bridge of righteousness into a hundred pieces! Recall how Bhishma, my father, Karna, and now Duryodhana were slain. No! Tonight, I shall slay all the survivors of the Pandava army—with or without help from the two of you!"

After some hesitation, Kripa and Kritavarma agreed to help Aswatthama achieve his goal. They discussed how to proceed, and when they decided on a specific plan, they set out for the Pandava encampment.

• • • • •

When Krishna and Satyaki arrived in Hastinapura, they went directly to the palace. They saluted Dhritarashtra and Gandhari, and Krishna said, "You know, O King, how your sons persecuted the Pandavas, and how Yudhisthira did everything possible to bring about peace. Instead of insisting on the return of his entire kingdom, he even offered to accept just five villages. All the other Kuru elders solicited you for peace, but you did not follow their counsel. So do not blame the Pandavas for this war or harbor malice toward them over the loss of your sons. The fault is yours."

Dhritarashtra remained silent. He could not dispute what Krishna had said.

Krishna turned to Gandhari. "Remember, O Queen, what you told Duryodhana in the assembly: Where there is dharma, there is victory. That is what has happened: dharma has prevailed, nothing more. Therefore, do not seek to destroy the Pandavas, though I know you could do that."

Those words calmed Gandhari's anger, although she still grieved deeply over the loss of her sons.

Suddenly, Krishna became intuitively aware of Aswatthama's plan. He told the king and queen of the imminent assault on the Pandava camp, and they urged him and Satyaki to leave immediately and protect the Pandavas. So the two heroes set out in great haste for the Pandava army's encampment.

• • • • •

Aswatthama, Kripa, and Kritavarma arrived outside the camp late at night while all the surviving Pandava warriors were sleeping soundly after their victory celebration. Krishna and Satyaki were still on their way back from Hastinapura, and the five Pandavas were asleep, some distance away on the banks of a stream.

Aswatthama said to his two companions. "Stay here at the gate and slay anyone who tries to escape. I shall worship Lord Shiva, that he may give me the strength to accomplish my purpose."

Aswatthama then set up an altar and began to perform intense worship. After a time, Shiva appeared and said, "No one is dearer to me than Krishna. To honor him, I have used my powers of illusion to protect the Pandava warriors. But their karma to live has now run out." He handed Aswatthama an excellent sword that glowed with power and beauty, saying, "I will enter into your body so you will be invincible in battle. I will also send many fierce invisible beings to help you."

Aswatthama smiled and bowed deeply to Shiva. Then, sword in hand, infused with Shiva's power, and assisted by those invisible beings, Aswatthama entered the camp and commenced the carnage. Amid much confusion, screaming, and fighting, he and his invisible accomplices killed all the camp's occupants, including Dhrishtadyumna, Shikhandin, and the five sons of Draupadi. Only one person survived: Dhrishtadyumna's charioteer managed to slip past Kripa and Kritavarma as they were slaughtering others trying to escape. He immediately set out to find the Pandavas and tell them of the massacre.

> Swami Kriyananda pointed out that this disturbing episode allegorically underscores a basic spiritual truth: To know God, we must transcend even our positive qualities, symbolized by the Pandava army. That does not mean we should cease to be peaceful, generous, or humble and instead become angry, selfish, or arrogant. Rather, it means we are not free as long as we *identify* with any human quality — even a positive one. It is spiritually helpful to be peaceful, generous, or humble, but we need to transcend the limiting thought, "I am peaceful (or generous or humble)." We must identify solely with the source of those qualities: our blissful soul nature.
>
> As has been wisely said, "Chains, though of gold, still bind."

* * * * *

When morning came, the three perpetrators returned to where Duryodhana lay on the lakeshore, now barely conscious. Like him, they were covered with blood. But unlike him, the blood was not their own.

As Aswatthama described what they had accomplished, Duryodhana became alert and said, "You have done what neither Bhishma nor Karna nor your father could do. I am highly gratified. May prosperity be yours! All of us will meet again in Heaven!" Then he smiled, closed his eyes, and gave up his life breath.

Thus, finally, The Great War truly came to an end. The only surviving chariot warriors were Aswatthama, Kripa, and Kritavarma on the Kuru side and the five brothers, Krishna, and Satyaki on the Pandava side.

· · · · ·

The sun had risen by the time Dhrishtadyumna's charioteer found the Pandavas at their makeshift camp. When he told them the devastating news, Yudhisthira was overcome by grief. "Alas, our glorious victory has turned to bitter defeat. We and our army have been heedless in celebrating our success. Prosperity abandons the careless person, and every kind of misery overtakes him.

"I have lost my sons, grandsons, and friends. My four brothers must endure the same losses. But I grieve even more for Draupadi. She will be plunged into an ocean of grief over the loss of her sons and brothers. Nakula, go to her. She has been staying with the royal women of Panchala. Bring her to the battlefield. Your brothers and I will meet her there."

While Nakula went to find Draupadi, the other Pandavas returned to Kurukshetra and, with deep sadness, surveyed the carnage. Strewn far and wide across the landscape were broken weapons and armor, smashed chariots, slain elephants and horses, countless human bodies, and parts of human bodies. Swarms of crows, jackals, dogs, and insects were feasting on the remains. Yudhisthira was overwhelmed by the tragedy of it all. He sat and wept for a long time.

Later, Nakula arrived with Draupadi, who was deep in sorrow and rage over the news of the midnight massacre. Her eyes blazed with angry tears as she said to Yudhisthira, "By good luck, O King, you are happy to have won the entire kingdom. Never mind what has happened to all your sons and nephews, as well as to my brothers. Listen to my vow: If the wicked Aswatthama does not reap the fruits of this horrible deed, if you do not kill him and his followers, I vow to fast and meditate until I leave this body!"

Yudhisthira said, "Your sons and brothers died nobly. Do not grieve for them. Aswatthama has gone away, and we know not where."

Draupadi replied, "Then you must find him, O King! I have heard that he was born with a magical gem on his head. If you take that gem from him, it will be as good as killing him. I shall give up my vow only if I can place that gem on your head." She turned to Bhima and said, "You must come to my rescue once more, Bhima. Slay the wicked Aswatthama! Bring me that gem!"

Without a word, Bhima and Nakula climbed into Bhima's chariot. Nakula took the reins as charioteer, and they set off in great haste to find Aswatthama.

Soon, Krishna and Satyaki arrived. When Krishna heard what had happened, he said, "The wicked-souled Aswatthama has the Brahma weapon. With it, he can destroy the entire world. Bhima is in grave danger. He must be protected!"

Arjuna understood. He climbed into Krishna's chariot, and they departed in great haste. They caught up to Bhima just as he came upon Aswatthama, who was sitting on the bank of the Ganga in the company of Narada, Vyasa, and other great rishis.

Aswatthama instantly became afraid of what Bhima and Arjuna might do, so he plucked a blade of grass and inspired it with mantras that converted it into the Brahma weapon. With great anger and bitterness, he declared, "For the destruction of the Pandavas!"

Instantly, a mighty fire erupted from that blade of grass and spread out over a vast expanse of the heavens. Krishna said, "Arjuna, you must use the Brahma weapon to neutralize Aswatthama's weapon, or else it will destroy the entire world!"

Arjuna leaped out of the chariot and fixed an arrow on Gandiva. He then invoked that mighty astra with its special mantra, softly wished good unto Aswatthama, himself, and his brothers, and bowed to the gods and all his superiors. Then he shot that fearsome arrow into the sky while thinking of the welfare of the three worlds and saying, "Let this weapon neutralize Aswatthama's weapon."

Fierce flames erupted from Arjuna's arrow, and the two Brahma weapons filled the sky with fire and thunder, causing the entire earth to tremble. Narada and Vyasa flew up into the sky between the two weapons and held them apart to prevent the ultimate conflagration. They called to Arjuna and Aswatthama, "O heroes, your actions are very rash! No great warrior should ever use the Brahma weapon against human beings. You must withdraw your weapons."

Arjuna replied, "I used this weapon only to neutralize his weapon. If I withdraw it, the energy of the sinful Aswatthama's weapon will consume us all. O great ones, you are like gods. You must find a way to save the three worlds from destruction." He then withdrew his weapon.

Vyasa said, "Aswatthama, now you must withdraw your weapon."

But Aswatthama did not have the inner purity required to do that. He knew that if one as impure as he tried to withdraw that weapon, it would cut off his own head. So he replied, "I invoked that weapon only out of fear that Bhima would take my life. He has already shown his sinfulness in killing Duryodhana."

Vyasa shook his head. "Withdraw your weapon, Aswatthama, and give the Pandavas the gem you wear on your head. Then, they will let you live."

Aswatthama said, "Whoever wears this gem will always be protected from weapons, disease, and hunger. I see that I have no choice but to relinquish it. Very well. But I cannot withdraw this mighty weapon. I will instead direct it into the wombs of the Pandava women so *there will be no more Pandavas!*"

"Stop!" cried Vyasa. "You must not do that!"

But Aswatthama did precisely that, and his fiery weapon disappeared.

Krishna said, "O wicked wretch, the victory of your sinful action will be short-lived. Before the war, a great rishi told Abhimanyu's wife, 'A son will be born to you, and his name will be Parikshit.' His words are binding on the universe, and they shall be fulfilled. There will be another Pandava!"

Aswatthama replied with an angry smile, "That will not happen, O Krishna. My words will be fulfilled, for my weapon will fall upon that unborn child."

"Yes, it will," conceded Krishna, "and the child in the womb of

Abhimanyu's wife will indeed die. But I will ensure that it lives again. He will reign as king of the Kurus for sixty years.

"As for you, vile creature, because of your unrighteous act, you shall wander the earth for three thousand years, racked with disease and without a friend, without being able even to speak. Now, remove that gem and give it to Bhima."

Krishna's curse plunged Aswatthama into deep despair. Nevertheless, he removed the gem and reluctantly placed it in Bhima's hand.

Krishna, Arjuna, Bhima, and Nakula gave reverence to the rishis and returned to Kurukshetra. Bhima gave the gem to Draupadi, and with a fierce smile, she presented it to Yudhisthira. When he placed that sparkling gem on his head, he resembled a tall mountain with the full moon above its peak.

Draupadi said, "I now give up my vow to fast and meditate until death."

CHAPTER 26

Reunions

I N HASTINAPURA, DHRITARASHTRA WAS LOST in grief over the
outcome of the war and the death of his sons. He was barely able
to stand up or even speak. But as a father, he had an obligation, and
Sanjaya reminded him of it: "Sire, you should order the funeral rites
to be performed for your sons."

That was too much for Dhritarashtra—he fell to the floor and
lay motionless, overcome by emotion. Vidura coaxed him back to
upright and helped him collect himself enough to call for a chariot
to take Gandhari, Kunti, and himself to the Ganga for the ceremo-
nies. Vidura also helped him arrange chariots for the many grieving
Kaurava wives who had lost husbands, brothers, and sons.

When Yudhisthira received word that Dhritarashtra and Gandhari
were on their way to the Ganga, the five brothers and Draupadi set
out to meet them, accompanied by Krishna and Satyaki.

As soon as they reached the river, the wailing Kaurava wives surrounded Yudhisthira and demanded, "Where is your virtue, O King?
Where is dharma, truth, and compassion? How can your heart be
calm when you have caused the slaughter of fathers and sons and
uncles and friends and Bhishma and Drona?!"

Yudhisthira passed by the Kaurava wives without responding, for
he had no answers to their questions. He and his brothers went directly to Dhritarashtra to present themselves. Dhritarashtra embraced
Yudhisthira, but only reluctantly, for he regarded the eldest Pandava
as the cause of all his grief.

Then, the blind king reached out his arms and said, "I wish to
embrace Bhima. Where is Bhima?"

Dhritarashtra's anger was evident, a blazing fire fanned by the
wind of his grief, ready to burn everything it would touch.

Krishna said, "Bhima is here, O King."

Bhima stepped forward to be embraced, but Krishna held him
back and presented to the blind king an iron statue of Bhima—

the very statue on which Duryodhana had practiced with his mace for thirteen years.

Dhritarashtra was so enraged he did not realize he was embracing a statue. With all his colossal strength, he crushed that statue into tiny fragments. His chest became bruised and bloody, and he fell down once again.

Sanjaya raised the king upright, saying, "Do not act like that." An attendant stepped forward and began to clean the king's body.

Having released his anger, Dhritarashtra then began to feel remorse. "Alas, oh Bhima, alas! I have killed him!"

Krishna said, "Grieve not, O King. You did not slay Bhima. I recognized your anger and gave you an iron statue to embrace instead of Bhima.

"Why do you cling to anger when all your sorrows are your own fault? Through your grief over the death of your sons, your mind has fallen from dharma. Others and I tried to help you avoid this on many occasions, but you would not listen. Recall your evil actions, as well as those of Duryodhana. They are the cause of your grief. The Pandavas are perfectly innocent."

Dhritarashtra replied, "You are right, Krishna. My sorrows are all due to parental affection. By good luck, you saved Bhima from death. Now, I am free of anger, and I wish to embrace him with love. My welfare now depends totally on the Pandavas." He warmly embraced Bhima and blessed him, then did the same to Arjuna and the twins.

The Pandavas and Krishna next approached Gandhari. As always, she was wearing a blindfold. Vyasa also had come to see her, for he knew what was about to happen: Even though Krishna had pacified her earlier, Gandhari was again angry and grieving over the deaths of her sons. And for that, she intended to curse the Pandavas.

So Vyasa tried to soothe her. "O Gandhari, set your heart on peace. Do not utter the words that want to fall from your lips. You censured Duryodhana before the entire assembly when Krishna tried to bring peace. You knew that he walked the path of unrighteousness, whereas the Pandavas have always behaved righteously. You, too, must tread the path of righteousness."

"O Holy One," she replied, "I do not blame Yudhisthira, Arjuna, or the twins. But I cannot forgive Bhima for striking Duryodhana below the navel."

Afraid for his life, Bhima said, "I acted out of fear, O Queen. No one could slay Duryodhana in fair and righteous combat. You know of all his wicked behavior. At the dice game, I vowed to kill him for that. To fail to fulfill my vow would be to swerve from the duties of a Kshatriya. Furthermore, you did not restrain your sons in the past. How, then, can you blame us now?"

Gandhari protested, "Could you not have spared even one of my sons?" She began to tremble visibly with rage and asked, "Where is Yudhisthira?"

With great trepidation, the eldest Pandava stepped forward. "I deserve your curse, O Queen, for I am the sole cause of all this destruction. I no longer need wealth, kingdom, or even life. I have proved myself to be a great fool and a hater of friends."

Gandhari said nothing, but from behind her blindfold, she directed her gaze at the tip of Yudhisthira's toe. Using her ascetic power, she caused him to have a sore toe and unsightly toenail. Seeing this, Arjuna hid behind Krishna, and the other three Pandavas shuffled about nervously. But Gandhari had spent her anger, and she began to comfort the Pandavas as a mother would.

The five brothers then went to Kunti. She was weeping uncontrollably, overwhelmed by both relief that they were alive and grief to see their many wounds. Some time passed before she could collect herself enough to embrace them.

She then went to comfort Draupadi, who had lost all her children and was now lying on the bare earth, weeping and wailing. Kunti gently lifted Draupadi to her feet, and together with the Pandavas, they returned to where Gandhari was.

Beholding Draupadi's incessant tears, Gandhari said, "Do not grieve so, daughter. I, too, am grief-stricken over the loss of my sons. I do not think this dreadful slaughter had a human cause; it was ordained by Time itself. Do not grieve over that which was inevitable. All of this is my fault."

Then, they and all the Kaurava wives went to the battlefield to witness the carnage and see jackals and vultures feasting on the lifeless bodies of their husbands and sons. The Kaurava ladies could not bear the shock, and they either fainted or began shrieking and running about like madwomen. With her spiritual vision, Gandhari could see the gruesome results of the mayhem. It was exceedingly painful for her, and she, too, broke into pitiable weeping.

After a time, Gandhari's spiritual vision led her to the lakeshore where Duryodhana's body lay. Seeing her son lying on the ground, covered with blood, with crows beginning to feast on his body, she fainted. Krishna revived her, and she began to wail loudly. Tears poured out from beneath her blindfold onto Duryodhana's body.

She said, "O Krishna, on the eve of the war that has exterminated this Kshatriya caste, Duryodhana came to me and said, 'O Mother, wish me victory.' I knew that a great calamity was upon us, and I said to him, 'O Son, where there is dharma, there is victory. Since your heart is set on war, you will without doubt obtain the regions of those who die in battle, and you will sport there like one of the celestials.'

"He ruled the earth, yet now this foolish, wicked prince sleeps on the bare ground. He who was formerly fanned by beautiful ladies is now fanned by the flapping wings of carnivorous birds."

She continued for a long time, lamenting the deaths of her sons and Bhishma, Drona, and Karna. Finally, she fell to the earth, deprived of her senses by grief.

But soon, Gandhari again began to boil with rage—this time toward Krishna. She got to her feet and said, "You have eloquence, O Krishna, and you have power. You could have prevented this slaughter, but you did not care. Therefore, you shall reap the fruits of your conduct. Spending what little good karma I have earned through my austerities, I curse you: Thirty-six years hence, you shall be the slayer of your own kinsmen! And you shall perish in a disgraceful manner!"

Krishna smiled faintly. He had been born to cause the war; through it, he had relieved the Earth of Her great burden of evil. He said, "My kinsmen now have the world's only army. They are the ultimate earthly power—and that is a worry, for power can be misused. They must be exterminated. Your curse has aided me in that task, for when the time is right, I shall incite them to kill one another."

The Pandavas were aghast, but Krishna continued. "Do not grieve, O Gandhari. This vast carnage is your own fault. Duryodhana was wicked, envious, and arrogant. Yet you applauded his evil actions. Why, then, do you ascribe your faults to me?"

When Gandhari made no reply, they all returned to the Ganga to perform the funeral rites for the slain warriors. The Kaurava ladies, weeping and wailing, offered oblations of water to their late husbands, sons, brothers, and kinsmen.

Kunti broke down and again began to weep uncontrollably. Something more was troubling her. When she recovered, she said softly to the Pandavas, "You, too, should offer oblations of water. Offer them to that great archer, that warrior distinguished by every mark of heroism and who was slain by Arjuna. He was your eldest brother, Karna."

The Pandavas were stunned, especially Yudhisthira. He said, "Mother! How could you have concealed this for so long? Because of it, we are undone. The grief I feel over this new knowledge is a hundred times greater than the grief I feel over the deaths of Abhimanyu and Draupadi's sons. Without your concealment, this horrible war never would have happened!"

He began to wail with grief. But he had a duty to perform, so once he regained his composure, Yudhisthira summoned Karna's wives and other family members. Together, they performed the water rite in honor of his departed eldest brother, Karna.

The Pandavas remained at the river for an entire month of mourning. During that time, many great rishis came to visit them. Rishi Narada told Yudhisthira the life story of Karna, and that plunged him even deeper into grief.

Kunti said to him, "Do not grieve, my son. I told Karna that he was your brother and that he should unite with you. His father, Surya, also told him. But he was fully resolved to hurt you, so I gave up trying to change his mind."

With tears in his eyes, Yudhisthira replied, "Your concealment has brought this great affliction upon me. I therefore curse the women of this world: Henceforth, no woman shall ever succeed in keeping a secret!"

> Yes, Vyasa's account clearly states that Yudhisthira uttered that curse. I have not invented any part of this entire story.

* * * * *

The Pandavas, Draupadi, and Kunti took up residence in the Hastinapura palace. Krishna and Satyaki stayed with them as honored guests.

For a long time, Yudhisthira grieved over the tragedy of the war and the thought that it had all been his fault. In his grief, he wanted to retire to the forest. He asked Arjuna to take over as king of the Kurus. His brothers and Draupadi pleaded with him not to go, but they could not convince him. He even wanted to starve himself to death.

He began to waver only when Vyasa and Krishna tried to talk him out of his plan. But still, he was filled with doubts. He said to them, "It seems to me that the practice of virtue is always inconsistent with the duties of a king. Pray, help me reconcile the two."

Vyasa replied, "For that, Yudhisthira, you should go to Bhishma, who is still alive on the battlefield. He will teach you what you wish to know—and much more."

Yudhisthira asked, "But how could I approach him after all I have done? He always fought fairly, yet we brought him down through deceit. How can I ask him about duties and morality?"

Krishna said, "Do not cling to grief, O King. Do as Vyasa told you. The Brahmins and your brothers stand before you beseechingly, as do the Kuru people. For everyone's sake, do what will benefit the world."

Yudhisthira acceded to Krishna's request. Although he no longer desired to be king, he realized his *duty* remained. The world needed healing, so he was installed on the throne of the newly reunited Kuru kingdom.

After the coronation, Yudhisthira said to Krishna, "My Lord, it is through your grace, your might, and your intelligence that my ancestral kingdom has been returned to me. You are the soul of the universe, and the universe has sprung from you. You are the Cause of all creation, its Sustainer, and its Dissolver. I bow to you again and again."

* * * * *

The brothers, Krishna, and Satyaki returned to Kurukshetra, where Bhishma lay, still alive, on his bed of arrows. As they arrived, many rishis and Brahmins were worshipping him. Bhishma saluted Krishna as well as his mangled body would allow.

Krishna told him, "O foremost of men, soon you shall leave your body, and the priceless wisdom you have acquired will depart with you. That is why the Pandavas have come here to listen to you teach them about duty and morality."

Bhishma replied, "O Krishna, what can I tell them that you have not already told far better than I ever could? You are the repository of all knowledge. Besides, how can I teach when my mind is agitated by pain from all these arrows? My very vitals are burning. My mind is unclear, and my strength is abandoning me.

"Therefore, O Lord, it behooves you to teach King Yudhisthira. When You, the Creator of the universe, are present, how could I teach, like a disciple teaching in the guru's presence?"

Krishna said, "Those words are worthy of you, great soul that you are. Nevertheless, you should be the one to teach Yudhisthira, for he needs to overcome his grief.

"I shall bestow on you a boon: As you teach him, no pain, weakness, hunger, or thirst shall cloud your perceptions or memory. Your understanding will penetrate every subject of duty, morality, and profit. You will have divine sight, and everything will come to your remembrance."

The rishis and Brahmins then began to worship Krishna, and a shower of celestial flowers fell around the area where Bhishma lay. The Apsaras sang, accompanied by many celestial instruments played by the Gandharvas. A pleasant and auspicious breeze blew, bearing every kind of sweet fragrance. The entire battlefield of Kurukshetra grew quiet, and a profound stillness prevailed.

After a time, the sun set. The rishis and Brahmins saluted Krishna, Bhishma, and Yudhisthira, then returned to their homes. Krishna, Satyaki, and the Pandavas reverenced Bhishma by walking around him several times, then bade him farewell. They mounted their chariots and rode back to Hastinapura like tired lions seeking their dens.

They would return the following day, and the teaching would begin.

CHAPTER 27

The Grandfather's Wisdom

THE NEXT DAY, THE PANDAVAS, Krishna, and Satyaki returned to Kurukshetra. Bhishma was feeling the blessings of Krishna's boon as he lay on his bed of arrows: His wounds no longer caused him pain, fatigue, or mental unclarity.

He said, "O Krishna, I now clearly see all the wisdom of the scriptures and kingly statecraft. Through your grace, I have received a deeper understanding. Still, why do you not give this teaching yourself?"

Krishna replied, "My fame is infinite and eternal. I wish that your fame may be enhanced and endure undiminished for as long as the world shall last. Do share the wisdom you have acquired."

Bhishma understood. He turned to Yudhisthira and said, "O King, what do you wish to know?"

Yudhisthira touched Bhishma's feet in reverence and received his blessings. Then he said, "Those who know duty and morality say that kingly duties constitute the highest dharma. Yet those duties are an exceedingly heavy burden. O Grandfather, please speak in detail about the duties of kings."

Bhishma then began to teach Yudhisthira every aspect of kingly behavior. Over the course of nearly two months, he spoke of duty, conduct, morality, virtues and vices, statecraft, strategy, politics, administration, the yugas, high spiritual teachings, and much more.

* * * * *

At one point, Yudhisthira asked, "O Grandfather, when a king is surrounded by foes, how should he decide who is a foe and who is, in fact, a friend? With whom should he make peace, and with whom should he make war?"

Bhishma replied, "Listen now to the duties that should be practiced in seasons of distress, when a foe may become a friend, and a friend a foe. One should make peace even with one's foes when one cannot otherwise save his life, and sometimes one must wage war against one's friends. In this regard, I will tell you the story of the mouse and the cat.

"There was a large banyan tree in the midst of a forest. It was home to many creatures. Among them was a mouse that lived in a hole at the base of the tree. A cat lived happily among its branches, often feasting on the birds that visited the tree.

"Not far away lived a hunter who set his traps every evening, then returned the next day to check them. One morning, in a moment of carelessness, the cat was caught by one of the traps. Seeing that, the mouse emerged from his hole and roved about fearlessly. He climbed upon the trap that held the cat, laughing as he nibbled on the bait the hunter had set in it. He did not notice, until it was too late, that a mongoose had seen him. It was standing on its haunches, licking the corners of its mouth with its tongue in anticipation of eating the mouse. The mouse then spied yet another foe: An owl was perched in the tree, peering down at him with clear intent.

"The mouse thought, 'Death is staring me in the face. What shall I do? If I step off this trap, the mongoose will eat me. If I stay on this trap, the owl will seize me. And if the cat can escape the trap, he will devour me. But a person of my intelligence should never lose his wits. I must think of a plan.'

"He reasoned, 'At present, although this cat is my natural enemy, he is my only refuge. The mongoose and owl will not attack when he is near. Yet he is in distress, and I can free him. A person in great danger should make peace even with an enemy. Therefore, let me help this foolish creature understand his own interests so I may escape from all three of my foes.'

"The mouse gently said, 'O cat, I desire the good of us both. I am sure you have seen the mongoose and the owl, who seek to eat me. You, on the other hand, are caught in this trap, and the hunter will soon come for you. But I will cut the net that holds you if you will abstain from killing me. Then we will both be happy.'

"Hearing these well-chosen and highly acceptable words, fraught with reason, the cat said, 'Bless you who wish me to live. Both of us are in distress, but we can help each other. Let us be friends.'

"The mouse replied, 'Here is my idea: I will crouch beneath your body so you can protect me while I cut the strings that are holding you.'

"The cat said, 'O mouse of great wisdom, you are indeed a friend. Tell me what I can do for you now, and I will do it. Let there be peace between us. Freed from this distress, I shall always worship and honor you.'

"The mouse, having made the cat understand his own interests, crouched trustingly beneath the body of his enemy. Seeing him thus protected, the mongoose and the owl lost all hope of seizing their prey, and they went away.

"The mouse then proceeded very slowly to cut the strings of the net that held the cat. The cat became impatient and pleaded, 'O friend mouse, why do you dawdle? Will you forget me now that you are safe? Do cut those strings quickly, before the hunter comes.'

"The mouse replied, 'Be patient, O friend! If I free you too soon, I shall be in great danger from you. But as soon as I see the hunter approach, I shall cut the last strings. You will be free to dash up the tree, and I shall take shelter in my hole.'

"The cat said, 'An honest person never treats his friends like this. I promptly rescued you from great danger. You should do the same. O wise one, do work more quickly. If I have ever unintentionally harmed you, I beg your forgiveness.'

"The mouse replied, 'O cat, if I cut the last string before the hunter arrives, you will forget what I have done for you, and you will eat me. That is why I have cut all but one of the strings that hold you. When I cut that string at the last moment, you will flee for your life without thinking of seizing me. Then we will both be safe.'

"Soon, the hunter arrived, and the cat became agitated with fear. But the mouse promptly cut the last string as promised, and the cat bolted up the banyan tree while the mouse fled into his hole. Seeing his hopes frustrated, the hunter soon went away, carrying his ruined trap with him.

"The cat called down to the mouse, 'O friend, why did you run away? I hope you do not suspect me of any evil intent. You have done me a great service, and I am grateful. You inspired me to trust and gave me my life. At such a time, friends should enjoy the sweetness of their friendship. He who makes friends and then forgets them is considered wicked. He never gains friends in times of danger and need. O mouse, it behooves you to enjoy the company of my poor self. All that I have is yours. I swear by my life that you have nothing to fear from me.'

"The mouse replied sweetly: 'O cat, I have heard your soothing words. Listen now to me. There is no such thing as a friend or a foe. It is circumstances alone that create friends and foes. Two persons are friends as long as their interests do not clash. But there is neither permanent friendship nor permanent hostility. Blind trust or mistrust is foolhardy. A foe becomes a friend, and a friend becomes a foe, always due to considerations of self-interest.

"'Besides,' the mouse added, 'You climbed down the tree earlier and did not see the trap. How can a person who fails to protect himself protect others?

"'You tell me sweetly that I am dear to you. But this whole world is moved by self-interest. You seek your interests, and others seek theirs. A person becomes dear for the purpose he may serve. Today, you were my foe, then my friend, and now once more my foe. There was a reason for our friendship: We freed each other from grave danger. Now that we are safe, there is no need for friendship. I am weak, and you are strong. Those who are weak always know that those of greater strength are foes.

"'I understand your thinking, O cat. Having been rescued from the trap, you applaud me so you may easily make a meal of me. Hunger tempted you into the trap. Now, you have been freed from the trap, but not from the hunger. What person of any wisdom would make himself vulnerable to a powerful foe who is not distinguished for righteousness, who is hungry and on the lookout for prey? I shall not mingle with you, so do not persist!'"

Bhishma concluded, "Thus did the wise mouse live a long and happy life."

* * * * *

Another time, Yudhisthira asked, "Tell me, O Best of Kurus, if a person fails to find the wealth he needs, what must he do to obtain happiness?"

Bhishma said, "He must regard everything—joy and sorrow, honor and insult, triumph and failure—with an equal eye. He must never run after earthly possessions. He must practice truthfulness. He must be ever calm. And he must live without attachment. That, O King, is a happy man. The ancients say that those five practices lead to perfect tranquility and emancipation. They are Heaven. They are Religion. They constitute the highest happiness.

"In this connection, I shall relate the story of Manesh, who desired wealth yet was repeatedly disappointed. He would gain it, then lose it, again and again. Finally, he acquired enough money to purchase two young bulls and a yoke to harness them to labor.

"One day, Manesh yoked the bulls together and took them into the field for training. A camel was lying nearby, and when the bulls saw it, they ran toward it and attacked. But the camel stood up and ran away, with the bulls still yoked together, dangling from either side of its neck.

"Seeing that, Manesh thought, 'If Destiny (past karma) wills that one not be wealthy, he surely cannot acquire wealth, even if he is clever and acts with full attention, confidence, and skill. Alas, my dear bulls are lost to me, dangling like gems from the camel's neck. That might seem to be an accident, but Destiny is at the root of all that happens. If Destiny is too powerful, our efforts cannot change it. Only a person with no attachments or desire for wealth can sleep happily.

"'Truly, one who casts off all desires is superior to one who satisfies his desires, for there is no end to desire. O my Soul, you have repeatedly been deceived by desire. Abstain from it now. Become tranquil by freeing yourself from all attachments. How is it that you have not yet done so? If I do not deserve destruction at your hands, if I should be sporting with you in delight, then do not tempt me toward greed. You have repeatedly lost your hoarded wealth. When will you free yourself from that desire?

"'Shame on my foolishness! I have been a slave. But I have finally been roused from sleep and am now fully awake. Without doubt, the desire for wealth can never bring happiness. The acquisition of wealth is always uncertain. Even if one acquires wealth, it is never enough; he always wants more. He also feels great anxiety over his wealth, and if it is lost, he feels as though he is dead.

"'Desire has been my destruction, but now I have awakened. Leave me, O Desire! Go where you will and live as you like. You are not of the Soul. I have no joy in you, for you follow the lead of misery and greed. I shall abandon you and take refuge in Goodness. I shall devote my mind to Yoga, my life to the guidance of the wise, and my soul to God. I shall rove happily in this world without attachment or calamities, so you can never again plunge me into sorrow.

"'If I continue to be agitated by you, O Desire, I shall be lost. You are the source of grief, needless toil, and fatigue. The paltry happiness brought by wealth is mingled with pain and sorrow. Robbers assault wealthy people or fill them with fear of losing their wealth. At last, I have understood that the desire for wealth is fraught with sorrow.

"'O Desire, you are a fool, never content, never satisfied. You burn like fire. Once you set yourself upon acquiring something, you pursue it without considering whether it is easy or difficult to obtain and whether it is beneficial or detrimental to happiness. You can never be satisfied. You wish to plunge me into sorrow.

"'From this day forth, O Desire, I shall not live with you. At first, I felt despair over the loss of my property, but I have now attained perfect freedom from attachments. I am no longer ignorant. I can rest, free from every fever of desire. I cast you off with all the passion of my heart. I shall never again allow you to dwell with me.

"'I shall forgive those who speak ill of me. I shall not injure, even when I am injured. If anyone speaks disagreeably of me, I shall disregard those words and respond only with agreeable words.

"'I shall rest content, with my senses at ease, living upon what comes to me. I shall not pursue your wishes, O Desire, for you are my foe. I have adopted the path of Goodness. Now I have contentment, tranquility, Truth, self-restraint, forgiveness, and universal compassion. Great is my happiness now, having cast off desire and greed.

"'One obtains happiness according to the measure of the desires he can cast aside. Like a person who has plunged into a cool lake on a hot day, I have entered into God. Pure happiness has now come to me. The happiness that comes from the gratification of Desire, or even that higher happiness that one enjoys in Heaven, does not amount to a sixteenth part of the bliss that arises from the abandonment of Desire. Having freed myself from Desire, I have entered the immortal city of God and shall pass my days there in happiness like a king.'"

Bhishma concluded, "Thus did Manesh free himself from attachments and cast off all desires. Indeed, as a result of losing his two bulls, he cut the very roots of desire and thereby attained immortality and the highest happiness."

•   •   •   •   •

On a third occasion, Yudhisthira said, "O Grandfather, all persons applaud virtuous behavior. I desire to learn what it is and how to acquire it."

Bhishma said, "O King, after your Rajasuya ceremony in Indraprastha, Duryodhana burned with jealousy over your prosperity. He asked Dhritarashtra how to attain such wealth and importance.

"Dhritarashtra replied, 'O Son, if you want to win prosperity equal to, or even greater than, Yudhisthira's, you must behave virtuously. Without doubt, one may conquer the three worlds by behavior alone. Nothing is impossible for those of virtuous behavior.'

"Duryodhana asked, 'How can I acquire virtuous behavior?'

"In answer, Dhritarashtra recounted an ancient story of Lord Indra and the Asura Prahlada. I shall tell you that story.

"By the merit of his behavior, Prahlada had snatched from Lord Indra his heavenly sovereignty and was now the ruler of the three worlds. Indra became despondent over his loss. He went to Vrihaspati, the guru of the Devas, and asked, 'What is the source of happiness?'

"Vrihaspati answered, 'Knowledge that leads to liberation is the source of happiness.'

"Indra asked, 'Is anything higher than that?'

"Vrihaspati said, 'Yes, but you should ask the rishi Bhrigu to tell you about it.'

"Indra then asked Bhrigu, who told him to ask Prahlada, saying that Prahlada had better knowledge of it.

"Hearing that, Indra smiled with delight. He immediately assumed the form of a Brahmin, went to Prahlada, and asked, 'What is the source of happiness?'

"Prahlada said, 'I have no time to answer you. I am fully occupied in ruling the three worlds.'

"The Brahmin said humbly, 'O King, when you have time, I beg to hear your instructions about the path that leads to happiness.'

"The Brahmin then stayed with Prahlada and behaved toward him as a disciple would behave toward his guru. For a long time, he did wholeheartedly whatever Prahlada desired. On many occasions, the Brahmin asked, 'O King, how did you win the sovereignty of the three worlds?' Yet he received no answer.

"Finally, one day, Prahlada was willing to answer the Brahmin's question. He said, 'I feel no pride in being a king. I follow the counsels of the Brahmins, who restrain me from unrighteous or improper actions. I am ever obedient to their teachings. I serve them and my seniors. I bear no malice. I am of righteous soul. I have conquered wrath. I am self-restrained, and all my senses are under control. The Brahmins pour beneficial instructions upon me as bees drop honey into the cells of their comb. Even so, I taste the nectar from those learned persons, and I live among my people like the moon among the stars.'

"Prahlada continued, 'O Brahmin, I am exceedingly gratified by your dutiful behavior toward me. Ask of me a boon.'

"The Brahmin said, 'O King, I desire the boon of acquiring your behavior.'

"That filled Prahlada with fear, for he knew that anyone who asked for such a boon could not be an ordinary person. What was going to happen next? Whatever it might be, he had to honor his offer, and he said, 'So be it.' Then he began to grieve deeply.

"The Brahmin went away, while Prahlada became very anxious and did not know what to do. As he sat brooding over the matter, a flame of light issued from his body. It had a shadowy form of huge proportions and great splendor. Prahlada asked the form, 'Who are you?'

"The form answered, 'O King, I am the embodiment of your Behavior. Cast off by you, I shall henceforth dwell in the Brahmin who became your devoted disciple.' And the form departed.

"Then, another lustrous form of similar size and shape issued from the body of Prahlada, and he asked it, 'Who are you?'

"The form replied, 'O Prahlada, know me as the embodiment of Dharma. I reside where Behavior dwells, so henceforth I shall dwell in that Brahmin.' And the form departed.

"Then a third form issued from Prahlada's body, blazing with splendor. Again, Prahlada asked who it was, and the form answered, 'I am Truth. I leave you now, for I always follow the way of Dharma.' And Truth went away.

"Next, another glowing form issued out of Prahlada's body. In reply to Prahlada's question, that mighty being said, 'I am the embodiment of Good Deeds. Know that I live where Truth lives.' And Good Deeds departed.

"Then, with a mighty roar, yet another shining form emerged from Prahlada's body. When Prahlada asked who it was, the form answered, 'Know that I am Strength. I dwell where Good Deeds are.' Then Strength set forth to follow Good Deeds.

"After that, a radiant goddess issued out of Prahlada's body. Prahlada asked her, 'Who are you?' She answered, "I am the embodiment of Prosperity. I dwelt in you, but you have cast me off, so I shall follow in the wake of Strength.'

"Prahlada began to tremble, and he asked, 'Where will you go, O Goddess? You are ever devoted to Truth, and you are the foremost of deities. Who is that Brahmin who was my disciple? I wish to know the Truth.'

"The goddess of Prosperity replied, 'That Brahmin was Indra. It was by your behavior that you subjugated the three worlds. Knowing this, Indra robbed you of your behavior and now rules the three worlds once again. Dharma, Truth, Good Deeds, Strength, and myself are all rooted in Behavior.' With those words, the goddess of Prosperity left Prahlada.

"When Dhritarashtra finished recounting this history, Duryodhana said, 'I wish to know the Truth about Behavior. Tell me how I may acquire it.'

"Dhritarashtra said, 'I shall tell you in brief, O Son. Abstain from injuring any creature by thought, word, or deed. Practice compassion and generosity. Never perform actions that do not benefit others or that shame you. Do that by which you may win praise in society. If persons of wicked behavior ever do win prosperity, they do not enjoy it for a long time because they are soon exterminated, down to the root. Knowing all this, O Son, be of good behavior if you wish to obtain prosperity greater than Yudhisthira's.'"

Bhishma concluded by saying, "O Yudhisthira, as you know all too well, Duryodhana did not follow those precepts and has therefore been slain. Dhritarashtra, too, now suffers the consequences of wicked behavior. You, however, have always followed virtue, and you shall surely obtain its fruits."

. . . . .

In his answers to these and many other questions, Bhishma conveyed to Yudhisthira the wisdom of how to be king of the Kurus — and king of himself.

Bhishma's teaching occupies almost a quarter of the Mahabharata.

CHAPTER 28

Farewells

AFTER NEARLY TWO MONTHS OF teaching, Bhishma had answered all of Yudhisthira's questions. The sun had finally turned its course to the north, so it was an astrologically auspicious time for the grandfather to leave his body. He asked Krishna and the Pandavas for permission to depart from this world, and they readily gave it. He then took control of his life force and left his body through the crown of the head. Celestial drums beat, and flowers rained from the sky as Ganga's son returned to his heavenly home. His very, *very* long incarnation had finally come to a close.

The Pandavas built a funeral pyre and cremated his body. They then wrapped the remains in a silken cloth, decorated it with flower garlands, and took it to the Ganga. There, along with many rishis and Kuru citizens, they made offerings of water to the departed grandfather.

As the ceremony concluded, Bhishma's mother, the goddess Ganga rose out of the waters, weeping sorrowfully. She lamented, "My son was noble, wise, devoted to his father, and of high vows. No one could ever defeat him. But alas, he was slain by Shikhandin. Without doubt, my heart must be stone that it does not break into a thousand pieces."

Krishna said, "O goddess, do not yield to grief. Your son was slain by Arjuna, not by Shikhandin. He has gone to the highest region of felicity. Let the fever of your heart be dispelled."

Hearing those comforting words, Ganga cast off her grief and regained her equanimity.

> Why was Ganga comforted by Krishna saying that Arjuna, not Shikhandin, killed her son? Was it that she did not want Amva to have her revenge?
>
> In fact, several passages in Vyasa's account declare it really was Shikhandin who killed Bhishma. Even Arjuna said so. During the battle,

however, Bhishma repeatedly said of the arrows lodged in his body, "These are Arjuna's arrows, not Shikhandin's." What is the truth?

With so many arrows from both men piercing his body, how could it be said that either killed Bhishma? Allegorically, we could say that overcoming ego (Bhishma) requires a combination of the human quality of self-control (Arjuna) and the divine quality of self-transcendence (Shikhandin).

Everyone offered the goddess due honor and received her permission to depart. Yudhisthira staggered up the riverbank, then collapsed in grief over the tragedy of the war.

As others gathered around him, Dhritarashtra scolded him, "O King, get up and tend to your duties. Enjoy this world you have conquered. It is Gandhari and I who should mourn, for we have lost one hundred sons. I ignored Vidura's wise counsel and followed the wicked Duryodhana, and now I am plunged into misery. You have no reason to grieve."

Krishna said, "O Yudhisthira, you did what you should have done. It was all destined to happen. Do not walk the path of ignorance. You must now bear the burden of the Kuru empire on your shoulders."

Yudhisthira responded, "Krishna, allow me to retire to the forest, that I may purify my mind and free myself from this sin."

Vyasa said, "O King, your mind is not yet calm, and therefore, you are once again stupefied by childish sentiment. In waging this war, you did what was needed, nothing more and nothing less. Over these last two months, Bhishma has been teaching you the way to salvation, but clearly, you have forgotten it already. God is the Doer of all actions, yet you think you were the doer. Very well, then expiate your supposed sinful action by performing the Aswamedha ceremony."

Yudhisthira replied, "O Holy One, the wealth we recovered from the Kuru camp is not nearly enough to perform such a grand ceremony. Duryodhana exhausted the Kuru treasury. How can I now tax the citizens to refill the treasury when it was I who brought about this destruction?"

Vyasa said, "Fear not, for the treasury shall once again be full. Long ago in the Himalayas, a vast amount of gold was left behind after a sacrifice." And he told Yudhisthira how to find that gold.

Krishna said, "O King, the war is over. You have fought and won the physical battle. But enemies still lurk within you. Now, it is time to fight with the mysterious mind and win that war as well. Merely retiring to the forest will not accomplish that.

"You dwell constantly upon your mistakes and your many persecutions and humiliations. You must stop that and take charge of your mind. Above all, you must redirect your desires toward virtue, for ungoverned desire ruins all spiritual aspiration."

Yudhisthira then did as Krishna counseled: Instead of retiring to the forest, he remained on the Kuru throne. He also began fighting the battle of the mind. After a time, he did as Vyasa suggested and led a mighty army to the Himalayas to recover the abandoned gold.

While they were gone, Abhimanyu's wife, Uttara, gave birth to a son. The child was stillborn because Aswatthama had directed his Brahma weapon into the wombs of the Pandava wives. But Krishna fulfilled his pledge to restore the child to life, and he was given the name Parikshit.

Soon afterward, the Pandavas returned from the Himalayas with the gold, and Yudhisthira performed the Aswamedha ceremony. The power of that ceremony, added to Yudhisthira's efforts to govern his mind, finally freed him from grieving over the war. He proceeded to rule the kingdom with calmness, kindness, and righteousness.

* * * * *

For the next fifteen years, the Pandavas humbly served Dhritarashtra and Gandhari. Bhima, however, held back; he nursed a grudge against them over their support of Duryodhana. For their part, Dhritarashtra and Gandhari became deeply affectionate toward their nephews—although not toward Bhima, because they could not forgive him for killing their sons.

Then Dhritarashtra, Gandhari, Sanjaya, Vidura, and Kunti decided to retire to the forest for the remainder of their lives. The Pandavas, Draupadi, Subhadra, and many others escorted them to their forest abode and remained with them for a time.

After they had been living there for nearly a month, Vyasa arrived and said to Dhritarashtra, "O King, I know the sorrow that burns in your heart and the hearts of all the mothers here. What boon can I give you?"

Dhritarashtra answered, "O Father, I deeply love my children, and I miss them sorely. I am tortured by Duryodhana's many sins and by having supported him in his evil deeds. I long for peace of mind."

Gandhari said to Vyasa, "O Holy One, Kunti, Draupadi, Subhadra, and countless others have also been grieving the deaths of their sons and brothers and fathers. Please reveal to them what happened to their loved ones after the war."

Vyasa said to everyone, "Do not grieve. It was all destined to happen. Those heroes came to Earth to accomplish the purpose of the gods. Come with me to the Ganga, and you shall be reunited with them."

Everyone's eyes were wide with anticipation as they followed Vyasa to the Ganga. Upon arriving, they performed their evening worship and sat on the banks until nightfall. Then Vyasa entered those sacred waters and summoned all the deceased warriors.

A deafening roar sounded as thousands of great heroes emerged from the holy waters, radiant with light and robed with celestial garments. They were now free from all hatred, pride, and jealousy. With her divine sight, Gandhari beheld her one hundred sons, as did Dhritarashtra, for Vyasa gave divine sight to him as well. Kunti and the Pandavas reconciled with Karna. Draupadi rejoiced to meet her father, brothers, and five sons. Bhima embraced his son, Ghatotkacha. Arjuna and Subhadra had a loving reunion with Abhimanyu.

All persons—the living and the dead—passed the night in boundless happiness. They cast off all grief, and a great reconciliation occurred. When the sun rose, the deceased warriors plunged back into the Ganga and returned to the regions from whence they had come.

The joy of the reunion had revitalized everyone. Yudhisthira wanted to live permanently in the forest with his elders, but Dhritarashtra told him, "O King, it is time for you to go back. You have a kingdom to rule."

So the Pandavas returned to Hastinapura. Over the years that followed, the Kuru people enjoyed peace, harmony, and prosperity under Yudhisthira's benevolent rule.

• • • • •

Thirty-six years after the war, many strange events occurred in the Kuru realm. Powerful winds showered the kingdom with gravel. Great rivers began to run uphill. Every day, fierce circles of light surrounded the sun and moon. These and many other omens foretold danger, filling everyone's heart with anxiety.

Far away in Dwaraka, a fight broke out between Satyaki and Kritavarma. Satyaki had long resented Kritavarma for having aided the slaughter of the sleeping survivors of the Pandava army. When Satyaki killed him, friends and kinsmen began to take sides, and a general brawl ensued. By the time it ended, they had all killed one another. That fulfilled one part of Gandhari's curse.

Krishna sent his charioteer to Hastinapura to tell Arjuna of the carnage. As soon as Arjuna heard the devastating news, he set out for Dwaraka, eager to see Krishna. But before he arrived, Krishna decided to return to Heaven, for he had finished his work on Earth.

He went out into the forest and sat in deep meditation. A hunter mistook him for a deer and shot an arrow that pierced his heel. When the hunter approached and saw what he had done, he was mortified — and terrified of the consequences. But Krishna comforted him, then left his body and rose heavenward, filling the sky with splendor and light. Upon reaching Heaven, he received the worship of all the deities. Thus, the second part of Gandhari's curse was fulfilled.

When Arjuna reached Dwaraka, he was met by thousands of women who were weeping and wailing in distress over the loss of their beloved Krishna. Arjuna collapsed upon hearing the news of Krishna's passing. He wept for a long time.

Arjuna realized that neither he, his brothers, nor Draupadi could bear life without Krishna. The time had come for them, too, to depart.

When Arjuna learned that Krishna had foretold that the sea would soon consume Dwaraka, he organized a long caravan of wagons and chariots to take the widows, children, and elders to Indraprastha. As the procession left Dwaraka, Krishna's prediction came true: the sea rushed in and swallowed the city.

Arjuna and some Dwaraka warriors protected the caravan as it moved slowly through the countryside and entered a region infested with bandits. Soon, thousands of bandits descended upon the caravan. Arjuna smiled and called out, "Stop, or I will take your lives! " But they ignored his warning.

Arjuna quickly began to string Gandiva, but he found it strangely difficult. He succeeded only after great effort. He then tried to bring to mind his astras, but he could not remember them. He shot many arrows at the robbers, and his inexhaustible quivers were soon empty. The bandits completely overwhelmed the caravan's protectors and carried off many of the women.

Arjuna was ashamed and sorrowful. How could this have happened to him, The Invincible One? When the caravan finally reached Indraprastha, he sought consolation and understanding from Vyasa. The master told him, "Do not grieve, Arjuna. It is all the work of Time. You and your brothers have accomplished the great purpose of your lives. Now it is time for you to depart this world and attain the highest goal."

Arjuna returned to Hastinapura to rejoin his brothers and Draupadi. When he told them what had happened and what Vyasa had said, they resolved to leave this world together.

Yudhisthira installed Arjuna's grandson, Parikshit, on the Kuru throne. He appointed Yuyutsu, Dhritarashtra's only surviving son, as Parikshit's guardian and Kripa as Parikshit's guru. The Pandavas gave away much wealth to the Kuru people. They and Draupadi then discarded their royal robes and dressed themselves in tree bark.

As they departed Hastinapura, the citizens begged them not to go, fearing this was a repeat of the Pandavas' exile to the forest after the dice game. But the Pandavas and Draupadi did not change their minds, and they left with cheerful hearts.

They traveled far to the west, then to the south, then east, and finally north into the Himalayas. From the outset, a stray dog accompanied them.

One day, as they ascended into those holy mountains, Draupadi fell to the earth, dead. Bhima was shocked and brokenhearted. He asked Yudhisthira, "Why has she fallen, O King? She never did anything sinful."

Yudhisthira answered, "Though she married us all, she was greatly partial toward Arjuna. Death is the fruit of that conduct."

Some days later, as they were climbing farther up into the mountains, Sahadeva dropped to the ground, also dead. Bhima asked Yudhisthira, "Sahadeva served us with such great humility. Why has he fallen?"

Yudhisthira answered, "He thought no one to be his equal in wisdom. For that, he has fallen."

They continued to climb until Nakula dropped dead. Bhima said, "Now the ever-obedient and righteous Nakula has fallen. Why?"

Yudhisthira replied, "He thought no one was as handsome as he. For that, he has fallen."

Arjuna could not bear life without his brothers and Draupadi, and before long, he, too, collapsed in death. Bhima said, "Now Arjuna, who has never lied and was invincible in battle, has fallen. Why?"

Yudhisthira answered, "Arjuna declared that he would vanquish all our foes in a single day, but he did not do it. He died because, in his pride, he disregarded all other warriors."

After a time, Bhima, too, fell to the earth. He looked up plaintively at Yudhisthira. "Now I, who am your darling, have fallen. Why, O King?"

Yudhisthira said, "You always boasted too much of your strength. Also, you were a gluttonous eater, and you never attended to the wants of others while you were eating. That is why you have fallen."

With those words, Bhima collapsed in death.

Without looking back, Yudhisthira continued to climb, still accompanied by the stray dog. Soon, there was a tremendous thunderclap. Yudhisthira looked up and beheld a celestial chariot swooping down toward him. It landed nearby, and he saw that, along with the driver, it carried a being who glowed with supernatural light. The being said, "I am the Lord Indra, O King. Come with me. You have earned the right to go to Heaven in your physical body."

> Swami Kriyananda pointed out that going to Heaven in the physical body is a metaphor for being able to exit the body consciously at death. It is a sign of spiritual advancement, in contrast to the unconscious, sleep-like exit that most people make.

Yudhisthira replied to Indra, "My heart is full of compassion for this dog, who is devoted to me. He should go with me."

Indra was puzzled. "You have won immortality and a position equal to mine, O King, with all the prosperity and felicities of Heaven. You should leave this dog behind."

Yudhisthira replied, "I cannot act unrighteously. I do not desire the prosperity of Heaven if it means leaving one who is devoted to me."

"There is no place in Heaven for persons with dogs," countered Indra.

Yudhisthira insisted, "I say again, it would be unrighteous of me to leave him. I can never abandon one who is destitute or devoted to me."

Indra argued, "You have renounced everything, O King. You are ready to abandon even your brothers and Draupadi. Why then do you not renounce this dog?"

Yudhisthira replied, "My brothers and Draupadi are dead, and I can do nothing about that. But I did not abandon them while they were alive, nor will I abandon this dog."

Suddenly, the dog transformed into Yudhisthira's father, the god Dharma.

"I am proud of you, my son. You have renounced everything in favor of dharma. O King, no one in Heaven can equal you. Great shall be your happiness."

Yudhisthira firmly insisted, "Happy or miserable, I wish to go where my brothers and Draupadi are."

Indra said, "Enjoy that which you have earned, O King. Why do you still cherish human affection? Your brothers and wife have reached regions of felicity. Do not concern yourself about them. You are going to Heaven."

Yudhisthira: "I care not to dwell anywhere except where my brothers and Draupadi dwell."

"Very well," sighed Indra. "Climb into my chariot. I will take you there."

Yudhisthira mounted the magnificent flying chariot, and Indra took him to Heaven. There, he beheld all the ineffable wonders and beauties of the celestial realm. They went to a place where many celestials had gathered around someone. When Yudhisthira moved closer, he saw that person seated on an excellent throne, shining with all the glory that belongs to great heroes and being worshipped by many deities. It was *Duryodhana*!

Yudhisthira turned away in a rage, crossed his arms, and shouted at the celestials: "I do not wish to share these regions of felicity with Duryodhana, stained as he was by greed and sin. He caused friends and kinsmen to be slaughtered! He caused the noble Draupadi to be humiliated before the assembly! I do not wish even to *see* Duryodhana! I wish to go where my brothers are."

The divine rishi, Narada, said, "Be not so, O King. In Heaven, all hostilities cease. Even though he always persecuted you, Duryodhana is worshipped by the gods because he died heroically in battle. It does not behoove you to remember grievances here. Now, *do* greet Duryodhana with politeness."

Yudhisthira replied, "If these are the regions attained by the wicked Duryodhana, then I wish to see the regions attained by my brothers and Draupadi. Where they are, that is Heaven! This place, in my opinion, is *not* Heaven!"

Indra shrugged and said, "If that is where you wish to go, you shall be taken there."

Indra summoned a celestial messenger, who led Yudhisthira along a dark and treacherous path, bordered on one side by a blazing fire and on the other by a boiling river. They entered a region polluted with stench and filled with stinging insects. The leaves on the trees were sharp razors. All over that region, sinful people were being tortured.

Yudhisthira asked the messenger, "How far must we go? Where are my brothers and Draupadi? And what celestial region *is* this?"

The messenger replied, "This is where I must leave you, O King. You may return with me if you wish."

He turned to go, and Yudhisthira turned to accompany him.

Suddenly, a voice piteously cried, "Wait, O son of Dharma, stay with us for a moment. At your coming, a delightful breeze has begun to blow, bearing the sweet scent of your person."

Another voice called, "Great is our relief and happiness. As long as you are here, O King, our torments cease to afflict us."

A third voice said, "Do stay with us, even for a short time."

Yudhisthira became filled with compassion. He said, "Alas, how painful! These voices seem familiar, but I cannot recognize them." He called out, "Who are you? Why are you here?"

Voices answered from all sides: "I am Karna!" — "I am Bhima!" — "I am Arjuna!" — "I am Nakula!" — "I am Sahadeva!" — "I am Draupadi!"

Yudhisthira was shocked, then outraged. "What perverse destiny is this? These high souls were devoted to truth. Why have they been assigned to this stinking region of woe? And how could that wretch Duryodhana gain such prosperity? Am I asleep or awake? Is this all the delusion of a diseased mind?"

He reflected briefly, then angrily censured all the gods, including his father, Dharma. He turned to the messenger. "Tell the gods I shall not return to them. I shall stay here because my presence comforts my afflicted brothers and Draupadi."

The messenger went back to the Devas and told them what had happened.

Immediately, the Devas came to where Yudhisthira was. The repulsive scenes disappeared, and a cool, sweet-smelling breeze began to blow.

Indra said, "Yudhisthira, do not yield to anger. The illusions have ended. You have obtained success and eternal felicity.

"Every king should behold Hell. He whose sinful actions outnumber his good actions first enjoys Heaven. Afterward, he must endure Hell. He whose good actions outnumber his sins must suffer Hell for a time before he can enjoy Heaven.

"You went to Hell first, O King, because you deceived Drona into thinking his son was dead. Your brothers and Draupadi also had to endure Hell for a time. But now, all of you have been cleansed of sin. Come with me to your own region of high reward. The gods themselves will wait upon you."

Dharma said, "O Son, I am greatly pleased with your devotion to me and your truthfulness, forgiveness, and self-restraint. All this was an illusion, my final test of you. Neither you nor any of your brothers nor Draupadi could ever deserve that place of sinners for a long time. Come with me, and bathe in the heavenly River Ganga."

Yudhisthira followed his father and entered the healing waters of the celestial river. He immediately found himself cleansed of all enmity and grief, even that of having caused Karna's death. Casting off his human body, he assumed a celestial form and joined his brothers. There, he beheld Krishna, blazing in glory and being worshipped by

Arjuna. He saw Karna with his father, Surya. Bhima was with his father, Vayu. Nakula and Sahadeva were with the twin Aswin gods. And he saw Draupadi in her subtle form: that of Sri Herself, Lakshmi, the goddess of grace.

And it was all exceedingly wonderful.

So ends the magnificent tale of the Mahabharata.

The Descent of Consciousness

Paramhansa Yogananda explained that the generations of Kuru royalty symbolize how divine consciousness descends into this material world. Each successive generation represents further descent into a more limited and outward-focused expression of that consciousness. I will minimize the story details to make the process easier to understand. Follow along with the graphic "The Descent of Consciousness."

The First Stage of Descent

Yogananda taught that the Supreme Spirit manifested creation by vibrating a portion of its consciousness to produce the cosmic sound vibration of AUM, the Divine Mother. That vibration is both creation and the creative power. It has two aspects: Paraprakriti is the subtle, hidden aspect that underlies material creation, and Aparaprakriti is the outward-manifesting aspect that is the physical universe.

King Shantanu represents the Father aspect of God, the portion of divine consciousness that is not vibrating and is uninvolved with creation. In contrast, the Mother aspect of God is intimately involved with creation. Indeed, She *is* creation!

Shantanu's first wife, Ganga, represents Paraprakriti. His second wife, Satyavati, represents Aparaprakriti. Both aspects of AUM have power, intelligence, and intention. Paraprakriti subtly attracts us inward toward soul consciousness. Aparaprakriti attracts us outward into material reality through *maya*, the delusive power that makes the infinite, indivisible Spirit appear finite and fragmented. Maya inclines us to feel separate from everything and everyone, including God.

Divine consciousness descends further into creation through Paraprakriti and Aparaprakriti.

The Descent of Consciousness

The qualities that the characters represent are in italics.

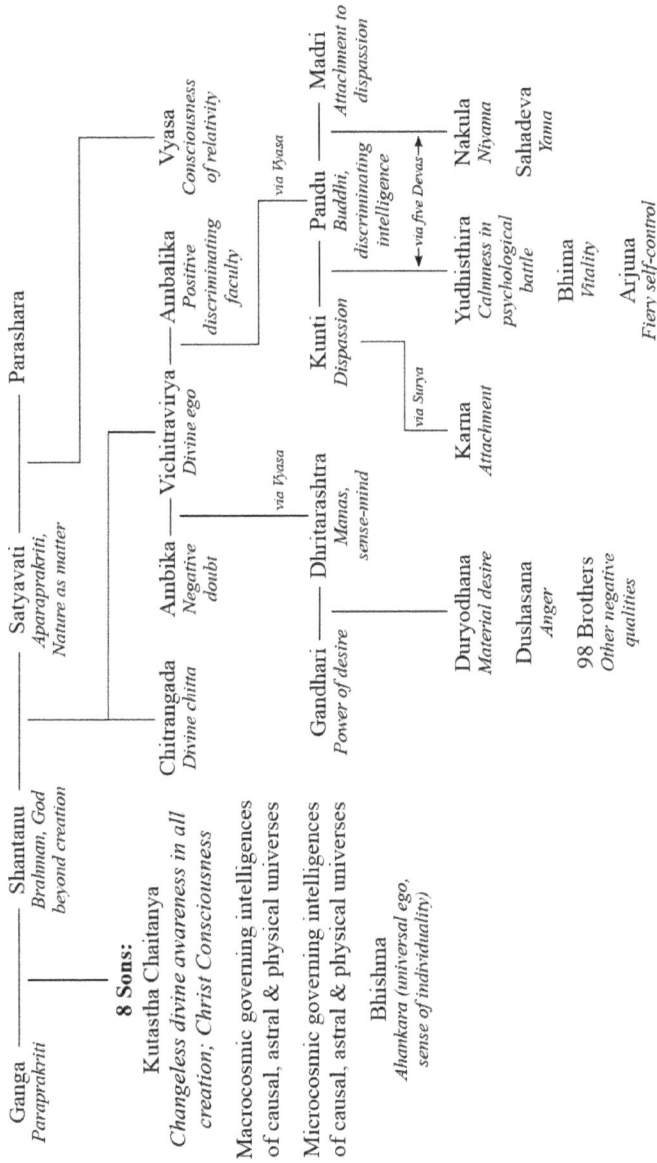

Ganga — Shantanu — Satyavati — Parashara
Paraprakriti *Brahman, God* *Aparaprakriti,*
beyond creation *Nature as matter*

8 Sons:

Kutastha Chaitanya
Changeless divine awareness in all creation; Christ Consciousness

Macrocosmic governing intelligences of causal, astral & physical universes

Microcosmic governing intelligences of causal, astral & physical universes

Bhishma
Ahamkara (universal ego, sense of individuality)

Chitrangada
Divine chitta

Ambika — Vichitravirya — Ambalika
Negative *Divine ego* *Positive*
doubt *discriminating faculty*

Vyasa
Consciousness of relativity

via Vyasa

Gandhari — Dhritarashtra
Power of desire *Manas, sense-mind*

via Vyasa

Kunti — Pandu — Madri
Dispassion *Buddhi,* *Attachment to discriminating dispassion*
intelligence

via Surya

Karna
Attachment

Duryodhana
Material desire

Dushasana
Anger

98 Brothers
Other negative qualities

←—*via five Devas*—→

Yudhisthira
Calmness in psychological battle

Bhima
Vitality

Arjuna
Fiery self-control

Nakula
Niyama

Sahadeva
Yama

The Descendants of Ganga (Paraprakriti)

Paraprakriti differentiated Herself into eight intelligences that are the subtle underpinnings of creation, represented by Ganga's eight sons:

- The *Kutastha Chaitanya*—God's unchanging consciousness within every atom of creation, also known as the Christ Consciousness.
- The macrocosmic governing intelligences of the three universes of thought (causal universe), energy (astral universe), and matter (physical universe).
- The three universes' microcosmic governing intelligences, which work at the level of individual beings.
- *Ahankara*, ego—the intelligence that gives all created beings a sense of individuality. Bhishma represents ahankara.

Ganga's drowning of her first seven sons symbolizes that the corresponding intelligences are hidden from ordinary consciousness. Bhishma's survival represents ego's presence in ordinary consciousness: We believe we *are* the body and personality, so we cater to them. The story reflects that belief through Bhishma's conviction that his purpose in life was to preserve the Kuru dynasty.

Paraprakriti did not descend into creation beyond those eight intelligences. Aparaprakriti did, however, as symbolized by several Kuru generations descended from Satyavati. Each represents a more limited expression of divine consciousness than the previous.

The Descendants of Satyavati (Aparaprakriti)

First Generation: Divine Faculties

Satyavati's three sons were the first generation of her descendants. They symbolize three divine faculties. The eldest, Vyasa, represents the consciousness of relativity: the power to see through the delusive force of maya and perceive the underlying divine unity.

Satyavati's next son, Chitrangada, represents divine *chitta*, which Yogananda translated as "primordial feeling," the bedrock of consciousness. It is our inborn ability to perceive Truth directly through soul intuition. Chitrangada died young, symbolizing that soul intuition is hidden from most people by maya and their karma, desires, attachments, and emotions.

Satyavati's youngest son, Vichitravirya, represents divine ego: identification with all creation, in contrast to human ego, which identifies only with the body and personality. Vichitravirya, too, died young, symbolizing that their innate oneness with all creation is hidden from most people. Instead, they identify with what is most apparent: the body and personality.

Second Generation: Human Faculties

When Chitrangada and Vichitravirya died childless, Satyavati asked Vyasa to produce the next generation of Kuru royalty through Amvika and Amvalika. The resulting births of Dhritarashtra and Pandu symbolize divine consciousness descending further into the world of matter—and further into limitation—as the human faculties of sensory awareness and intellect, respectively.

The elder wife, Amvika, represents negative doubt: using intellect to negate rather than understand. She closed her eyes during her union with Vyasa, symbolizing that negative doubt amounts to "closing our eyes" to the underlying unity of all creation. Her son, Dhritarashtra, was born blind as a result. He represents the "blind mind" or sense-mind—the part of our awareness that relays sensory data to the intellect but cannot understand what that data means.

Dhritarashtra's birth as the eldest Kuru prince of his generation reflects Yogananda's term for the senses: "the oldest child." They are our first—and for a long time, only—means of relating to the external world after birth. Consequently, habits of sense-gratification become deeply ingrained, symbolized in the story by Dhritarashtra's inability to deny Duryodhana (material desire) whatever he wanted.

Amvalika represents the positive discriminating faculty: using intellect to ask questions and gain understanding. Her union with Vyasa produced Pandu, who symbolizes discriminating intellect: the ability to understand sensory data, perceive differences, and reason one's way to a decision.

THE FOUR ASPECTS OF HUMAN CONSCIOUSNESS

With the births of Dhritarashtra and Pandu, all four fundamental aspects of human consciousness appear in the Kuru family tree. Yogananda stated that each aspect has a specific location within the body:

- *Manas* (sense-mind), represented by Dhritarashtra, is at the top of the head.
- *Buddhi* (discriminating intellect), symbolized by Pandu, is in the brain's prefrontal cortex, just interior to the point between the eyebrows.
- *Ahankara* (ego), represented by Bhishma, is located in the medulla oblongata at the base of the brain.
- *Chitta* (primordial feeling), symbolized by Chitrangada, is in the heart chakra, in the astral spine opposite the physical heart.

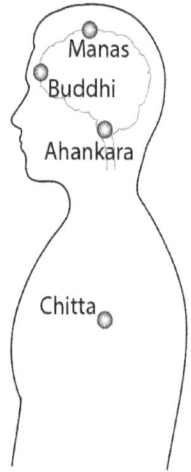

To summarize how these aspects interrelate, consider the image of a horse reflected in a mirror. The mirror is manas, which relays the visual data to buddhi without knowing it describes a horse. Buddhi interprets the data and concludes, "That is a horse." Ahankara tells us how the horse relates to our sense of self: "That is (or is not) my horse." Chitta then expresses how we feel about it; for example, "I am happy to see my horse" or "I wish that horse were mine."

Swami Kriyananda explained further, saying, "*Chitta* is more than an aspect of consciousness: It is consciousness. In man, *chitta* is far more than the reactive feelings in his heart: It is deep, intuitive feeling, which defines the very consciousness of self. In divine consciousness, *chitta* becomes cosmic feeling—not that of the ego, but of the divine Self: Absolute Bliss."

When the heart chakra is calm, our intuitive faculty enables us to perceive Truth. However, the heart is also where desires, attachments, and emotions originate. Those agitate chitta, causing our intuitive faculty to show us only a distorted expression of Truth. It is like trying to see what is at the bottom of a pool of water when the surface is agitated: the stronger the desire, attachment, or emotion, the greater the agitation, and the more distorted our view.

When intuition is distorted or blocked, our only hope for happiness is for discriminating intellect (Pandu) to rule our inner kingdom, supported by dispassion (Kunti, his primary wife). Discrimination and dispassion are valuable faculties, but they are of the conscious mind, which is vulnerable to the influences of maya and subconscious habits and desires. That vulnerability is symbolized by Pandu's passion for hunting and sexual gratification, which resulted in his death.

Dhritarashtra became acting king, symbolizing that sense-mind takes over in the absence of discrimination and intuition. We are then under the sway of maya and our habits and desires, and our inner kingdom is in a precarious state.

Third Generation: Human Qualities

The Pandavas and Kauravas were Satyavati's third generation of descendants. They symbolize divine consciousness descending into an even more limited state: human qualities. The Kauravas and their allies represent the many negative qualities that keep us in delusion. The Pandavas and their allies symbolize positive qualities (both human and divine) that give us the clarity, strength, and determination to confront those negative aspects.

The battle begins when we try to reclaim our divine birthright of bliss. The battlefield is Kurukshetra, the field (*kshetra*) of action (*kuru*). As Krishna states in the Gita (13:1), the body—and, by extension, the mind—is the battlefield.

Yogananda and all great masters have promised that the drama will end happily for each of us: We will reclaim our blissful soul nature. And the more fully we *live* our positive qualities and attune ourselves to God's grace, the sooner grace will lift us into that happy ending.

SUPPLEMENT 2

Excerpts from the
Unabridged Mahabharata

I mentioned in the preface that Vyasa's account includes many
lengthy monologues and descriptions that bog down the action.
Nevertheless, they add a delightful, often charming, flavor to the epic
and help weave the magical aura of this great scripture.

To give you a taste of that, below are three brief examples from
Ganguli's literal translation into nineteenth-century British English. I
will not explain the various clans and mythological characters mentioned
here, as they are beside the point. Also, Ganguli used the word "car" for
chariot; the modern car did not exist when he made his translation.

I hope you will enjoy these excerpts as much as I do.

1. How did the Kurus feel when Bhishma fell?

Sanjaya's account of the Kurukshetra War, from the Bhagavad
Gita through the end of the conflict, is a series of long replies to
Dhritarashtra's questions. In the following example, Dhritarashtra
has asked Sanjaya how the Kurus reacted to the fall of Bhishma on
the tenth day of the war. Sanjaya could have replied, "They were really sad and afraid," but instead he said this:

> The Kurus, deprived of Devavrata [Bhishma], were filled
> with great anxiety, and resembled a herd of goats and sheep
> without a herdsman, in a forest abounding with beasts of
> prey. Indeed, after the fall of that foremost one of Bharata's
> race, the Kuru host looked like the firmament divested of
> stars, or like the sky without the atmosphere, or like the
> earth with blasted crops, or like an oration disfigured by
> bad grammar, or like the Asura host of old after Vali had
> been smitten down, or like a beautiful damsel deprived of

husband, or like a river whose waters have been dried up, or like a doe deprived of her mate and surrounded in the woods by wolves; or like a spacious mountain cave with its lion killed by a *sarabha* [a powerful, eight-legged mythical creature that is part lion, part bird].

Indeed, O chief of the Bharatas, the Bharata host, on the fall of Ganga's son, became like a frail boat on the bosom of the ocean, tossed by a tempest blowing from every side. Exceedingly afflicted by the mighty and heroic Pandavas of sure aim, the Kaurava host, with its steeds, car-warriors, and elephants much troubled, became exceedingly distressed, helpless, and panic-stricken.

2. What is it like to face Arjuna in battle?

Recall that Vyasa gave Sanjaya the ability to know what the warriors were experiencing inwardly as well as witness the outward events of the war. At one point, Dhritarashtra asked Sanjaya a question that he could have phrased, "How did it feel to be attacked by Arjuna?" Instead, his question was so long that the following lengthy sentence was but a small part of it:

When that car-warrior of exceeding energy, viz., Vibhatsu [Arjuna], looking like a mass of clouds, came, emitting thunderbolts like the clouds themselves, shooting showers of arrows like Indra pouring rain, and making all the points of the compass resound with the slaps of his palms and the rattle of his car-wheels, when that hero whose bow was like the lightning's flash and whose car resembled a cloud having for its roars the rattle of its wheels (when that hero came), the whiz of whose arrows made him exceedingly fierce, whose wrath resembles an awful cloud, and who is fleet as the mind or the tempest, who always pierces the foe deep into his very vitals, who, armed with shafts, is terrible to look at, who like Death himself bathes all the points of the compass with human blood in profusion, and who, with fierce uproar and awful visage, wielding the bow Gandiva incessantly pours on my warriors headed by Duryodhana shafts whetted on stone and furnished with vultures' feathers, alas, when that hero of great intelligence came upon you, what became the state of your mind?

3. Krishna's reply to Vidura's warning

War seemed inevitable when Duryodhana refused to return the Pandavas' kingdom after they had completed their thirteen years of exile. Nevertheless, Krishna traveled to Hastinapura to make one last attempt at a peaceful resolution. Upon his arrival, Vidura lectured him at length on what an evil wretch Duryodhana was, how he would never return the Pandavas' kingdom, and how Krishna had put himself in grave danger by coming to Hastinapura. Here is Krishna's response:

> That, indeed, which should be said by a person of great wisdom; that, indeed, which should be said by one possessed of great foresight; that, indeed, which should be said by one like thee to a friend like me; that, indeed, which is deserving of thee, being consistent with virtue and profit, and truth; that, O Vidura, hath been said by thee, father-and mother-like, unto me.

> That which thou hast told me is certainly true, worthy of approbation and consistent with reason. Listen, however, with attention, O Vidura, to the reason of my coming.

> Well knowing the wickedness of Dhritarashtra's son and the hostility of the Kshatriyas that have sided with him, I have still, O Vidura, come to the Kurus. Great will be the merit earned by him who will liberate from the meshes of death the whole Earth, with her elephants, cars and steeds, overwhelmed with a dreadful calamity. If a man striving to the best of his abilities to perform a virtuous act meets with failure, I have not the least doubt that the merit of that

act becomes his, notwithstanding such failure. This also is known to those that are conversant with religion and scripture, that if a person having intended mentally to commit a sinful act does not actually commit it, the demerit of that act can never be his.

I will sincerely endeavour, O Vidura, to bring about peace between the Kurus and the Srinjayas who are about to be slaughtered in battle. That terrible calamity (which hangs over them all) hath its origin in the conduct of the Kurus, for it is directly due to the action of Duryodhana and Karna, the other Kshatriyas only following the lead of these two. The learned regard him to be a wretch who doth not by his solicitation seek to save a friend who is about to sink in calamity. Striving to the best of his might, even to the extent of seizing him by the hair, one should seek to dissuade a friend from an improper act. In that case, he that acteth so, instead of incurring blame, reapeth praise. It behoveth Dhritarashtra's son, therefore, O Vidura, with his counsellors, to accept my good and beneficial counsels that are consistent with virtue and profit and competent to dispel the present calamity.

I will, therefore, sincerely endeavour to bring about the good of Dhritarashtra's sons and of the Pandavas, as also of all the Kshatriyas on the face of the Earth. If while endeavouring to bring about the good (of my friends), Duryodhana judgeth me wrongly, I shall have the satisfaction of my own conscience, and a true friend is one who assumeth the functions of an intercessor when dissensions break out between kinsmen.

In order, again, that unrighteous, foolish, and inimical persons may not afterwards say that though competent, still Krishna did not make any attempt to restrain the angry Kurus and the Pandavas from slaughtering one another, I have come here. Indeed, it is to serve both parties that I have come hither. Having striven to bring about peace, I will escape the censure of all the kings.

If after listening to my auspicious words, fraught with virtue and profit, the foolish Duryodhana accept them not, he will only invite his fate. If without sacrificing the interests of the Pandavas I can bring about peace among the Kurus, my conduct will be regarded as highly meritorious, O high-souled one, and the Kauravas themselves will be liberated from the meshes of death. If the sons of Dhritarashtra reflect coolly on the words I shall utter—words fraught with wisdom, consistent with righteousness, and possessed of grave import—then that peace which is my object will be brought about and the Kauravas will also worship me (as the agent thereof). If, on the other hand, they seek to injure me, I tell thee that all the kings of the Earth, united together, are no match for me, like a herd of deer incapable of standing before an enraged lion.

The Mahabharata's principal narrator concluded the episode with this:

Having said these words, that bull of the Vrishni race and delighter of Yadavas [Krishna], then laid himself down on his soft bed for sleep.

Krishna's response could have been much shorter: "I know Duryodhana is wicked, but for everyone's sake, I must try for peace. I can protect myself."

But aren't you glad to have experienced his full response?

SUPPLEMENT 3

Humor in the Mahabharata

In the storytelling, I shared a number of amusing episodes, such as:
- Many instances of Bhima's impulsiveness, mischievousness, and immense appetite
- Arjuna's discomfiture when the Apsara Urvasi tried to seduce him in Heaven
- Duryodhana's humiliation at the hands of the Gandharvas
- Draupadi's sarcastic jabs at her unsympathetic husbands when Kichaka harassed her in Matsya
- The Kuru chariot warriors' frequent squabbling, highlighted by Kripa's putdown of Karna: "Anyone who wants single combat with Arjuna is a fool who needs to take a sedative!"
- The exchange of insults between Salya and Karna as they charged toward the long-awaited duel with Arjuna. In the unabridged Mahabharata, the exchange is much longer—and even funnier—than what I shared.

These episodes contribute to character development and storyline, so they have a natural place in the Mahabharata. But might it also be that Vyasa could not resist adding a bit of lighthearted entertainment to his epic?

In any case, he took humor even further in the following two episodes. I did not include them in the storytelling because they diverge from the storyline—and as you will discover, they are quite preposterous.

The Foolish Vow

On the seventeenth day of the war, Karna wounded Yudhisthira so severely that his charioteer had to take him to the Pandava camp for medical treatment. As I told the story, Arjuna immediately went after Karna when he learned of Yudhisthira's injuries. In the un-abridged Mahabharata, however, he first had Krishna take him to see Yudhisthira. Here is a brief summary of that encounter:

Arjuna and Krishna entered Yudhisthira's tent as surgeons were painstakingly removing many arrows from his body. Upon seeing the uninjured Arjuna, Yudhisthira brightened and said, "I am overjoyed that you have slain the evil Karna without being wounded! Tell me how you did it."

Arjuna replied, "I fought long and hard against Aswatthama, who had to flee to Karna for protection. Then Karna attacked me with fif-ty chariots, and I destroyed them all. But I avoided combat with him so I could come to see you. Now that I have seen you, I will return to the field and slay him. Bless me that I will be victorious."

Yudhisthira instantly began to boil with rage. "You have aban-doned Bhima on the field, leaving him to fight Duryodhana and Karna alone! You have pledged many times to kill Karna. Why has your fear of him brought you here now? You have a divine chariot, the celestial bow Gandiva, and Krishna as your charioteer, yet still you do not fight! You should give Gandiva to Krishna and become his charioteer, or give it to some other king more capable than you. O wicked soul, it would have been better if you had never been born!"

Arjuna's eyes grew wide with fury, and he drew his sword to kill Yudhisthira. But Krishna caught his arm, took him aside, and whis-pered urgently, "Arjuna, why draw your sword? There is no one here to fight. You came to see Yudhisthira. Now you have seen him. You should rejoice that he is well enough to see you."

Arjuna was breathing as heavily as an angry snake. "O Krishna, I made a vow that I would cut off the head of anyone who told me to give Gandiva to someone else. By slaying him, I will fulfill my vow."

Krishna said, "For shame, Arjuna! How could you think of slay-ing your eldest brother? You are not even in combat with him! That is ignorance. Your vow was foolish, and now you think to perform a sinful act. No one who knows dharma would do this!"

Arjuna sagged visibly. "You are right, Krishna. If I slay him, I will not be able to live, even for a moment. But how can I honor my vow without killing him?"

Krishna said, "Yudhisthira spoke as he did because he is exhausted and badly wounded. He was only trying to provoke you into killing Karna. Yet it is true that you must keep your vow."

Krishna thought for a moment, then continued, "It is said that if a person who deserves respect is treated with disrespect, he is considered dead. Yudhisthira certainly deserves respect. You should show him disrespect in some small way. He will not be angry with you."

Arjuna nodded, turned back to Yudhisthira, and said fiercely, "Do not speak to me this way as you relax in the luxury of your tent! Bhima is fighting heroically; he has a right to criticize me, but you do not! You are strong in words but not in battle! I find no pleasure in the thought of restoring you to sovereignty. You are addicted to the evil practice of gambling. You caused all of us to fall into this hell for the past thirteen years! Do not criticize me again lest you provoke my wrath!"

Arjuna felt great remorse for having spoken so harshly to his beloved eldest brother, and he said quietly to Krishna, "I will kill myself."

Krishna pulled him aside again and whispered, "By killing yourself, you would sink into a lower hell than if you had killed Yudhisthira. What you must do now is boast about yourself. That is the same as slaying yourself."

Arjuna nodded and began to praise himself enthusiastically and at great length for his tremendous prowess and magnificent accomplishments. He then sheathed his sword, bowed his head, and said to Yudhisthira, "Please forgive me, brother."

Yudhisthira replied, "You are right, Arjuna. I have acted wickedly. I am the worst of men—foolish, cruel, ignorant, and addicted to vices. Let Bhima become king. Strike off my head right now! Or perhaps I should retire to the forest."

Despite being in severe pain, he tried to stand up to leave. But Krishna stopped him by bowing at his feet and saying, "O King, you told Arjuna to give Gandiva to a better man, and he had vowed to kill anyone who said such a thing. I have been trying to untangle this delicate situation. You must forgive me. I swear that today, the earth will drink the blood of Karna."

Yudhisthira raised Krishna to his feet. "Arjuna and I have been stupefied by folly, and you have rescued us. O Krishna, you are our guru." He turned to Arjuna. "Come and hold me close, dear brother. You are forgiven."

After they tenderly embraced, Yudhisthira said, "Now, go and slay that villainous Karna!"

Memory Lapse

After the war and Bhishma's teaching of Yudhisthira (Chapter 27: "The Grandfather's Wisdom"), Krishna and Arjuna took an extended vacation. They roamed far and wide, enjoying beautiful woodlands, majestic mountains, and sacred pilgrimage sites. It was a period of great happiness for them.

Their travels concluded in Indraprastha, where they spent many hours enjoying the Pandavas' magnificent, magical assembly hall. They whiled away their days in merriment and recounted the many stirring incidents of the war and the sufferings of the past.

One day, as they sat relaxing amid the celestial beauty of that assembly hall, Arjuna said, "O Krishna, your greatness became known to me before the battle when you drove me in my chariot between the two armies. You shared with me many great truths and revealed your form as the Lord of the universe."

> Of course, he was speaking of Krishna's matchless teachings and the divine vision, as recounted in the Bhagavad Gita.

Arjuna continued, "However, due to the fickleness of my mind, I have forgotten everything you said. I yearn to know those marvelous teachings. Please tell them to me again."

Krishna was taken aback. He said, "I revealed to you great mysteries. I taught you the eternal truths, religion in its true form. Those truths are more than sufficient for knowing God. It is highly disagreeable to me that you did not receive what I imparted to you! Without doubt, Arjuna, you are destitute of faith, and your understanding is not good!

"It would be impossible for me to repeat everything I said on that occasion. I shall instead recount an old story that gives the same teaching. Listen closely this time, Arjuna, that you may attain the highest."

> Krishna proceeded to tell that story, which did indeed address many of the Gita's main points. Unlike with the Gita, however,

Krishna's retelling was only a lecture — there was no interaction with Arjuna — and the story was impersonal, rather tedious, and devoid of the Gita's sweetness. No wonder that few people are aware of that "second Gita."

Did Arjuna really forget the first Gita? And was Krishna truly unable to repeat it? Or did Vyasa fabricate their humorous exchange — and perhaps other amusing elements of the Mahabharata as well — to emphasize that joy is a vital part of the spiritual path?

Acknowledgements

I am deeply grateful to everyone who helped this project happen. I must begin with Kisari Mohan Ganguli for his boundless dedication and conscientiousness in translating the Mahabharata into English. What a labor of love! I wanted to base my storytelling only on "the real thing," and he provided it.

I offer heartfelt thanks to Nayaswami Rambhakta for his excellent editorial help, Nayaswami Lakshman for his expert proofreading skills, and fellow Mahabharata aficionado Nayaswami Omprakash for his many suggestions for improvement.

I am grateful to Nayaswami Narayan and Nayaswami Dharmadevi of Crystal Clarity Publishers for their unswerving support for both the written and audiobook versions—and their patience with the process. I also thank Vincent Perrone for lending his superb audio-editing skills.

Thanks also to the many people who have persistently yet kindly urged me over the years to give them a longer—but not too long!—and more satisfying taste of the Mahabharata. Your encouragement has been a source of inspiration and motivation for me.

I also want to thank my wife, Nayaswami Diksha, for her unwavering support for this project. Your encouragement and belief in me have been a great blessing.

Most of all, I am grateful to Paramhansa Yogananda and Swami Kriyananda for their matchless teachings, example, inspiration, and support. You have been the guiding lights of this project and my life. I humbly offer everything at your feet.

Glossary of Characters

For the central characters, the descriptions below include the (italicized) psychological/spiritual qualities that Paramhansa Yogananda said they represent. Their allegiance — Pandavas or Kauravas — is indicated for those who fought in the Kurukshetra War. Yogananda also offered qualities for some less-central characters not included in this storytelling.

Abhimanyu — *self-mastery* — the great warrior son of Arjuna and Subhadra. His wife was Princess Uttara of Matsya; their son was Parikshit. Pandava side.

Amva — the eldest Princess of Kashi. Bhishma abducted her and her sisters Amvika and Amvalika from their swayamvara as brides for Vichitravirya. She sought and received the boon from Lord Shiva that she would get revenge by killing Bhishma in her next life (as Shikhandin).

Amvalika — *positive discriminating faculty* — the youngest Princess of Kashi. Her husband was Vichitravirya; their son (by Vyasa) was Pandu.

Amvika — *negative doubt* — the middle Princess of Kashi. Her husband was Vichitravirya; their son (by Vyasa) was Dhritarashtra.

Arjuna — *self-control* — the great warrior son of Kunti and Indra (chief of the Devas). Third Pandava brother. Great disciple of Krishna and favorite pupil of Drona. His wives included Draupadi and Subhadra. He was a former incarnation of Paramhansa Yogananda.

Asura — demon. The Asuras were the enemies and martial equals of the Devas. They incarnated on Earth so they could rule here. The Mahabharata tells how the Earth was cleansed of them.

Astra — an intelligent force of nature that an accomplished warrior could infuse into ordinary weapons, making those weapons far more powerful. One invoked an astra by uttering its particular mantra with deep concentration and attunement with that force.

Aswamedha—a great yagya (sacred ceremony). Yudhisthira performed the Aswamedha after the Kurukshetra War to help cleanse himself of feelings of guilt over the war.

Aswatthama—*attraction; desire born of past habits*—the immortal son of Drona. Kaurava side. Aswatthama carried out the nighttime massacre in the Pandava camp after the Kurukshetra War.

Balarama—the elder brother of Krishna. Indian spiritual tradition has it that Balarama was an incarnation of Ananta (also called Adishesha), the manifestation of Vishnu in the form of a giant cobra that supports the world on its head.

Bharata—*cosmic consciousness*—one of the great kings of Indian history. He was a descendant of Kuru and an ancestor of Shantanu and the Pandavas and Kauravas.

Bhima—*the power of vitality*—the son of Kunti and Vayu. Bhima was the second oldest Pandava, one year younger than Yudhisthira. He was famed for his strength, prowess with the mace, and appetite. His wives included Draupadi and Hidimbi the Rakshasi.

Bhishma—*ego*—the eighth son of Shantanu and Ganga. His given name was Devavrata. Bhishma means "the terrible," referring to his awe-inspiring oath to live a celibate life and never occupy the Kuru throne, which was his birthright. Bhishma commanded the Kuru army for the first ten days of the Kurukshetra War.

Bhuminjaya—Prince of Matsya. His father was Virata. When Arjuna defeated the entire Kuru army in Matsya, Bhuminjaya served as Arjuna's charioteer.

Brahmin—the highest of the four main castes, traditionally those fully dedicated to knowing God.

Chitrangada—*divine primordial element (chitta)*—the elder son of Shantanu and Satyavati. He was king of the Kurus until his untimely death. Vichitravirya was his brother; Bhishma and Vyasa were his half-brothers.

Chitrasena—the Gandharva king and close friend of Arjuna during Arjuna's time in Heaven. Chitrasena later helped humiliate Duryodhana by defeating and capturing him.

Deva—demigod, minor god. Although the Devas usually ruled Heaven, their age-old rivals, the Asuras, were occasionally able to conquer Heaven for a time.

Dhrishtadyumna—*calm inner light*—Prince of Panchala. His father was Drupada, his sister was Draupadi, and Shikhandin was his brother. He was born full-grown from a sacrificial fire to fulfill Drupada's desire for a son who would kill Drona. Dhrishtadyumna commanded the Pandava forces in the Kurukshetra War.

Dhritarashtra—*blind mind*—the son of Vyasa and Amvika. Pandu and Vidura were his younger half-brothers. Dhritarashtra served as acting king of the Kurus after Pandu's death. His wife was Gandhari; their sons were Duryodhana (eldest), Dushasana (second oldest), and 98 others. His consort was a Vaishya woman; their son was Yuyutsu. Dhritarashtra was known for his great strength.

Draupadi—*kundalini power*—Princess of Panchala, she became the Pandavas' queen. Her father was Drupada, and her brothers were Dhrishtadyumna and Shikhandin. When she was born, full-grown from a sacrificial fire, heavenly voices declared that she would cause the destruction of all Kshatriyas.

Drona—*past tendency, habit*—preceptor of the Kuru princes, Karna, Dhrishtadyumna, and others. His son was Aswatthama. He was the second Kuru army commander at Kurukshetra and the archenemy of Drupada. He was also called Dronacharya, acharya meaning "teacher."

Drupada—*extreme dispassion*—King of Panchala. His children included Dhrishtadyumna, Draupadi, and Shikhandin. He was the archenemy of Drona. Pandava side.

Duryodhana—*material desire*—Kuru prince, the eldest son of Dhritarashtra and Gandhari. He was the primary villain of the Mahabharata. He was born on the same day as Bhima, amid evil omens that he would be the destroyer of the Kurus.

Durvasa—a great rishi, known for his explosive anger. He insisted on giving Kunti the mantra through which she could summon Devas and have children through them.

Dushasana—*anger*—Kuru prince, the second son of Dhritarashtra and Gandhari. Dushasana was one of the four main conspirators bent on destroying the Pandavas. The other three were Duryodhana, Shakuni, and Karna.

Dussala—a Kuru princess, the only daughter of Dhritarashtra and Gandhari. Her brothers were the Kauravas. Her husband was Jayadratha.

Ekalavya—Prince of the Nishadha kingdom. Although Drona refused to teach him, he became a great archer through attunement with Drona. As *gurudakshina*, he willingly cut off his thumb, ensuring that Arjuna would be the greatest archer.

Gandhari—*power of desire*—Princess of Gandhara. Her husband was Dhritarashtra; their sons were Duryodhana, Dushasana, and 98 others. Her younger brother was Shakuni.

Ganga—*AUM, Paraprakriti, Divine Mother*—the goddess of the River Ganga. Her husband was Shantanu; their sons were Bhishma and seven others. She drowned those seven at birth.

Ghatotkacha—the great and noble warrior son of Bhima and Hidimbi the Rakshasi. Pandava side. Karna killed him at Kurukshetra with Indra's infallible spear.

gurudakshina—the obligatory gift of the disciple to the guru in return for the guru's training.

Jayadratha—*body-bound inclination, fear of death*—King of Sindhu. His wife was Dussala. Kaurava side.

Karna—*attachment; also greed*—the son of Kunti and Surya. Dearest friend of Duryodhana, who made him King of Anga. He was a great warrior, taught by Drona and Parashurama. Karna was one of the four main conspirators bent on destroying the Pandavas, the others being Duryodhana, Dushasana, and Shakuni. He was the third Kuru commander at Kurukshetra.

Kauravas (also known as Kurus)—a generic name for the descendants of Kuru. Technically, the sons of both Pandu and Dhritarashtra were Kauravas, but "Kauravas" usually refers to the sons of Dhritarashtra and Gandhari, not those of Pandu and his wives.

Kripa—*delusion, ignorance*—the first teacher of the Kuru princes. Kaurava side. Immortal. Yudhisthira appointed him the guru of Parikshit when the Pandavas and Draupadi went to the Himalayas to end their incarnations.

Krishna—*God/guru*—"Krishna" refers to his dark complexion. The Mahabharata portrays him as an incarnation of Vishnu/Narayana, born to cleanse the world of evil. Krishna was younger than Yudhisthira and Bhima and some months older than Arjuna. His many wives included Rukmini and Satyabhama. His brother was Balarama. He was a former incarnation of Babaji, the guru of Yogananda's guru's guru.

Kritavarma—a cousin of Krishna's wife Satyabhama. He commanded the army that Krishna gave to Duryodhana for the war. Kaurava side. His death at the hands of Satyaki ignited the fatal brawl among Krishna's kinsmen.

Kshatriya—the caste of rulers and warriors, the second highest of the four main castes.

Kunti—*the power of dispassion, renunciation*—the elder wife of Pandu. Kunti was the mother of Yudhisthira, Bhima, and Arjuna and the stepmother of Nakula and Sahadeva. As the sister of Krishna's father, she is the link that made Krishna and the Pandavas cousins.

Kuru—a great ancient king who was an ancestor of Bharat, Shantanu, and the Pandavas and Kauravas.

Madri—*attachment to dispassion*—the younger wife of Pandu. Her sons were Nakula and Sahadeva via the Aswini twins. She was the stepmother of Yudhisthira, Bhima, and Arjuna.

Nakula—*the power to practice niyama*—the son of Madri and an Aswin twin. He was the fourth oldest of the Pandavas (Sahadeva's twin), known for his beauty.

Narada—the celestial rishi, son of Brahma and Saraswati, and the consummate devotee of Narayana. Narada tends to appear whenever something momentous is about to happen or has happened.

Narayana—Vishnu, the preserving force of the Brahma/Vishnu/Shiva trinity. Krishna is popularly said to be an incarnation of Narayana, but Yogananda said that is a myth; see "Krishna" above.

Pandavas—the five brothers: Yudhisthira, Bhima, Arjuna, Nakula, and Sahadeva. They were called Pandavas, after Pandu, even though five Devas, not Pandu, were their biological fathers.

Pandu—*pure discriminating intelligence*—King of Hastinapura. He was the son of Vyasa and Amvalika. He was Dhritarashtra's younger half-brother and Vidura's older half-brother. His wives were Kunti and Madri, with whom he had no children. Still, the wives' five children (by various Devas) were known as the Pandavas, after Pandu.

Parashara—great rishi who was the father of Vyasa.

Parashurama—an immortal Brahmin warrior. His disciples in the science of weaponry included Bhishma, Drona, and Karna.

Parikshit—the son of Abhimanyu and Uttara. When the Pandavas and Draupadi departed for the Himalayas to give up their bodies, Yudhisthira crowned Parikshit the new Kuru king.

Rajasuya—a great *yagya* (sacred ceremony) in which a king celebrates sovereignty over the entire world, thus ensuring his place in Heaven. Yudhisthira performed the Rajasuya.

Rakshasa—a type of Asura possessing superhuman strength and magical powers, including the ability to change shape and grow tremendously in strength at night.

Rishi—a general term for a highly advanced Brahmin sage. Vyasa, Vasishtha, Durvasa, and Parashurama were rishis who played significant roles in the Mahabharata.

Sahadeva—*the power to practice yama*—the son of Madri and an Aswin twin. Youngest of the Pandavas, he was Nakula's twin, renowned for his wisdom.

Sanjaya—*introspection*—an adviser and charioteer of Dhritarashtra. Vyasa gave him divine sight so he could report to Dhritarashtra the entire Kurukshetra War, including the warriors' thoughts.

Shantanu—*God the Father*—King of the Kurus and husband of Ganga; their son was Bhishma. After Ganga left him, he married Satyavati; their sons were Chitrangada and Vichitravirya. Shantanu was the great-grandfather of the Pandavas and Kauravas.

Satyaki—*devotion*—a dear friend and cousin of Krishna. Pandava side. He began the post-war internecine conflict that resulted in the deaths of all Krishna's kinsmen.

Satyavati—*Aparaprakriti, Nature as matter*—the second wife of Shantanu; their sons were Chitrangada and Vichitravirya. She had a son, Vyasa, by Parashara before she met Shantanu.

Shakuni—*material attachment*—Prince of Gandhara. The younger brother of Gandhari. He was Duryodhana's uncle and scheming advisor. His co-conspirators against the Pandavas were Duryodhana, Dushasana, and Karna. Kaurava side.

Salya—*material pride*—King of Madra. He was Madri's brother and, therefore, the uncle of the Pandavas, yet he fought on the Kaurava side. Salya was the Kuru commander for the last day of the Kurukshetra War.

Shikhandin—*the will to perform uplifting actions; self-transcendence*—born Drupada's daughter and sister of Dhrishtadyumna and Draupadi, she convinced a Yaksha (magical nature-spirit) to change her into a man. In his previous life, Shikhandin had been Amva. He was born to kill Bhishma, and he partnered with Arjuna to accomplish it. Pandava side.

Subhadra—the sister of Krishna. Her husband was Arjuna; their son was Abhimanyu.

Sudra—peasant caste, the lowest of the four main castes.

Susharma—King of Trigarta. Kaurava side.

Swayamvara—a wedding ceremony for a princess. It means "ceremony of self-choice," indicating that the princess could choose her preferred husband from among the kings and princes invited to the ceremony.

Uttara—Princess of Matsya. Daughter of Virata. Her husband was Abhimanyu; their son was Parikshit.

Vaishya—*attachment due to desires*—a consort of Dhritarashtra; their son was Yuyutsu. Vaishya was her caste; the Mahabharata does not state her name. Vaishya is the caste of farmers and merchants, the third of the four main castes.

Vasishtha—an immortal son of Brahma. He was one of the great ancient rishis and the heavenly guru of the young Bhishma. It was he who cursed Bhishma to incarnate and have a long life.

Vichitravirya—*divine ego*—the younger son of Shantanu and Satyavati. King of the Kurus after his older brother Chitrangada died. His elder half-brothers were Bhishma and Vyasa.

Vidura—the principal minister of Hastinapura, known for his wisdom and virtue. Vidura was the son of Vyasa and Amvika's maidservant. His older half-brothers were Pandu and Dhritarashtra.

Vikarna—*repulsion; also greed*—Kuru prince, the only son of Dhritarashtra and Gandhari to protest the winning of Draupadi at the game of dice and the recall of the Pandavas for a second game.

Virata—*oneness, samadhi*—King of Matsya, where the Pandavas spent their thirteenth year of exile and prepared for the Kurukshetra War. Pandava side. His queen was Sudeshna, and their children included Bhuminjaya and Uttara.

Vyasa—*consciousness of relativity*—the immortal avatar son of Parashara and Satyavati. His half-brothers were Chitrangada and Vichitravirya, and his sons were Pandu, Dhritarashtra, and Vidura. He authored the Mahabharata and the Srimad Bhagavatam (which recounts the lives of the so-called incarnations of Vishnu, with special emphasis on Krishna).

Yudhisthira—*calmness in psychological battle*—the son of Kunti and Dharma (the god of righteousness and death, also called Yama). He was the eldest Pandava by one year, famed for his devotion to dharma and Truth.

Yuyutsu—*desire to give psychological battle*—the son of Dhritarashtra and Vaishya. He was the only son of Dhritarashtra to survive the Kurukshetra War, having defected to the Pandava side. He was appointed guardian of Parikshit when Parikshit became king of the Kurus.

About the Author

Nayaswami Gyandev, PhD

For more than thirty years, Nayaswami Gyandev has retold the Mahabharata to audiences all over the world. He is a senior teacher with Ananda Sangha Worldwide and has taught all aspects of the Yoga tradition for more than forty years. He is a Kriyacharya (teacher of Kriya Yoga) and a longtime disciple of Paramhansa Yogananda, author of *Autobiography of a Yogi*. He has authored numerous books and videos, including *Spiritual Yoga: Awakening to Higher Awareness* and the forty-eight videos of *The Ananda Yoga Series*. Gyandev is director of Ananda Yoga worldwide and a co-founder of Yoga Alliance.

FURTHER EXPLORATIONS

CRYSTAL CLARITY PUBLISHERS

If you enjoyed this title, Crystal Clarity Publishers invites you to deepen your spiritual life through many additional resources based on the teachings of Paramhansa Yogananda. We offer books, e-books, audiobooks, yoga and meditation videos, and a wide variety of inspirational and relaxation music composed by Swami Kriyananda.

See a listing of books below, visit our secure website for a complete online catalog, or place an order for our products.

crystalclarity.com

800.424.1055 | clarity@crystalclarity.com

1123 Goodrich Blvd. | Commerce, CA 90022

ANANDA WORLDWIDE

Crystal Clarity Publishers is the publishing house of Ananda, a worldwide spiritual movement founded by Swami Kriyananda, a direct disciple of Paramhansa Yogananda. Ananda offers resources and support for your spiritual journey through meditation instruction, webinars, online virtual community, email, and chat.

Ananda has centers and meditation groups in over 45 countries, offering group guided meditations, classes and teacher training in meditation and yoga, and many other resources.

In addition, Ananda has residential communities in the US, Europe, and India. Spiritual communities are places where people live together in a spirit of cooperation and friendship, dedicated to a common goal. Spirituality is practiced in all areas of daily life: at school, at work, or in the home. Many Ananda communities offer internships during which one can stay and experience spiritual community firsthand.

For more information about Ananda communities or meditation groups near you, please visit ananda.org or call 530.478.7560.

THE EXPANDING LIGHT RETREAT

The Expanding Light is the largest retreat center in the world to share exclusively the teachings of Paramhansa Yogananda. Situated in the Ananda Village community near Nevada City, California, the center offers the opportunity to experience spiritual life in a contemporary ashram setting. The varied, year-round schedule of classes and programs on yoga, meditation, and spiritual practice includes Karma Yoga, personal retreat, spiritual travel, and online learning. Large groups are welcome.

The Ananda School of Yoga & Meditation offers certified yoga, yoga therapist, spiritual counselor, and meditation teacher trainings.

The teaching staff has years of experience practicing Kriya Yoga meditation and all aspects of Paramhansa Yogananda's teachings. You may come for a relaxed personal renewal, participating in ongoing activities as much or as little as you wish. The serene mountain setting, supportive staff, and delicious vegetarian meals provide an ideal environment for a truly meaningful stay, be it a brief respite or an extended spiritual vacation.

For more information, please visit expandinglight.org or call 800.346.5350.

ANANDA MEDITATION RETREAT

Set amidst seventy-two acres of beautiful meditation gardens and wild forest in Northern California's Sierra foothills, the Ananda Meditation Retreat is an ideal setting for a rejuvenating, inner experience.

The Meditation Retreat has been a place of deep meditation and sincere devotion for over fifty years. Long before that, the Native American Maidu tribe held this to be sacred land. The beauty and presence of the Divine are tangibly felt by all who visit here.

Studies show that being in nature and using techniques such as forest bathing can significantly reduce stress and blood pressure while strengthening your immune system, concentration, and level of happiness. The Meditation Retreat is the perfect place for quiet immersion in nature.

Plan a personal retreat, enjoy one of the guided retreats, or choose from a variety of programs led by the caring and joyful staff.

For more information or to place your reservation, please visit meditationretreat.org, email meditationretreat@ananda.org, or call 530.478.7557.

The 1946 Unedited Edition of Yogananda's Spiritual Masterpiece

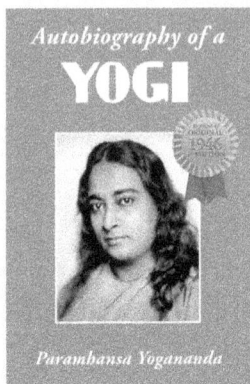

AUTOBIOGRAPHY OF A YOGI
Paramhansa Yogananda

Autobiography of a Yogi is one of the world's most acclaimed spiritual classics, with millions of copies sold. Named one of the Best 100 Spiritual Books of the twentieth century, this book helped launch and continues to inspire a spiritual awakening throughout the Western world.

Yogananda was the first yoga master of India whose mission brought him to settle and teach in the West. His firsthand account of his life experiences in India includes childhood revelations, stories of his visits to saints and masters, and long-secret teachings of yoga and Self-realization that he first made available to the Western reader.

This reprint of the original 1946 edition is free from textual changes made after Yogananda's passing in 1952. This updated edition includes bonus materials: the last chapter that Yogananda wrote in 1951, also without posthumous changes, the eulogy Yogananda wrote for Gandhi, and a new foreword and afterword by Swami Kriyananda, one of Yogananda's close, direct disciples.

Also available in Spanish and Hindi from Crystal Clarity Publishers.

The Original Writings of Paramhansa Yogananda

SCIENTIFIC HEALING AFFIRMATIONS
Paramhansa Yogananda

Yogananda's 1924 classic, reprinted here, is a pioneering work in the fields of self-healing and self-transformation. He explains that words are crystallized thoughts and have life-changing power when spoken with conviction, concentration, willpower, and feeling. Yogananda offers far more than mere suggestions for achieving positive attitudes. He shows how to impregnate words with spiritual force to shift habitual thought patterns of the mind and create a new personal reality.

Added to this text are over fifty of Yogananda's well-loved "Short Affirmations," taken from issues of *East-West* and *Inner Culture* magazines from 1932 to 1942. This little book will be a treasured companion on the road to realizing your highest, divine potential.

METAPHYSICAL MEDITATIONS
Paramhansa Yogananda

Metaphysical Meditations is a classic collection of meditation techniques, visualizations, affirmations, and prayers from the great yoga master, Paramhansa Yogananda. The meditations given are of three types: those spoken to the individual consciousness, prayers or demands addressed to God, and affirmations that bring us closer to the Divine.

Select a passage that meets your specific need and speak each word slowly and purposefully until you become absorbed in its inner meaning. At the bedside, by the meditation seat, or while traveling — one can choose no better companion than *Metaphysical Meditations*.

SONGS OF THE SOUL
Paramhansa Yogananda

Yogananda preferred to express his wisdom not in dry intellectual terms but as pure, expansive feeling. To drink his poetry is to be drawn into the web of his boundless, childlike love. In one moment his *Songs of the Soul* invite us to join him as he plays among the stars with his Cosmic Beloved. Then they call us to discover that portion of our own hearts that is eternally one with the Nearest and Dearest. This volume is a bubbling, singing wellspring of spiritual healing that we can bring with us everywhere.

More about Paramhansa Yogananda

PARAMHANSA YOGANANDA
A Biography with Personal Reflections and Reminiscences
Swami Kriyananda

Paramhansa Yogananda's life was filled with astonishing accomplishments. And yet in his classic autobiography, he wrote more about the saints he'd met than about his own spiritual attainments. Yogananda's direct disciple, Swami Kriyananda, relates the untold story of this great master and world teacher: his teenage miracles, his challenges in coming to America, his national lecture campaigns, his struggles to fulfill his world-changing mission amid incomprehension and painful betrayals, and his ultimate triumphant achievement.

Kriyananda's subtle grasp of his guru's inner nature and outward mission reveals Yogananda's many-sided greatness. Includes many never-before-published anecdotes and an insider's view of the Master's last years.

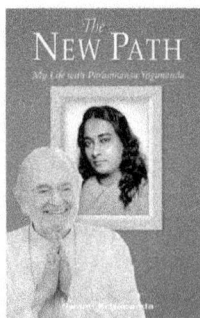

THE NEW PATH
My Life with Paramhansa Yogananda
Swami Kriyananda

Winner of the 2010 Eric Hoffer Award for Best Self-Help/Spiritual Book
Winner of the 2010 USA Book News Award for Best Spiritual Book

The New Path is a moving revelation of one man's search for lasting happiness. After rejecting the false promises offered by modern society, J. Donald Walters found himself (much to his surprise) at the feet of Paramhansa Yogananda, asking to become his disciple. How he got there, trained with the Master, and became Swami Kriyananda makes fascinating reading.

The rest of the book is the fullest account by far of what it was like to live with and be a disciple of that great man of God.

Anyone hungering to learn more about Yogananda will delight in the hundreds of stories of life with a great avatar and the profound lessons they offer. This book is an ideal complement to *Autobiography of a Yogi*.

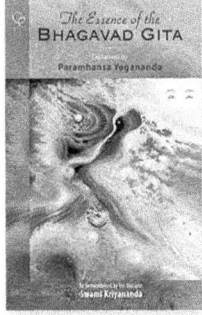

THE ESSENCE OF THE BHAGAVAD GITA
Explained by Paramhansa Yogananda
As remembered by his disciple, Swami Kriyananda

Rarely in a lifetime does a new spiritual classic appear that has the power to change people's lives and transform future generations. This is such a book. This revelation of India's best-loved scripture approaches it from a fresh perspective, showing its deep allegorical meaning and down-to-earth practicality. The themes presented are universal: how to achieve victory in life through union with the Divine; how to prepare for life's final exam — death — and what happens afterward; and how to triumph over all pain and suffering.

Swami Kriyananda worked with Paramhansa Yogananda in 1950 while the Master completed his commentary. At that time, Yogananda commissioned him to disseminate his teachings worldwide.

"Millions will find God through this book!" Yogananda declared upon completion of the manuscript. "Not just thousands — millions. I have seen it. I know."

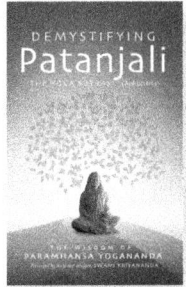

DEMYSTIFYING PATANJALI: THE YOGA SUTRAS
The Wisdom of Paramhansa Yogananda
Presented by his direct disciple, Swami Kriyananda

For millennia this fascinating series of yoga sutras, or aphorisms, by the great Indian sage Patanjali has baffled scholars and mystics alike. Today, these powerful writings stand newly revealed as a practical, concise handbook that redirects all sincere seekers swiftly towards their true home in the Divine.

Demystifying Patanjali represents the confluence of three great yoga teachers. Patanjali, the first exponent of the ancient teachings of yoga, presented his system of inner contemplation, meditation practice, and ethics. Paramhansa Yogananda, perhaps the greatest of all yoga masters to live and teach in the West, revealed with deep insight the meaning behind Patanjali's often obscure aphorisms. Finally, Yogananda's direct disciple, Swami Kriyananda, the author of nearly 150 spiritual books in his own right, compiled his guru's explanation into a clear, systematic presentation.

These three great souls combine to give us a modern scripture that will enlighten the mind, expand the heart, and inspire the soul of every seeker.

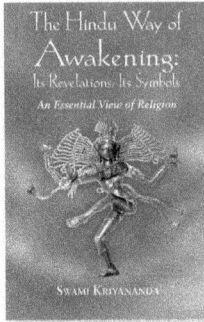

THE HINDU WAY OF AWAKENING
Its Revelation, Its Symbols: An Essential View of Religion
Swami Kriyananda

Hinduism, as it comes across in this book, is a robust, joyful religion, amazingly in step with the most advanced thinking of modern times, in love with life, deeply human as well as humane, delightfully aware of your personal life's needs, for the teaching in this book is no abstraction: It is down-to-earth and pressingly immediate.

This book brings order to the seeming chaos of the symbols and imagery in Hinduism and clearly communicates the underlying teachings from which these symbols arise.

Wisdom Stories Series

As a universal medium, stories reach into the hearts of all God's children — young and old — delivering timeless truths in ways easy to digest and assimilate. Perhaps, more than anything, this is why Paramhansa Yogananda wove stories into all of his teachings through his lectures and books and why his close disciple, Swami Kriyananda, did the same.

Presented in an easy-to-find format based on their spiritual principles, the Wisdom Stories series presents these tales, as told by Yogananda, the master storyteller himself. Such stories allow people to relax, be fully present and receptive, and understand truths and subtleties they might otherwise miss.

STORIES FROM INDIA, VOLUME 1
First in the Wisdom Stories series
Paramhansa Yogananda

STORIES FROM INDIA, VOLUME 2
Second in the Wisdom Stories series
Paramhansa Yogananda